L A K E
MICHIGAN

A guide to
small towns, rural areas
and natural attractions

by

Donna Marchetti

GLOVEBOX
GUIDEBOOKS
OF AMERICA
1112 Washburn Place East
Saginaw, MI 48602-2977

Published by: **Glovebox Guidebooks of America**
1112 Washburn Place East
Saginaw, Michigan 48602-2977
(800) 289-4843 or (517) 792-8363

Library of Congress, CIP

Donna Marchetti, 1953-

Lake Michigan
(A Glovebox Guidebooks of America publication)

ISBN 1-881139-25-5

Printed in the United States of America

10 9 8 7 6 5 4 3 2 1

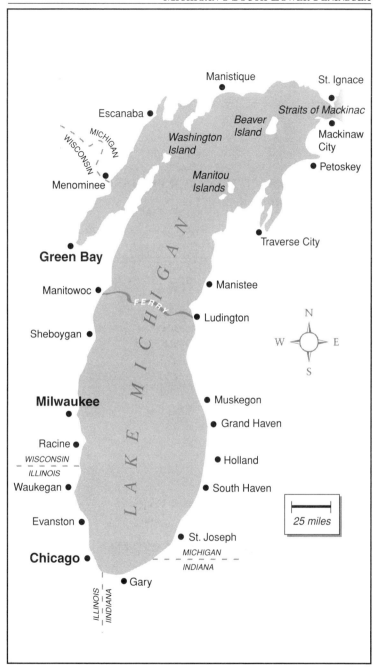

Manistique

St. Ignace

Escanaba

Beaver
Island

Straits of Mackinac

MICHIGAN

WISCONSIN

Washington
Island

Mackinaw
City

Menominee

Manitou
Islands

Petoskey

Green Bay

LAKE MICHIGAN

Traverse City

Manitowoc

Manistee

FERRY

Ludington

Sheboygan

N

W — E

S

Milwaukee

Muskegon

Grand Haven

Racine

WISCONSIN
ILLINOIS

Holland

Waukegan

South Haven

25 miles

Evanston

St. Joseph

MICHIGAN
INDIANA

Chicago

Gary

ILLINOIS
IINDIANA

3

Table of Contents

NATURAL ATTRACTIONS

Chapter 3
MICHIGAN'S NORTHERN LOWER PENINSULA
Cherries, Dunes and Old Money 117

PLACES

NATURAL ATTRACTIONS

Chapter 4
MICHIGAN'S UPPER PENINSULA
Five Miles and Half a World Away 207

Chapter 5
THE WISCONSIN SHORE
Brats, Beer and Hard-working Industry 237

Chapter 6
DOOR COUNTY
Wisconsin's Vacationland

Seul Choix Lighthouse near Manistique, Mich.

Introduction

Lake Michigan, 307 miles long and 118 miles wide, has 1,640 miles of shoreline. Its surface area is 22,300 square miles, making it the largest lake entirely within the borders of the United States and the sixth-largest natural lake in the world. Its average depth is 279 feet, with its deepest point 923 feet below the surface. It rivals Lake Erie in age: like that much smaller lake, Lake Michigan was formed about 10,000 years ago when glaciers moved ponderously across North America, gouging out the contours of these Great Lakes. So much water is contained within the shores of Lake Michigan that it takes 70 years for it to turn over completely.

What all these facts and figures don't tell you is how incredibly beautiful Lake Michigan is. From midnight blue to deep green to Caribbean turquoise, the colors of the lake vary, but all are astounding to first-time visitors. Sunrises and sunsets are dramatic affairs, the water dancing with flame-toned hues from an expansive sky. Though it has many moods, when the lake is serene it is remarkably clear, the outline of fossils and many-colored agates distinct even through waist-deep water. But what may be the biggest surprise of all, to anyone who hasn't been there before, are the wide, fine-grained, can't-wait-to-walk-on-them-barefoot beaches.

From the Indiana/Michigan border up along Michigan's Lower Peninsula all the way to Mackinaw City is a long line of almost uninterrupted beach, much of it framed by spectacular dunes, the largest stretch of freshwater coastal sand dunes in the world. Even these magnificent beaches are rivaled by some of the wild, beautiful stretches of sand in the Upper Peninsula. Moving down the Wisconsin side of the lake, you'll still find beaches galore, though generally smaller than those in Michigan.

But of course the original lakeside inhabitants – the Native Americans – knew about the clear, cold water and the pale sandy beaches ringed with towering forests. It was the Ojibwa who named the lake "Michigan," meaning "Great Water" in their language. They depended on the lake for transportation and on its rich fishing grounds for nourishment.

The coming of Europeans changed the lake forever. Lake Michigan was the second of the Great Lakes to be seen by French explorers. In the early 1600s Samuel de Champlain visited Lake Huron, where he heard tales of a land to the west, beyond a great body of water where the "People of the Sea" dwelt beside the "Stinking Water." This could mean only one thing – that beyond the land of the Huron was the ocean, and beyond that lay China. Back home in Quebec, Champlain became caught up in his duties, and never had the opportunity to forge on to the Orient.

That task fell to Jean Nicolet, 20 years old in 1618 when he arrived in the New World from his home in France. By 1634 he was well practiced in the art of diplomacy, and when word reached Quebec that there were warring tribes to the west, Nicolet was dispatched to make peace. Certain that his journey would take him to China, he packed a magnificent robe of Chinese damask.

He donned it when he arrived at Green Bay, which turned out to be the famed "stinking water." Dressed to meet an emperor, he was well received, then dined on beaver meat and other decidedly non-Oriental fare. He returned to Quebec with the news that the New World was larger than expected, and that it would be no easy task to find China.

His journey nonetheless opened up the westward path, and voyageurs and traders soon followed. After them, in the 1800s, came the lumberjacks, who cut the vast forests surrounding the lake to build Chicago, Milwaukee and other cities of the Midwest. The fishing industry thrived, with a seemingly never-ending supply from the lake in which 149 species have been found.

When the forests were gone and the fish depleted, what remained were the great cities concentrated on the lake's southern edges, and the depressed lumber towns everywhere else. Most of them recovered by turning their attention to other kinds of activity, and for many of them it was tourism.

This is, to a large degree, what you will find today – the busy industrial cities of Gary, Chicago, Racine and Milwaukee sprawled across the lower part of the lake, with much of the remaining shoreline devoted to resort areas and tourist towns. There are forests again, and an abundance of fish. This vast stretch of shoreline north of the cities is the focus of this book.

The attractions along the way are many and diverse: art enclaves, historic forts, lumber baron mansions, dozens of lighthouses, cherry orchards and grape vineyards, fascinating museums, trails, forests, islands and more — all against the backdrop of one of the most beautiful lakes anywhere.

USING THIS BOOK

The book is divided into six chapters, each covering a different geographic region. Each chapter is further broken down into towns within that area. Historical information is included, not with the intention of providing a comprehensive history, but to give some perspective on how each town fit into the general pattern of growth along the lake. There is information on attractions – and these are more likely to be museums or light-houses than miniature golf or go-cart tracks, which may be here today but gone tomorrow. Many of these attractions are closed during the winter or have abbreviated hours, so it is always best to call when planning a visit.

With most towns, there is also a listing of where to stay and where to eat. Many of the accommodations are bed and breakfasts. If you have not stayed in a bed and breakfast before, you are in for a treat. But you should also know that there's some special etiquette involved. A bed and breakfast is, after all, someone's home. The owners are friendly, helpful and eager to please. But they do set their own rules. Some welcome children, but many do not – not because they don't like them, but because their home may be filled with expensive antiques, or their clientele comes to their B & B specifically for the quiet, romantic environment, easily shattered by a two-year-old's wail. Some B & B owners accept credit cards, others don't. A few do not permit alcohol on the premises. Many prohibit smoking. Be sure to ask if any of these is a concern. While most places remain open all year, a few close for the winter.

Included in each chapter is a section called "Natural Attractions." This is where you will find information about the many state and national parks and forests along the lake. Smaller attractions, such as municipal parks and beaches, are covered in the sections on each specific town.

WHAT YOU WON'T FIND

This is a book about the smaller towns and resort areas along the lake. You will not find anything about Chicago, Milwaukee, Gary or Racine. If it's got a population over 50,000, it's not covered here. Information about these and other big cities is abundant and easy to find in other guidebooks and from the Visitors and Convention Bureau in each location. What this means is that beginning at the southern Michigan border, this book covers the area along the lake all the way up Michigan's Lower Peninsula, across the Upper Peninsula and down the Wisconsin coast just shy of Milwaukee. The only city on this stretch of coastline not covered is Green Bay.

Something else you will not find in this book is a chain or franchise anything. The accommodations and restaurants listed are all one-of-a-kind, with a special emphasis on those with waterfront locations. If you have an attachment to a particular fast food chain, chances are you'll find it in most of these towns, but the aim of this book is to let you in on some of the great surprises that await you. Likewise, if you can't find accommodations listed here to suit your needs, rest assured that most places have one or more chain motels. Just contact the chamber of commerce listed with each town.

The final thing you won't find is any shortage of fun-filled and interesting activities in this tour along the lake. And it doesn't matter if you plan to explore by bike, car or by foot – or for a day, a week of a month. You'll find plenty to appreciate. *Enjoy*.

Traditional Icelandic church on Washington Island, Wis.

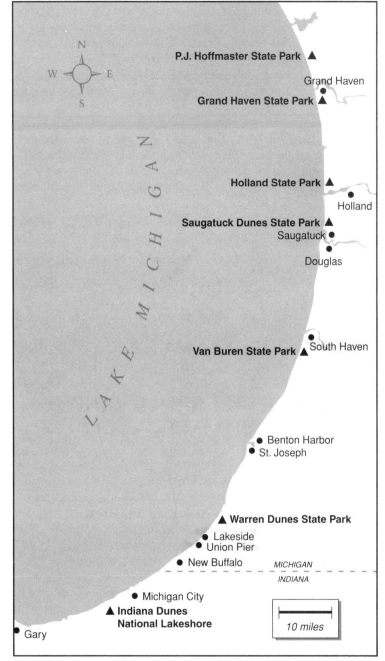

N
W   E
S

P.J. Hoffmaster State Park ▲

Grand Haven ●

Grand Haven State Park ▲

LAKE MICHIGAN

Holland State Park ▲

Holland ●

Saugatuck Dunes State Park ▲

Saugatuck ●

Douglas ●

LAKE MICHIGAN

Van Buren State Park ▲ ● South Haven

Benton Harbor ●
St. Joseph ●

▲ **Warren Dunes State Park**

● Lakeside
● Union Pier

● New Buffalo   *MICHIGAN*
                     INDIANA

● Michigan City
▲ **Indiana Dunes**
National Lakeshore

● Gary

10 miles

14

Near the waterfront at New Buffalo.

Chapter

O N E

MICHIGAN'S SOUTH LOWER PENINSULA

Chicago's Playground

Within a couple hours' drive of Chicago are some of the most beautiful beaches and picturesque lakeside towns in the United States. Windy City folks discovered this nearby paradise in the 1900s and have been coming in droves ever since. The result is a very popular, sometimes crowded tourist mecca that is filled with great restaurants, places to stay, shops and galleries, geared to the tastes and often the pocketbooks of the sophisticated city dweller in search of fun and relaxation.

This is most evident in Harbor Country, just over the Indiana border. The small-town streets are lined with specialty shops

Fishing from the lighthouse pier at St. Joseph.

and eateries, and the harbor at New Buffalo is filled with Chicago yachts. For places like Union Pier and New Buffalo, tourism is the main industry.

The same can be said for South Haven, a town of just 5,600 permanent residents. This is the quintessential beach town; whereas Harbor Country draws the shoppers and diners, South Haven draws the fun and sun crowd who come to enjoy beaches that even a Caribbean-spoiled tourist would rave about.

Pretty, charming Saugatuck, too, is geared primarily to tourism. Its calling card is its profusion of galleries; this is, after all, the Art Coast of Michigan.

The larger towns of St. Joseph and Grand Haven have some degree of industry in addition to tourism, but each is a wonderful place to visit — Grand Haven for its long waterfront boardwalk lined with attractions and St. Joseph for its beautiful parks and outdoor sculptures.

Holland is in a category all its own. At 30,000, it is second in population only to Muskegon among the Michigan towns on the lake. Too far inland to be a beach town (though there is a gorgeous beach at Holland State Park), Holland's appeal is its beautiful downtown and its Dutch heritage, which is evident all the time but flowers particularly during the annual Tulip Time Festival.

The great thing about these towns is that each has a unique appeal, something that sets it apart from the next town just a few miles down the road. And because these places are so close together, it's easy to hop from one to the other, indulging whatever whim the day might bring.

For nature lovers, there are seven state parks and one national park. Indiana Dunes National Lakeshore, the only Indiana attraction in this book, is one of only two national lake shore parks on Lake Michigan. Don't let its proximity to industrial Gary scare you away. It is 15,000 acres filled with beauty and history.

Whether your passion is nature, hiking, fishing, cycling, cross-country skiing, shopping or just plain eating well, you will find it along Lake Michigan's southeast coastline.

Just a reminder: This is vacationland, and places to stay or eat are far too abundant to offer a complete list here. Those included are distinctive in some way, but certainly not the only options. For the entire rundown, contact the chambers of commerce in the individual towns.

Harbor Country

This string of small communities is the first stop after the Indiana-Michigan border. Only 90 minutes from Chicago, Harbor Country is a favorite spot among Windy City folks for weekend getaways and summer homes. The largest of the towns, New Buffalo, has a population of about 2,300; the rest — Michiana, Grand Beach, Union Pier, Lakeside, Harbert, Sawyer and Three Oaks — number in the hundreds for year-round population but swell with visitors during the busy summer months. Much of the shore here is lined with private homes, so beaches — though certainly available — are not the primary attraction. What draws people to Harbor Country is the small town atmosphere coupled with sophisticated dining, a plethora of great places to stay, galleries, boutiques, antiques stores, country markets and wineries. Just look for the Red Arrow Highway, lined on either side by eateries and shops.

Of the Harbor Country towns, New Buffalo is where the most action takes place. This is where you'll find the harbor and marina, and a explosion of expensive condos along the water-front.

The town was actually named for Buffalo, New York, by Captain Wessel Whittaker, a Buffalo native, whose schooner Post Boy went aground here in a storm in October 1834. He discovered a natural port at the mouth of the Galien River as he was traveling along the shore to report his ship's loss to the owners in Buffalo. Seeing the possibilities the protected port could offer, he envisioned another Chicago. After finishing business back in New York, Whittaker returned to the area, staying on to build the first structure in what would be the town of New Buffalo.

Fortune smiled on the town in 1849, when the Michigan Central Railroad completed its track as far as New Buffalo, making it a natural stopover for people traveling from Detroit to Chicago. Lodging houses, restaurants and saloons sprang up. The whiskey that flowed in great quantities was frequently a free reward to shop customers who made purchases. The town was booming, and real estate prices soared.

Things took a turn for the worse, though, when the railroad line was completed to Chicago, and travelers no longer needed to stop at New Buffalo. Ironically, Chicago was also responsible for New Buffalo's resurgence in the early 1900s. Wealthy Chicagoans with cars could now escape the city easily to breathe the fresh lake air.

The new resort hotels prospered and New Buffalo became known as the "Gateway of Michigan." Resorts also sprang up in nearby Lakeside and Union Pier, where John Dillinger was a frequent visitor. The Pere Marquette Railroad built a huge roundhouse and luxury hotel in New Buffalo in the 1920s, but all that's left now is the roundhouse, better recognized as Gold's Gym.

Visitors can learn about the railroad era at the **New Buffalo Railroad Museum**, 530 S. Whittaker (616-469-2090). Housed in a replica of the original depot, the museum contains a miniature train display of the New Buffalo area as well as many railroad artifacts, such as old poster-size ads for Pullman sleepers. On the grounds there's a restored World War II troop car and a 1935 Henschel steam locomotive used in Germany during the war. The museum has plans to convert an old box car into a reading room and research center.

In addition to shops, restaurants and the railroad museum, New Buffalo offers several recreational possibilities. The **New Buffalo Municipal Marina** (616-469-6887), at the mouth of the Galien River, has slips to accommodate transient boats. Nearby are public boat launches with access to Lake Michigan. Across the river at the end of Whittaker Street is the **New Buffalo Lakefront Park and Beach**, the most easily accessed and largest public beach in Harbor Country. Fishing charters and sailing excursions are available; information can be obtained from the chamber of commerce.

Cyclists will enjoy Harbor Country's many rural roads. Self-guided backroad or mountain biking routes are available from the **Three Oaks Spokes Bicycle Museum** (616-756-3361). The museum also rents bikes. For a brochure with maps, send a self-addressed, stamped envelope to: Backroads Bikeway, One Oak Street, Three Oaks, MI 49128, or stop in at the museum.

The rural areas of Berrien County, where Harbor Country is located, have long been an excellent place for growing fruit. Recently more land has been devoted to grapes, and the area has gained a reputation for its fine wines. There are two wineries nearby, and though they are not on the lake, they are well worth a drive inland.

Heart of the Vineyard Winery (800-716-9463), located in Baroda, offers a variety of well-made wines that can be sampled in the barn-turned-tasting-area. The offerings include chardonnay, cabernet, pinot gris, pinot noir, merlot and a refreshing sparkling rose. A few steps from the tasting room is an old Amish-built round barn, which is being converted into a brandy still. If you can't make it to the winery, Heart of the Vineyard has a tasting center in Union Pier on the Red Arrow Highway.

At **Tabor Hill Winery and Restaurant** in Buchanan (800-283-3363), visitors can sip excellent wines while enjoying a fine meal overlooking rolling vineyards. This is truly one of the most pleasant "wine" environments in the state. The winery produces a number of dry and semi-dry wines, including chardonnay, merlot, riesling and Michigan cherry wine. The Lake Michigan Shore Chardonnay Barrel Select is a winner. Tours and tastings are free. The winery is open daily during the summer; during the winter the tasting room is open daily and tours are given on the weekends. Weekday tours in winter are by appointment only. The restaurant is open for lunch and dinner Wednesday through Sunday during the summer. In winter, lunch is served Saturday and Sunday, and dinner is served Friday and Saturday. The winery also operates the Tabor Hill Champagne Cellar on the Red Arrow Highway in Bridgman.

St. Julian Winery in Paw Paw is Michigan's oldest and largest winery. It produces distinctive wines, many of which have won top awards. Their Michigan Raspberry Champagne has many fans, and the Solera Cream Sherry is a consistent prize winner. There is a St. Julian tasting room in Union Pier at 9011 Union Pier Road. (616-469-3150).

It's a rare weekend when there isn't a festival or special event happening in Harbor Country. And they go on all year round. There are parades, arts and crafts fairs, golf events, holiday festivals — the list goes on and on. Here are a couple of favorites: The annual **Art Attack** takes place in April. In this celebration of "all that is art," local businesses participate by sponsoring events like special film screenings, fashion shows, artist exhibits, arts and crafts demonstrations, book signings and readings. Each August brings the **Ship and Shore Festival**, which includes food, music, kids' games, arts and crafts sales, jewelry, a lighted boat parade and fireworks. In September there's the **Harbor Country Harvest Festival** with apple bobbing, quilting demonstrations and lots of farm-fresh produce like pumpkins, apples, blueberries and corn. Also in September is the **Apple Cider Century Bike Ride**, one of the Midwest's most popular bicycle events. More than 7,000 cyclists participate in this ride through Michigan's scenic countryside.

WHERE TO STAY:

Bauhaus on Barton, 33 N. Barton Street, New Buffalo, MI 49117; 616-469-6419. What a kick! A fifties B & B! Stacks of LPs (what are those? your kids would ask), '50s music playing. '50s knickknacks (poodles!), and that unique '50s invention — very weird lamps. These are the decor for this fun-loving place. There's the I Love Lucy Room, the Sky King Suite with full kitchen, and the Millionaire Suite. The Deluxe Suite includes the Jetsons Room and the Ozzie and Harriet Room (with — what a shocker — a king-size bed!). All rooms have a private bath. The furnishings throughout are authentic '50s; owners Roger and Beverly Harvey scoured the country looking for them. This swell B & B is a few blocks from the lake right in town on a residential street.

Gordon Beach Inn, 16220 Lake Shore Road, Union Pier, MI 49129; 616-469-0800. Built as an inn during the 1920s, Gordon Beach retains much of its original charm, now enhanced by modern conveniences. It is in a very quiet area, surrounded by towering trees, a couple of blocks from the beach. Hand-stenciled walls and lots of wood add to its charm.

There are 20 rooms, each with private bath, telephone, TV and air conditioning. Three deluxe rooms with whirlpool tubs, wet bars and private decks offer more spacious accommodations. Fanny's Restaurant on the premises serves full meals, including a children's menu. Full bar service is available.

Harbor Grand Hotel and Suites, 111 West Water Street, New Buffalo, MI 49117; 888-605-6800 or 616-469-7700. This is presently the only waterfront accommodation right in New Buffalo (though it is on the river, not Lake Michigan). Inspired by Frank Lloyd Wright's Prairie school of architecture, the hotel has a warm, comfortable feel. Accommodations range from rooms with no water view to harbor view rooms with fireplace and whirlpool tub. Also available are two-room suites with refrigerators and microwaves; these reasonably priced suites make a nice option for families. The hotel has an indoor pool and spa as well as a restaurant with harbor view.

The Lakeside Inn, 14281 Lake Shore Road, Lakeside, MI 49116; 616-469-0600. Owned by Devereux Bowly, who also owns the Gordon Beach Inn, this is a historic inn built in the 1920s. It sits high on bluff overlooking the lake from the opposite side of Lake Shore Road. Steep stairs lead down to a beautiful beach which stretches for miles in either direction. There are 30 rooms, each with private bath, telephone, TV and air conditioning. Five rooms have whirlpool tubs. The inn's spa features a sauna, exercise equipment and massage services. Common areas include a 100-foot porch overlooking the water and a large, comfortable lobby with fireplace. The Lakeside Cafe, a small, casual restaurant, serves food but has no liquor license.

 Pine Garth Inn, 15790 Lake Shore Road, PO Box 347, Union Pier, MI 49129; 616-469-1642. This B & B has a gorgeous location high on a bluff overlooking the lake, with stairs leading down to a private beach. The beautiful grounds and quiet atmosphere make it an ideal place for relaxation. There are seven guest rooms, each with private bath. Most overlook the lake, and some have whirlpool tubs or balconies. All have in-room VCRs. There is a screened porch overlooking the lake, and in the winter the Great Room fireplace helps ward off the chill. Full breakfast is served in the inn's dining room. The owners also rent cottages across the street from the inn.

Sandpiper Inn, 16136 Lakeview Avenue, Union Pier, MI 49129; 800-351-2080 or 616-469-1146. A Georgian-style inn with a private beach, the Sandpiper is quiet and elegant. The rooms, featuring beautiful lake views, are designed with luxury in mind — screened porches, fireplaces, private baths, whirlpool tubs, telephones and TVs. Full breakfast is served. This is an adult inn; no children are allowed.

Tall Oaks Inn, 19400 Ravine Drive, New Buffalo, MI 49117; 800-936-0034 or 616-469-0097. Built in 1914 as a lumber camp, the Tall Oaks Inn is now a beautiful country bed and breakfast. Set among towering trees on a four-acre lot in a quiet neighborhood, it is about a five-minute walk to Lake Michigan. There are 12 guest rooms, from single bedrooms with shared bath to suites with private bath, fireplace, Jacuzzi, sitting room and deck. Large common areas include extensive decks, garden room, and a cozy living room with fireplace. Host L. Julia Mead oversees a full breakfast each morning, which can be eaten in your room or in the inn's dining room. This is a lovely, tranquil place for a getaway.

WHERE TO EAT:

Hannah's, 115 S. Whittaker, New Buffalo; 616-469-1440. This large, homey place is a local favorite. Open for lunch and dinner seven days a week, Hannah's has something for just about everyone. There are plenty of meal-size salads, a host of pasta dishes, chicken, ribs and shrimp, plus the specialty — pork chops topped with apple brandy sauce, apples and walnuts. Burgers and stick-to-your-ribs sandwiches are also available.

Jenny's Restaurant, 15460 Red Arrow Highway, Lakeside; 616-469-6545. The eclectic food served at Jenny's has elements of Spanish, French, Italian, with a bit of Thai thrown in for good measure. Entrees include such tasty offerings as curry-coconut marinated chicken with Thai barbecue sauce or rack of

lamb with a Dijon mustard crust. The extensive wine list has
more than 75 offerings from around the world, including some
Michigan wines. Jenny's minimalist decor makes the place
open, bright and airy. A pleasant place with interesting, creative
cuisine, it hasn't gone unnoticed. Have a reservation or get
there early, especially in season. It's open seven days a week
during the summer, but closed on Tuesday and Wednesday during the off season. Dinner only is served.

Rosie's, 128 N. Whittaker, New Buffalo; 616-469-4382. A
great place for home-style, reasonable food, Rosie's is a popular place for breakfast or lunch. Start the day with Belgian waf-
fles or one of the many special omelets. Lunches are meant to
fill you up: hearty fare like pot roast or hot turkey sandwiches
accompanied by soup or salad.

*For more information contact the Harbor Country Chamber of
Commerce, 530 S. Whittaker St. #F, New Buffalo, MI 49117;
800-362-7251 or 616-469-5409.*
Internet: http://www.harborcountry.org

St. Joseph/Benton Harbor

Unlike the Harbor Country towns to the south, St. Joseph
depends on industry as well as tourism. With a population of
about 9,500, it has a small-town feel, but its proximity to
Chicago ensures that it satisfies sophisticated tastes as well. St.
Joseph is a pretty town, set high on a bluff overlooking the
lake, with a charming downtown shopping area and beautiful
parks. It's a great place for walkers, who enjoy evening prome-
nades along the bluff's edge and out to the lighthouse made
famous by a U.S. postage stamp.

Benton Harbor, on the other hand, is unfortunately a depressed
area with dilapidated buildings and many social and economic
woes. Nonetheless the stories of the two towns go hand-in-
hand, so both find a place in this book.

The towns are located on opposite sides of the St. Joseph River, which has had an effect on their history and development, for the river stretches more than halfway across the lower peninsula. It also provided easy access to the Mississippi River system, making it a natural place for goods to pass through.

It is one of the oldest settlements on Lake Michigan. Fort Miami was founded here in 1679 by Robert Cavalier Sieur de La Salle, best known for claiming New Orleans for France. The fort was the first white settlement in what is now southwestern Michigan and among the first in the entire state.

Settlement of the village of St. Joseph began in the 1830s. It soon became a busy port, handling goods headed for Chicago, Kalamazoo and towns in Indiana. Boat building and lumbering were also among the early industries. Fortune frowned on the port, though, when the Michigan Central Railroad designated New Buffalo as its lake terminus. Lumbering and sawmilling took the place of shipping.

Across the river, Benton Harbor, first known as Brunson Harbor, grew as a hard-living, hard-drinking lumber town. The two towns never really got along, squabbling over bridges, canals and other water issues.

As the wood ran out, fruit growing increased, and both towns became known for grapes, peaches, apples, pears and other fruit. After the turn of the 19th century, tourism became a part of the picture.

And Benjamin Purnell is largely to thank. These towns owe at least some of their early reputations as resort destinations to the smart business sense of Purnell, founder of the House of David, a religious colony that took up residence here in 1903. Members were required to give all their worldly goods to Purnell upon joining the church. But to supplement the colony's income, Purnell built a miniature railroad, a very successful amusement park and a tourist hotel. He also put together a top-notch baseball team that attracted visitors from far and wide. (Men of the colony were forbidden to cut their hair, and there are famous photos of the baseball team in their uniforms with hair flowing down to their waists.)

Purnell was the seventh and last "angelic messenger" recognized by the group. Many would argue that "angelic" wasn't one of his qualities. From most accounts he appears to have been a tyrant who exercised absolute control over his loyal followers. Children were not permitted to be educated. All property was held in common. Marriages were arranged without consent, but conjugal relations were often forbidden, and transgressions were severely punished. Purnell, though, had an apparent penchant for young girls, a weakness that proved to be his downfall.

Purnell's alleged sexual practices caught up with him and he was arrested in 1926, Thereafter followed a sensational trial, during which he died.

The colony lived on, though split in two, one half led by Purnell's widow, Mary. Mary's City of David, as it's now called, presently has nine members who live a quiet life in their small community. There is a museum and gift shop on the grounds, which are open late June through late September. Guides provide a one- to two-hour walking tour, which also includes a lecture with slide presentation. For more information contact **Mary's City of David Museum** (616-925-1601). The House of David community also still exits, but its numbers are even smaller.

There are many other things to do in and around St. Joseph, rain or shine. Downtown's **Lake Bluff Park** is a favorite place for walking. Perched along the top of the ridge above the lake, it offers a taste of the town's history as well as beautiful views of the lake. Strung out along its length are a series of monuments commemorating events such as the founding of Fort Miami and the Fireman's Monument, erected in honor of firemen who lost their lives in a 1896 blaze. Among the other monuments is the Maids of the Mist, a 1872 fountain depicting two maids, "Hope" and "Constance." Farther down the walkway is the town's Century Stone, which sits over a bronze box filled with information and memorabilia placed there in 1934.

It contains city documents, information on St. Joseph and its citizens, and a letter from the mayor in 1934 to the mayor in 2034. At one end of the park is the **John E.N. Howard Bandshell**, where free concerts are held throughout the summer.

Three parks offer beach access. **Tiscornia Park**, on the north side of the river channel, also attracts fishermen, who come to try their luck off the North Pier. The pier leads out to St. Joseph's two 1907 lighthouses, built along the same pier so that boat captains could line them up visually, similar to a gun sight, in order to navigate their way into the river channel. Though there were other similar piers along the lake, only St. Joseph and Grand Haven still have two towers standing with their catwalks intact. This was one of two Michigan lighthouses featured in a 1995 series of postage stamps honoring lighthouses of the Great Lakes. Both St. Joseph lights are still functioning, and both have their original Fresnel lenses.

On the other side of the river channel is **Silver Beach**, with a 1,600-foot fine sand beach, children's play equipment, bathhouses, and volleyball nets. During the summer there is a lifeguard on duty. Further south is the **Lions Park** beach, with picnic shelter and playground but no lifeguard. All three beaches charge for parking during the summer.

Nature lovers and walkers will enjoy **Sarett Nature Center** in Benton Harbor (616-927-4832), a wildlife sanctuary and educational center operated by the Michigan Audubon Society. The center has five miles of self-guided nature trails through woods and fields, and past marshes and ponds. Weekend nature programs and children's summer classes are also offered. During the winter trails are open to cross-country skiers. Call for hours and schedules.

If you happen to be in St. Joseph on a rainy day, don't worry — there are still things to do. One of the highlights is the **Krasl Art Center** on Lake Blvd. (616-983-0271). The center has three galleries that feature changing exhibits from various sources such as the Smithsonian Institution or the Detroit

Institute of the Arts. The center's permanent collection consists entirely of sculpture, most of it outdoors on the Krasl grounds. George Rickey's "Three Lines Diagonal," a kinetic sculpture on the outside of the building, is especially intriguing. The center is active in promoting the placing and care of outdoor sculpture, not just on their grounds, but elsewhere as well. "SculpTour," a brochure that outlines a self-directed tour of outdoor sculptures in the St. Joseph area, is available at the center. Open hours are Monday through Thursday, 10-4; Friday, 10-1; Saturday, 10-4; and Sunday, 1-4.

Children will enjoy the **Curious Kids Museum**, just down the street (616-983-2543), where they can explore science, history and culture via hands-on exhibits and special programs. Sound, the human body, rain forests, sailing and machines are just some of the things children can experience. A special wing is geared specifically to children ages four and under. For older kids there's a small-scale television studio. The museum is open year round, but the days and hours vary so call for information.

The **Josephine Morton Memorial Home Historic Museum**, 501 Territorial Road in Benton Harbor (616-982-0399), is the town's oldest home. Built in 1849 by early settler Eleazer Morton, the house was occupied by four generations of the Morton family. It is now a museum staffed by volunteers in period costume. Though the house itself has changed much since it was built, it has many authentic period furnishings. It is open mid-April through October, Sundays 2-4 and Thursdays 1-4.

St. Joseph celebrates several annual festivals and events, including the **Blossomtime Festival** in April-May, which draws more than 250,000 visitors to celebrate the coming of springtime blossoms, and the **Venetian Festival** along the St. Joseph River each July.

WHERE TO STAY:

The Boulevard Inn, 521 Lake Blvd., St. Joseph, MI; 616-983-

6600. This classy, modern all-suite inn is perched high on a bluff overlooking the lake in downtown St. Joseph. Though it seems geared primarily to business travelers, it would be a nice option for families traveling with children. There are 82 suites, of three different sizes, each with living room and bedroom, refrigerators and wet bars, cable TV and phones. The inn's restaurant, Bistro on the Boulevard, is excellent.

The Chestnut House Bed & Breakfast, 1911 Lakeshore Drive, St. Joseph, MI 49085; 616-983-7413. Hosts Frank and Elizabeth Caré lived in England for several years, an experience that has influenced the decor and feel of their pretty B & B. It sits high on a hill across the street from the lake, with nice views from the outdoor deck and swimming pool. There are five guest rooms, each with private bath (though one is across the hall). Some rooms have whirlpool tubs or skylights. Elizabeth's flowers grace the home, even arriving on the breakfast tray in delicate little eggshells. Frank, a terrific cook, enjoys making homemade scones and other English delights for guests. Breakfast is served on fine English china in the glassed-in front porch. Hors d'ouvres are served every evening.

South Cliff Inn Bed and Breakfast, 1900 Lakeshore Drive, St. Joseph, MI 49085; 616-983-4881. With a spectacular location overlooking the lake, this B & B is the perfect place to relax and enjoy the view. There are two large decks that allow you to do just that. The seven guest rooms each have a private bath; some have fireplaces or balconies overlooking the lake. One has a whirlpool tub in the bedroom. Homemade breakfast with fresh fruit is served.

WHERE TO EAT:

Bistro on the Boulevard, 521 Lake Blvd.; 616-983-6600. This sophisticated restaurant is located in the Boulevard Inn in downtown St. Joseph. When it's warm you can dine on the outdoor patio, with a view of the river and the lake from the top of the bluff. Indoor diners also have a view of the water. The draw here is excellent, creative food and top-notch service, but no stuffiness or pretension. Chef Ali Barker, who made a name for himself in the Cleveland restaurant scene before coming to the Bistro, offers a wonderful array of appetizers like spinach fettucine with wild mushrooms or caramelized leek and onion soup, and main courses such as confit of duck or sesame-crusted halibut.

Lighthouse Depot Restaurant and Brew Pub, 1 Lighthouse Lane; 616-98-BREWS (616-982-7397). Until 1917 this historic building was the storehouse facility for St. Joseph's lighthouse. Later it was used by the Naval Reserve, Army Reserve, then the National Guard. In 1997 it opened as a restaurant and brew pub. A bright, airy atrium now separates the old building from the new addition. The atmosphere is casual, the food a mix of traditional fare like pizza or steaks and more unusual offerings like smoked shrimp spring rolls. Diners can eat outside by the river or indoors. Boaters can tie up right by the restaurant and enjoy a nice dinner al fresco. And, of course, the Depot serves its own beer.

For more information contact St. Joseph Today, 520 Pleasant Street, Suite 214, St. Joseph, MI 49085; 616-982-0032.
Internet: http://www.sjtoday.org

Along the Black River at South Haven.

South Haven

This charming little town at the mouth of the Black River has only about 5,600 permanent residents, but it swells to bursting in the summertime when vacationers arrive in search of the perfect beach holiday. And they can be pretty sure to find it here. The town's sandy white beaches are among the most beautiful along this stretch of the lake. Long known as a resort area, the town is filled with grand old Victorian homes, many of which were built to house the first vacationers. Today's accommodations are numerous, ranging from romantic "adults-only" bed and breakfasts to family-oriented motels. Restaurants are plentiful and the shopping is good.

South Haven's first white settler arrived in 1831. The business of the day was timber: logs floated down the Black River were processed at the sawmills in South Haven before being loaded onto boats and shipped to ports along the lake. Fishing and shipbuilding also had important roles. By the turn of the century South Haven was a bustling port, with ferries taking people back and forth from places like Chicago and Milwaukee. The town became popular among Chicagoans wanting to get away from the city, and its reputation as a resort quickly grew.

One such excursion ended before it began, in the worst maritime disaster in Great Lakes history. On July 24, 1915, the steamer Eastland was docked in the Chicago River, taking on 2,500 employees of the Western Electric Company who were bound for a holiday at South Haven. The ship, which had been in service for ten years, began to list almost immediately. The captain was able to right it, only to have it tilt in the other direction. Panicked passengers began to jump overboard. They were the lucky ones. Within a half-hour of boarding, the Eastland slid over on its side, trapping passengers in the cabins which were plunged into the river. More than 800 people died. The cause was never determined.

Photos of the tragedy are on display at the **Michigan Maritime Museum**, on the river by the lift bridge in South Haven (800-747-3810 or 616-637-8078). Displays at the museum also depict the history of the first known inhabitants of the area. There are dugout canoes from the 1600s and 1800s as well as a birchbark canoe. Visitors can learn about the history of wooden boat building on the Great Lakes through displays of tools and photos. For kids (and curious adults) there's a hands-on display of marine knots. A fourth-order Fresnel lens from the Detroit River is also on display at the museum. A separate building on the grounds houses three restored Coast Guard boats: a 26-foot motor surfboat, 25.5-foot pulling surfboat and a 36-foot motor lifeboat that is designed to right itself so the cabins remain watertight. Also on the grounds is an original outbuilding from the U.S. Life Saving Service station.

The town's other historical museum is the **Liberty Hyde Bailey Museum** (616-637-3251), birthplace and home of Dr. Bailey, a famous botanist and horticulturist born in 1858. On display are many of Bailey's books and the family household items, as well as period furniture and tools.

For most summer visitors, though, the beach is the main event. The **North Beach** and the **South Beach** stretch along Lake Michigan on either side of the Black River channel. Both have beautiful fine sand. There is ample parking, though a fee is charged. (Several B & Bs are within easy walking distance to the North Beach, eliminating the parking hassle altogether.) Both beaches have lifeguards, picnic tables, volleyball, rest rooms and food concessions. If the waves are rough at one beach, try the other; because they're on opposite sides of the channel breakwalls, the conditions are often different.

The breakwalls are a favorite place for walking. The south breakwall leads out to the town's 1903 lighthouse. Built to replace the original wooden tower, the bright red cylindrical cast iron light is active though now automated. The catwalk originally used to access the light tower in bad weather still stands.

Another great place for walking is **Riverfront Park** along the south side of the river. This is also a pleasant place to picnic while watching the boats go back and forth in the channel. There are rest rooms, grills, tables and a pavilion. Shady, wooded **Stanley Johnston Park**, overlooking the harbor, has picnic tables, a shelter, playground, basketball court and rest rooms.

INFORMATION PLEASE...

Looking for more? Want to find out what's happening in South Haven next month? Or when Holland's tulips will be in full bloom? One of the best ways to get up-to-date travel information about the towns along the lake's eastern shoreline is through the West Michigan Tourist Association. The association publishes two full-color guides annually, both free for the asking. The *West Michigan Travel Guide* includes an events calendar and information on lodging, campgrounds, attractions, restaurants and shopping in each town along the lake, from New Buffalo in the south to Mackinaw City at the northern tip of the Lower Peninsula. The *Lake Michigan Circle Tour and Lighthouse Guide* also has information about the towns, but with a special emphasis on the dozens of lighthouses that line the shore, including those in Wisconsin, Indiana, Illinois and Michigan's Upper Peninsula. The association also offers free travel planning assistance. Call 800-442-2084 for help or to request printed information, or check out their website at *www.wmta.org* for up-to-the-minute travel information any time of the year.

For those who want to get out on the water instead of just looking at it, there are charters and rentals available from the harbor. Several fishing fleets take folks out in search of perch, salmon and trout. Visitors can take dinner cruises and other excursions on **The White Rose** (888-828-7673 or 616-639-8404), a 50-foot boat that sails on the Black River and Lake Michigan. Sailing cruises, parasailing and boat or waverunner rentals are also available at the harbor. Contact the chamber of commerce for current listings. If you've brought your own boat, there's a public launch at **Black River Park** on Dunkley Avenue.

Cyclists and hikers will enjoy the **Kal-Haven Trail**, a 33.5-mile all-purpose recreational trail that runs from South Haven to Kalamazoo along the old Penn Central/New York Central rail line. The surface of crushed stone makes it best negotiated by mountain or hybrid bikes. In the winter it is open to cross-country skiers and snowmobiles. A trail pass is required. For more information contact Kal-Haven Trail State Park, 23960 Ruggles Road, South Haven, MI 49090; 616-637-4984.

If shopping is more your idea of fun, be sure to stop at **Old Harbor Village** on the waterfront. Designed to look like an old New England port town, this picturesque district has restaurants and a variety of unique shops connected by cobblestone walkways and boardwalks.

South Haven hosts a number of festivals each year. An integral part of the town's identity is its title of Blueberry Capital of the World, an honor celebrated annually at the **Blueberry Festival** in August. The festive event features a parade, arts and crafts fair, sand sculpture contest and lots of blueberries. South Haven's agricultural prowess is recognized also at the **Strawberry Festival** each June. Other large celebrations are **Harborfest** in June and the **Fine Arts Fair** every July 4th weekend, featuring over 100 top-notch artists from around the country.

WHERE TO STAY:

Lake Bluff Motel, 76648 11th Avenue, South Haven, MI 49090; 800-686-1305 (reservations) or 616-637-8531. Overlooking the lake south of town, Lake Bluff Motel has 49 units, some with kitchenettes and two bedrooms. Some suites have whirlpool tubs and fireplaces. Facilities include adult and children's swimming pools, hot tub, sauna, outdoor grills and picnic tables, and a recreation building with video games and ping pong table. You'll have to drive to get to downtown shops and restaurants.

The Last Resort, 86 North Shore Drive, South Haven, MI 49090; (616) 637-8943. This is South Haven's first resort inn, now carefully restored. Located in a beautiful residential area across the street from the lake, the inn is close to beaches and restaurants. The atmosphere is beach casual, with several common rooms and a large porch. There are 15 accommodations, each different, ranging from rooms with bath and double bed to an apartment and cottage. Three large penthouse rooms, each with whirlpool tub, are great for a romantic getaway or for families. (The Last Resort is an exception to the general no-kids-at-B-&-Bs rule — kids love the place, with its non-fussy and comfortable ambiance.) Continental breakfast is included. The inn is decorated with original art by owner Mary Hammer.

Old Harbor Inn, 515 Williams Street, South Haven, MI 49090; 800-433-9210 or 616-637-8480. This 37-room modern hotel overlooks the harbor on the Black River in the center of downtown. Rooms vary from basic, with a street view, up to master suites that have two bedrooms, kitchenette and a deck overlooking the water. Other rooms may have sleeper sofas, whirlpool tubs, fireplaces, balconies, microwaves or refrigerators. There is an indoor pool and sauna. The prime location and modern amenities make this a bit more expensive than most other options in South Haven.

Victoria Resort Bed and Breakfast, 214 Oak Street, South Haven, MI 49090; 800-473-7376 or 616-637-6414. Built in the early 1900s as a resort, the Victoria Resort is an 11-room inn and six cottages on three acres. It's one-and-a-half blocks from the lake and close to restaurants and shops. Rooms at the inn range from simple to luxurious with whirlpool baths and fireplaces. The cottages are two- or three-bedroom with fully equipped kitchen, phone, TV and outdoor grill and picnic table. The resort has an outdoor pool and tennis courts. This affordable resort is perfect for families.

Yelton Manor Bed & Breakfast, 140 North Shore Drive, South Haven, MI 49090; (616) 637-5220. The first thing to notice about Yelton Manor is the grounds, beautifully groomed and exploding with roses. This is actually two Victorian mansions, each with a slightly different type of accommodation. Yelton Manor occupies one. This is a traditional bed and breakfast with 11 rooms or suites, each with private bath and TV/VCR. Many have whirlpool baths, and some have fireplaces or balconies with lake views. Full breakfast is served each morning and hors d'oeuvres each evening. The other mansion houses the Manor Guest House, a more private retreat with six guest rooms. Each room is furnished in antiques and has a fireplace, whirlpool tub and TV/VCR. Two have balconies. Continental breakfast is delivered to the rooms each morning. Both are elegant places for a romantic idyll. Better not to take the kids — they'll be uncomfortable and so will everyone else.

WHERE TO EAT:

The Idler Riverboat, 515 Williams; 616-637-8435. There are actually two restaurants aboard this restored 1897 riverboat (formerly owned, in turn, by Vincent Price's father and Nabisco) docked in the heart of the shopping district at Old Harbor Village. At the Bayou Beach Club the fare is casual, with items like burgers, sandwiches and coconut shrimp. The Magnolia Grille is for the slightly more discriminating, offering cajun-inspired seafood and prime rib. Both restaurants are named in honor of the Idler's past life as a Mississippi-plying sidewheeler that used to winter in New Orleans.

Pigozzi's North Beach Inn, 51 North Shore Drive; 616-637-6738. Housed in an 1800s mansion, Pigozzi's has been an inn or restaurant — and sometimes both — since the 1920s. Open for breakfast, lunch and dinner, it features good food in a casual atmosphere for reasonable prices. The focus of the entrees is Italian, with many types of pasta dishes offered. There is an outdoor deck overlooking the water. Pigozzi's does not accept reservations; it's a popular place, so get there early.

Three Pelicans Restaurant and Pub, 38 North Shore Drive; 616-637-5123. This lively spot features upscale food with a Caribbean flare, such as grilled tuna with tropical kiwi salsa and Jamaican jerk BBQ chicken or ribs. (Though their excellent blueberry vinaigrette is no doubt locally inspired.) There's an outdoor patio and pub downstairs from the main-level dining room. The beverage menu has a good selection of beers, including some Michigan brews.

Beautiful Oval Beach at Saugatuck.

For more information contact the Greater South Haven Area Chamber of Commerce, 300 Broadway, South Haven, MI 49090, 616-637-5117; or the Lakeshore Convention and Visitors Bureau, 415 Phoenix Street, South Haven, MI 49090; 616-637-5252.
Internet: http://www.southhavenmi.com

Saugatuck/Douglas

These two towns, with a combined population of 2,000 year-round residents, are on opposite sides of the Kalamazoo River near where it empties into Lake Michigan. Saugatuck in partic-ular is a favorite destination for many. And for good reason. This beautiful little town is jam-packed with galleries, bou-tiques, restaurants, charming inns and bed and breakfasts, all lined up along the riverbank. So packed, in fact, that in the summertime it can be hard to find a parking space. Keep trying — it's worth it.

The first permanent white settlers in the area were William Gay

Butler and his wife Mary, who came from Hartford, Connecticut, in 1830. They built a log cabin in the area that is now Butler Street in Saugatuck, and began their difficult life as pioneers. Their daughter, the first white child born in the area, died when she was a year old; Mary died shortly thereafter.

William Butler and a few fellow settlers struggled on in the town they had named Kalamazoo. (The name was later usurped by the city that now bears it. Saugatuck was known for a short period as Newark until it was given its permanent name by the first postmaster.) Another settlement, known as Singapore, sprang up nearby, next to stands of virgin timber. The first sawmill was up and running by 1837.

A third settlement, Douglas, grew on the opposite side of the river. Both Douglas and Saugatuck were occupied with the lumber trade, producing wood products such as barrels and shingles. Shipbuilding also became an important industry; at one time there were three shipyards in Saugatuck, and between 1870 and 1900 more than 200 boats were built here. Saugatuck was miraculously spared the devastation of fire during the drought of 1871, when Chicago burned to the ground and most of Holland, just to the north, was destroyed. The sawmills at Singapore, Saugatuck and Douglas were kept busy supplying wood for rebuilding.

But by 1875, there was little timber left, and the sawmill at Singapore was disassembled and shipped to St. Ignace in the north. The residents of Singapore left as well, many to Saugatuck and Douglas. Without the trees to hold the land in place, the sand took over and today the place is a ghost town.

Fruit growing and tourism began to take the place of lumbering. The first tourists arrived in the early 1900s, escaping the city life in Chicago. Then groups from St. Louis and Cincinnati established summer residences here.

There was, however, a problem. The sharp turns of the Kalamazoo River made it difficult for ships carrying goods or tourists to enter or leave the harbor. In 1906 the riverbed was

The historic passenger steamer S.S. Keewatin at Douglas.

moved, making the passage much easier to navigate. It was an endeavor that changed not only the course of the river but the path of Saugatuck's history.

Everyone was happy about the improvement except the fishermen who had settled near the mouth of the river in an area called Fishtown. In a few years, the old river had closed at either end, leaving them landlocked on a small body of water that came to be known as Ox-Bow Lagoon. They left, but the lagoon wasn't totally abandoned: a group of Chicago artists founded the Summer School of Painting at the location, setting Saugatuck on its course as the Art Coast of Michigan. The school still exists, now called the **Oxbow School of Art**, operated by the Art Institute of Chicago. People come to study a variety of arts, including drawing, painting, ceramics, writing, glassblowing and performance art.

It comes as no surprise, then, that Saugatuck is filled with art. The variety is astounding. In addition to fine arts galleries and arts and crafts boutiques, there are shops specializing in custom-made leather goods, art glass, sculpture, jewelry, Native

American art, stained glass and more. Perhaps because of the focus on art, the town itself is pleasing to look at — at every turn, there's a profusion of flowers, a beautifully restored building, a green-carpeted lawn or an artful window display.

But there are plenty of other things to do besides shop and admire the art. The **Star of Saugatuck**, an authentic sternwheel paddleboat, takes visitors on a one-and-a-half-hour narrated tour of the Kalamazoo River, and out onto Lake Michigan if the weather permits. Passengers learn about Saugatuck's history and see where the ghost town of Singapore once thrived. Cruises run May through October. Call 616-857-4261 for schedules and information.

The **City of Douglas**, a 60-foot excursion boat, also offers narrated tours. The boat has a glassed-in dining room and snack bar. Scenic, lunch or dinner cruises are available. Call 616-857-2107.

For a taste of what cruising the Great Lakes was like in its heyday, tour the **S.S. Keewatin**, permanently docked at Douglas. This 350-foot steamship was built in 1907 in Glasgow, Scotland, for service in the Great Lakes. For 57 years it carried passengers and cargo until its retirement in 1965. It is now a museum, and though it has deteriorated over the years, it offers a glimpse into a chapter of Great Lakes history that will never

Exploring the dunes with Saugatuck Dune Rides.

be reopened. The Keewatin is open from Memorial Day through Labor Day weekend. Call 616-857-2464 for information.

One of the prime attractions of any lakeside town is its beach, and Saugatuck has a gorgeous one. **Oval Beach** has long been lauded as one of the most beautiful in the Midwest. Because both Saugatuck and Douglas have developed along the Kalamazoo River, Oval Beach, on Lake Michigan, is isolated from the bustle of shops and restaurants. It is on the opposite side of the river from Saugatuck, so beachgoers must either drive around, crossing the bridge at Douglas, or take the unique hand-cranked chain ferry that crosses from downtown Saugatuck. Nearby is the sand dune **Mt. Baldhead**, which energetic visitors can climb for a panoramic view of the lake and surrounding dunes. Douglas also maintains a public beach south of Oval Beach.

For a completely different experience of the dunes try the **Dune Schooner Rides** (616-857-2253) just north of town. Not for the faint-hearted, these are like roller coaster rides over sand hills and through gullies, with fast turns and skids. Fun and informative, the ride takes visitors past the ghost town of Singapore and to the top of towering dunes for magnificent views. Take your camera but keep it in a sealed plastic bag until the photo stops — while the schooners are going sand flies everywhere.

WHERE TO STAY:

Saugatuck has more than 30 bed and breakfasts alone. Needless to say, they are not all listed here. The following were chosen for their waterfront locations or some other aspect that makes them special.

BaySide Inn, 618 Water Street, PO Box 1001, Saugatuck, MI 49453; 616-857-4321. Formerly a boathouse, this casual bed and breakfast inn has a premium location right on the Kalamazoo River in the heart of downtown Saugatuck. Most of the bright, breezy rooms overlook the water. All have decks,

Visiting the dunes near Saugatuck.

private baths, television and phone. The airy common area
includes a living room, dining area, outdoor deck and hot tub.
A continental breakfast of baked goods and fruit is served
daily, and fresh cookies come out of the oven every afternoon.
Ask for a waterfront room — they're more expensive but well
worth it. No smoking is allowed.

The BeachWay Resort and Hotel, 106 Perryman Street, PO
Box 1001, Saugatuck, MI 49453; 616-857-3331. This attractive
family-oriented hotel is away from the bustle of town, overlooking the river from the opposite side and close to the road
that leads to the beach. Accommodations range from hotel
rooms to three-bedroom apartments. Not all have a view of the
water, so ask if it's important. All rooms have telephone and
cable TV with VCR. There's a video library in the lobby.
Though it's only a short way to beautiful Oval Beach, the
BeachWay has an outdoor pool.

The Landings Inn and Marina, 726 Water Street, PO Box
935, Saugatuck, MI 49453; 800-353-4550 or 616-857-4550.
Located on the river at the end of the main commercial area,
The Landings was built originally as a fishing barn. Now it's a
charming inn that doubles as a marina for guests who have
their own boat. There are four rooms, three of which overlook
the water. One has a full kitchen. The upper floor is a two-bedroom suite that can accommodate up to four people. No break-

DUNE FACTS
Did you know...

- that the Great Lakes dunes have been around for 3,000 to 4,000 years?
- that they are the largest group of freshwater coastal dunes in the world?
- that the most common mineral in Great Lakes sand is quartz, followed by feldspar?
- that the black colored sand sometimes seen along the lake shore is the mineral magnetite?
- that when conditions are right, moist sand can make a "singing" sound when walked upon?
- that the state of Michigan has 275,000 acres of sand dunes?
- that dunes are among the most fragile of habitats, vulnerable even to human footsteps?

It takes just the right combination of sand, wind, vegetation and geography for dunes to develop. In the Great Lakes region the process was set into motion some 13,000 years ago when melting glaciers washed debris from eroded bedrock into the basins that eventually formed the Great Lakes. An amazing array of life thrives in the dunes — not just beautiful and sometimes rare plant species, but toads, snakes, spiders, turtles, warblers, hawks and more.

Want to know more? These facts were taken from *Discovering Great Lakes Dunes* by Elizabeth Brockwell-Tillman and Earl Wolf of the Michigan Department of Natural Resources. This 32-page booklet describes the geological history and formation of dunes, various dune types and locations, the dune zones, the value of the dunes and how to protect them. It is illustrated throughout with stunning photographs and informative graphics. The book is available for a nominal fee from the Gillette Sand Dune Visitor Center at P.J. Hoffmaster State Park (888-224-6806), Michigan State University Extension Service offices (517-355-0240), and The Michigan Sea Grant program offices (734-764-1118 or *msgpubs@umich.edu*).

Klompen dancers in Holland.

fast is served but coffee is available. Smoking is allowed only on the spacious outdoor deck.

Maplewood Hotel, 428 Butler Street, PO Box 1059, Saugatuck, MI 49453; 800-650-9790. This beautiful old hotel is not on the water, but located in the heart of downtown Saugatuck. The Greek Revival structure was built in the 1860s as a luxury resort. It has maintained its air of elegance, from the 15 graciously appointed guest rooms to the Mitchell Lounge with its comfortable furnishings and reproducing grand piano. All rooms have private baths, TV and phones. The larger suites have fireplaces and whirlpool tubs. Continental breakfast is served in the Burr Tillstrom Dining Room, which is available for privately catered events. Other amenities include an outdoor pool, a glassed-in sun room and a library.

Rosemont Inn Resort, 83 Lakeshore Drive, PO Box 214, Saugatuck, MI 49453; 800-721-2637 or 616-857-2637. Located in a quiet area near the Douglas municipal beach on Lake Michigan, the Rosemont is a romantic, adults-only retreat. Built in the early 1900s as a boarding house for the families of loggers, it now has 14 elegant guest rooms and several appealing common areas that combine the charm of the old with the comfort of the new. All rooms have air conditioning, private baths and phones. Some have gas fireplaces. Many that face the lake have nice views, especially after the summer leaves have fallen. One of the most pleasant amenities is the whirlpool and spa area with its floor-to-ceiling windows facing out to the pool. Continental buffet breakfast is served each morning.

WHERE TO EAT:

Chequers, 220 Culver Street; 616-857-1868. This casual eatery is acclaimed for its authentic English pub food. Got a yearning for bangers and mash? Shepherd's pie? Or just ordinary fish and chips? This is the place.

Coral Gables Restaurant, 220 Water Street; 616-857-2162. Back when the Coral Gables was the Hotel Saugatuck, rooms were $5. Though prices of everything have gone up since then, this is still a reasonable place to get a meal with a waterfront view. The restaurant, which has been in the Johnson family for over 40 years, serves sandwiches, salads, pizza, pasta, seafood and meat dishes in a casual atmosphere. A large outdoor deck accommodates diners in the warm months.

Mermaid Bar and Grill, 340 Water Street; 616-857-8208. The Mermaid offers creative food in a casual setting right on the water in the heart of town. There's a good variety of salads, sandwiches and dinner entrees like garlic-teriyaki glazed tuna, Jamaican chicken, Maryland crab cakes and pecan crusted walleye. A very reasonable children's menu makes this an attractive place for families. Outdoor dining overlooking the water is available in the summer.

For more information contact the Saugatuck/Douglas Convention and Visitors Bureau, PO Box 28, Saugatuck, MI 49453; 616-857-1701.
Internet: http://www.saugatuck.com

Holland

Don't get discouraged as you drive into town past dozens of

"DeZwaan" at Windmill Island Municipal Park in Holland.

unattractive strip malls and fast food places. Downtown Holland is a gem. Immaculately kept, this small city of about 30,000 has a history that is unique among the towns that developed near or on the Lake Michigan shore.

Look at the names of the surrounding small towns — Zeeland,

Graafschap, Vriesland — and you might wonder if you're in the wrong country. Stand on Windmill Island in Holland, Mich., and gaze at the 200-year-old windmill there, and you'll feel almost certain.

Rest assured you're still in Michigan. These Dutch-founded towns owe their existence to the potato famine that raged in Europe during the 1800s. Starvation combined with religious intolerance drove a small group of people led by their minister, Albertus Van Raalte, out of the Netherlands and into a new and uncertain life in the American Midwest. They set out in 1846 for a 55-day voyage across the Atlantic, arriving in November of that year. They were taken in by sympathetic members of the Reformed Dutch Church while Van Raalte scouted sites for their permanent home. After much investigation he chose a spot several miles inland from Lake Michigan along the shores of Black Lake (now known as Lake Macatawa), then inhabited by Ottawa.

It was February 1847 before the first small group set out for their new home, leaving most of the women and children behind until the first shelters were built. It was difficult work to do in the winter and they were unskilled as builders, but by

Watching candle making at Windmill Island Municipal Park, Holland.

47

mid-March their small number had grown to 43. There was, however, little food and few supplies, since no roads had yet been built. Over the months more Dutch immigrants arrived, some expecting to find comfortable homes with groomed lawns. Instead they were faced with rough log dwellings, malaria and cholera. Many died during the summer of 1847. Conditions continued to worsen.

By the spring of 1848 the food shortage in Holland was so acute that families sent their older children to work as domestics or farmhands for American families in Grand Haven and other neighboring communities. As they learned English and grew accustomed to the American way of doing things, the gap between the Dutch and their new neighbors began to shrink. Gradually some Americans moved into the community at Holland, some businesses were established and slowly the economic picture brightened.

The community grew, pushing the Ottawa farther north to the area around Grand Traverse Bay. Growth was further aided when roads were built and the harbor on Lake Michigan was dredged, allowing goods to be transported in and out of the area more easily.

By the time the Civil War broke out, the little town was well established. Its citizens reacted with horror to the practices of slavery and supported the Union cause with fervor. Four hundred men enlisted in the army, 399 of whom had been born overseas. Sixty of them lost their lives.

By 1871, Holland was thriving with a number of small businesses. But just as prosperity seemed assured, disaster struck. It had been an unusually dry summer, and the surrounding fields were parched and brittle. The wind picked up a spark from a brush fire on the outskirts of town and before long fire raged throughout the streets, consuming the vulnerable wooden buildings like kindling on a bonfire. When it was over, 310 homes and 76 businesses had been lost.

As fate would have it, Chicago's tragic Great Fire occurred the

same night. Efforts to rebuild Holland were slowed considerably as available building materials and supplies went instead
to the larger, more important city. Holland was in dire straits
until the call for help went out to neighboring communities.
Food and money to aid the stricken town came from as far
away as Massachusetts.

Today much of Holland looks like any other small Midwestern
city. Except in spring, when it bursts into bloom with millions
of tulips. The annual **Tulip Time Festival** each May draws
hundreds of thousands of visitors and features *klompen* (wood-
en clog) dancers, parades and fireworks in addition to the stars
of the show, the tulips. In a tradition that dates from the first
tulip festival in 1929, each morning the streets are scrubbed
ceremonially by townspeople in period costume.

Tulip time or not, you can get a flavor of Holland's Dutch legacy by visiting **Windmill Island Municipal Park** (616-355-
1030). Located on an island in the Macatawa River, the park is
an oasis of green grass and flowers. In the spring, 80,000 tulips
bloom here, followed by other flower varieties as the season
progresses. The central attraction, though, is "DeZwaan," a
working Dutch windmill that was brought to Michigan in 1965
for restoration. Many of its parts are original, dating from the
1700s. It is the only genuine Dutch windmill operating in the
United States today. The short guided tour of the windmill is
well worth taking.

Just outside the windmill you can watch *klompen* dancers give
demonstrations. Other attractions include a candle-making shop,
a fudge shop and a store where you can buy Dutch goods and
flour ground by DeZwaan. Also on the grounds is the Posthouse,
a reproduction of a 14th-century Dutch inn, where visitors can
watch a video and browse a small collection of Dutch artifacts.
The park is a beautiful place to have a picnic lunch. Bring your
own or buy a snack from the concession stand there.

Plans are underway to recreate a "terp," a traditional Dutch village using authentic Dutch buildings disassembled and brought
to Windmill Island.

Other local attractions follow the Dutch theme, but on a somewhat more commercial note. **Veldheer Tulip Gardens** (616-
399-1900) not only grows tulips, they sell them, along with
wooden shoes and pottery modeled on Delftware from the
Netherlands. There's also **Dutch Village** (616-396-1475), a
theme park with traditional Dutch buildings, gardens and
canals as well as specialty shops and a Dutch restaurant. At the
Original Wooden Shoe Factory (616-396-6513), you can
watch artisans make the wooden shoes favored by the Dutch
for their leak proof quality, then wander through the Dutch
Country Store for imported cheeses and chocolates.

For a historical look at the local Dutch tradition visit the
Holland Museum at 31 West 10th Street (888-200-9123 or
616-392-9084). Here you'll find early Dutch artifacts, including furniture brought over on ships by the Dutch immigrants.
Holland's maritime history is also a theme, with attention given
to the tragedy of the Alpena, a passenger steamer that went
down near Holland in a storm during the fall of 1880.
Considered one of the worst maritime disasters on the Great
Lakes, the sinking of the Alpena claimed everyone on board, an
estimated 60 to 101 people. The museum also looks at the history of manufacturing in Holland, with displays on the Chris
Craft boat company, which had a plant here from 1929 until
1988; the Holland Furnace Company; and the Prince
Corporation, manufacturer of automotive components. Other
artifacts include pieces created in the Netherlands for the 1939
World's Fair. World War II disrupted plans to return them to
Europe, and eventually they were given to the town of Holland.
Part of the museum is reserved for changing exhibits.

The town's other historical museum is the unique **Cappon
House Museum** at 228 West 9th Street (616-392-6740). This
Italianate-style home belonged to Holland's first mayor, Isaac
Cappon, who came to Holland from the Netherlands in 1848.
His first home was destroyed in the 1871 fire. In 1874 he built
the present house at a cost of $10,000. Filled with beautiful
walnut and ash woodwork and elegant antiques, the museum is
a historical treasure. What makes it so unusual is that almost all
of the furnishings are original to the Cappon family. (Most his-

torical museums of this type are furnished with same-era artifacts, often gathered from the surrounded community, but it is
rare to find a historical home with its original furnishings
intact.) Call for hours.

While in Holland be sure to spend some time just walking
around downtown. In addition to great shopping, the area has
interesting, unique architecture, much of which has been carefully restored. The entire downtown area is on the National
Register of Historic Places. Downtown's **Centennial Park** has
fountains and flowers on four acres of greenery. Scattered
throughout the downtown area are wonderful bronze statues
erected in the 1990s. These depict various themes, from the
pleasures of music to the tenderness of a shared valentine. One
statue, Ben Franklin, sits on a bench, waiting for someone to
chat with.

Don't worry if you plan a winter walking tour just as the snow
starts to fly. The white stuff never accumulates on Holland's
downtown streets and sidewalks. No, it's not magic, it's the
largest municipally owned snow melt system in the country.
Warm water is diverted from the town's water treatment plant
then run through 60 miles of underground plastic tubing, keeping ice and snow at bay.

Near downtown is **Hope College**, founded by Van Raalte,
which is still associated with the Reformed Dutch Church. The
school's beautiful 1927 Gothic-style chapel is worth a stop.

Second to its tulips, Holland is probably best known for its
lighthouse. "**Big Red**," as it's known, is a large square structure
that has gone through several incarnations before evolving to
its present appearance in the 1930s. The house-like portion of
the building once contained boilers to power the steam fog
horn. Though the boilers are gone, the lighthouse is still active.
The best view of Big Red is from Holland State Park, north of
town on Lake Michigan. This is also the primary beach for
Holland residents. (See "Natural Attractions" in this chapter.)

Just north of the state park on Lake Shore Avenue is **Tunnel**

Park, a popular spot with beach, dune climbs, overlooks, picnic facilities and children's play area. It is named for the tunnel that leads under a sand dune to the beach.

Further along Lake Shore Avenue, about halfway to Grand Haven, is **Kirk Park**, with 2,000 feet of Lake Michigan shoreline, picnic area with shelter, hiking trails and dune overlooks.

During the winter nearby **Pigeon Creek Park** has cross-country skiing on marked and groomed trails. Equipment rental and lessons are available. The park's lodge is open on weekends. For more information on these three county parks contact the Ottawa County Parks and Recreation Commission at 616-846-8117.

A bike path stretches for nearly 20 miles along the lake shore from Holland State Park north to Grand Haven. Running parallel to Lake Shore Avenue, the paved path offers access to Tunnel Park and Kirk Park, with great scenery along the way.

WHERE TO STAY:

Centennial Inn, 8 East 12th Street, Holland, MI 49423; 616-355-0998. Located on a residential street in the heart of the town near Hope College, this bed and breakfast inn was once Holland's first hospital. Later it was the location of the Netherlands Museum. Today it is an elegant place for visitors to stay. Eight rooms in two buildings offer a variety of accommodations, all with unique furnishings and decor. Each has a private bath, phone, TV and air conditioning; some have fireplaces, and one has a whirlpool tub. Hosts Rein and Kay Wolfert serve a full breakfast.

The Dutch Colonial Inn, 560 Central Avenue, Holland, MI 49423; 616-396-3664. This spacious, lovely 1928 home is located in a residential area close to downtown. There are four guest rooms, each with private bath and Jacuzzi tub, phone and TV. The large common sitting room has a fireplace and beautiful furnishings for atmosphere, and a refrigerator and microwave for convenience. Rooms are stocked with homemade cookies, and a full breakfast is served in the elegant for-

The lighthouses at Grand Haven.

mal dining room. Hosts Pat and Bob Elenbaas are warm and gracious. The many antiques and fragile items make this a place best suited for adults.

North Shore Inn, 686 North Shore Drive, Holland, MI 49424; 616-394-9050. A restored 1900s home, the North Shore Inn is on two quiet acres of Lake Macatawa waterfront. There are three guest rooms furnished with antiques and handmade quilts. Two rooms have a lake view; two have private baths. Hosts Beverly and Kurt Van Genderen serve a three-course gourmet breakfast. Bikes are available free of charge. This is a no-smoking inn not suited to children under 12.

WHERE TO EAT:

Holland has an impressive selection of restaurants serving great food. Here are just a couple:

Alpen Rose, 8th and Central; 616-393-2111. This popular downtown restaurant has three sections: the Cafe Konditorei for casual, fast service; the Kitzbuhel Room for family dining; and the Salzburg Room for a more formal atmosphere. The restaurant features American and Bavarian food, with unusual items like grilled wild boar chops or ragout of rabbit with wild mushroom sauce. Diners with less exotic tastes will probably lean more toward the wiener schnitzel and bratwurst.

Piper Restaurant, 2225 South Shore Drive; 616-335-5866. This is the place for waterfront dining. There's not a bad seat in the house in this restaurant overlooking Lake Macatawa. The ultra-modern interior comes as a pleasant surprise in a town filled with traditional design and architecture. The walls are covered with intriguing art, much of it for sale. The main attraction, though, is the food, and here you can't go wrong. The moderately priced menu features wood-fired pizza, appetizers like shrimp bruschetta or goat cheese torta, and seafood, steak and pasta entrees. Try the Bayside Stew, a tasty concoction of sea scallops, shrimp, mussels and yellowfin tuna in caramelized tomato broth with onions, mushrooms, garlic and redskin potatoes. Finally, DO NOT miss the rum vanilla caramel flan. Forget the diet just this once.

For more information contact the Holland Area Convention and Visitors Bureau, 76 East 8th Street, Holland, MI 49423;

800-506-1299 or 616-394-0000.
Internet: http://www.holland.org

Grand Haven

Located along the south shore of the Grand River near where it empties into Lake Michigan, Grand Haven is a lively town of about 12,000. Not dependent entirely on the tourist trade, Grand Haven has some manufacturing and its port is a working one. But the town is also well equipped for tourists, especially with its long boardwalk along the river leading out to the lighthouse pier.

The history of Grand Haven parallels that of many other lake towns. Before the arrival of Europeans, the area was inhabited by Ottawa, Chippewa and Potawatomi villages. Fur traders were the first white people to come, and soon thereafter a post was established for John Jacob Astor's American Fur Company. Permanent settlers arrived in 1834, and with them logging began. When the timber was gone fruit trees were planted. Agriculture still plays a big part in the local economy. Tourism's roots stretch back to the late 1800s, when magnetic mineral water was discovered underground here. Touted for its medicinal abilities, the water was the main appeal of several health spas that drew hundreds of visitors. The spas are gone, but other attractions have taken their place.

Many of these are by the **Boardwalk**, which runs for 2.5 miles along the river and out to the pier. The walkway begins at **Chinook Pier**, where charter fishing boats are docked, then leads past shops, restaurants, marinas, the beach and finally to Grand Haven's two lighthouses. The outer light is housed in a large square building, constructed in 1875, that once held giant boilers to power the fog signal. The inner light, erected in 1905, is the more common lighthouse shape — a conical tower — in this case built of cast iron. These are connected by a catwalk, originally used to move from one light to another during bad weather. The purpose of having two lights was so that boat captains could line them up visually in order to navigate into the channel. This is one of only two places on the lake, the other being St. Joseph, where two lighthouses remain. Both Grand Haven lights are painted a brilliant bright red.

On the boardwalk in town is the **Tri-Cities Museum** (616-842-0700), located in the old Grand Trunk Railroad depot built in 1870. The museum focuses on the history of Grand Haven and the other two communities that make up the Tri-City area — Spring Lake and Ferrysburg. In addition to displays depicting early settlers' lives in the area, the museum devotes attention to the U.S. Coast Guard, which has had a station in Grand Haven for more than 75 years.

A plaque along the boardwalk near the Coast Guard Station commemorates the Coast Guard cutter Escanaba, whose home port was Grand Haven. In 1943 the cutter was sunk by a German submarine in the North Atlantic while escorting a convoy from Greenland to Newfoundland. Only two crew members survived. The townspeople raised over a million dollars toward the commissioning of a second Escanaba. In 1987 the Escanaba III was commissioned at Grand Haven. It is now stationed in Boston. Every August Grand Haven celebrates its close ties to the Coast Guard with the **Coast Guard Festival**, a week-long event that features arts and crafts, family activities, a parade and fireworks.

It may not be a Coast Guard cutter, but the **Harbor Steamer** (616-842-8950) is one way to get out onto the water. Docked at Chinook Pier, this sternwheel paddleboat takes visitors for cruises along the Grand River and into nearby Spring Lake.

Also along the boardwalk is **Waterfront Stadium**, with seating for 2,400, the place to view Grand Haven's unique **Musical Fountain**. The fountain, constructed in 1953, is a synchronized music, light and water show that takes place every evening during the summer. Said to be the world's largest such fountain, it pumps 40,000 gallons of water through 8,000 feet of pipe to send streams 125 feet into the air. For more information and a schedule call 616-842-4910 or 616-842-2550.

Just off the boardwalk downtown is **Harbourfront Place**, a popular shopping and restaurant complex in a renovated Story and

Clark piano factory.

Beachgoers will find a sandy haven (though often crowded in summer) just south of the boardwalk at **Grand Haven State Park**. This small park consists entirely of a beach campground and a swimming beach with fine white sand. (For camping information see "Natural Attractions" at the end of this chapter.) The city also maintains a public beach with parking south of the state park.

Another park to visit, though not on the waterfront, is **Mulligan's Hollow**, south of the downtown area. In the winter it's alive with people skating on the outdoor rink or skiing down its slopes. During the summer it's a pleasant, shady place to picnic. It's also the location of the **Imagination Station**, a 10,000-square-foot play area designed by kids.

Across the Grand River from town is the 112-acre **Dunes Preserve**. This undeveloped dune wilderness was set aside in 1971. The **Connie Lindquist Trail** runs through the dunes. A brochure/guide is available from the City of Ferrysburg (616-842-5950).

Most attractions in Grand Haven and the communities of Spring Lake and Ferrysburg are connected by the convenient, inexpensive **Harbor Trolley**, which runs Memorial Day through Labor Day. For schedules or a route map call 616-842-3200.

For those who like to get around on their own two wheels, Ottawa County has more than 100 miles of bicycle paths. One popular route runs parallel to the Lake Michigan shoreline for nearly 20 miles from Grand Haven to Holland. For more information and a map of bike trails throughout Ottawa County contact the visitors bureau at 800-303-4096.

WHERE TO STAY:

Harbor House Inn, 114 S. Harbor Drive, Grand Haven, MI 49417; 800-841-0610 or 616-846-0610. This pretty, pastel Victorian inn overlooks the Grand River about a half-mile from the beach. There are 17 guest rooms, each with private bath. Some have whirlpool tubs or fireplaces. A continental breakfast buffet is served. This is a nice place to stay if you want to be right in town.

Khardomah Lodge, 1365 Lake Avenue, Grand Haven, MI 49417; 616-842-2990. Built in 1873, this charming rustic inn is recognized by the state of Michigan as a historical landmark. The interior exudes warmth, with its beautiful wood paneling and floors, open spaces and stone fireplace. There are 16 guest rooms, accommodating one to four people each, that share five bathrooms. The lodge can be rented by a family of other group, who then have the option of cooking meals in the lodge kitchen or arranging for catering. The lodge is in a quiet area within walking distance to restaurants, shops and the beach.

Lakeshore Bed and Breakfast, 11001 Lakeshore Drive, Grand Haven Twp., MI 49460; 800-3-Hansen or 616-844-2697. Dan Hansen has a passion for presidential memorabilia, which he has been collecting since high school. So it seems fitting that he and his wife Jaclyn have made it the theme of their luxuri-

Climbing Mt. Baldy at Indiana Dunes National Lakeshore.

ous lakeside bed and breakfast. There are three guest rooms in this large 1935 house, each spacious and beautifully decorated, with a private bath and Jacuzzi tub, CD player, TV with VCR and air conditioning. Former President Gerald Ford actually slept in the Ford Suite. If you can afford it, go for the Presidential Suite, which has a spectacular view of the lake from the extra-large whirlpool tub. The Hansens serve a full breakfast on White House china. Be sure to ask to see some of Dan's collection, including Ford's autographed golf ball and the lock of George Washington's hair. Lakeshore, which is located in a quiet residential area about five miles south of Grand Haven, has its own private beach. In addition to the B & B rooms, a cottage and bungalow are also available. A small, enclosed outdoor kitchen is perched at the edge of the hill over-looking the water. This cozy little amenity has a commercial grill, indoor table and deck.

The Looking Glass Inn, 1100 South Harbor, Grand Haven, MI 49417; 800-951-6427 or 616-842-7150. Once a summer cottage, the Looking Glass Inn is now a casual bed and breakfast. Perched high on a hill overlooking the lake, the dunes and the lighthouse, it has four guest rooms, each with private bath and cable TV. The large front deck has a beautiful water view. There's also a solarium with hot tub. Hosts Norma and Howie Glass serve a full buffet breakfast.

Seascape Bed and Breakfast, 20009 Breton, Spring Lake, MI 49456; 616-842-8409. This casual B & B is located on Lake Michigan on the north side of the Grand River. There are three accommodations, each with private bath and lake view. The Harborside Suite has two bedrooms and a sitting room with private access to a patio and path leading down to the private beach. Full breakfast is served.

WHERE TO EAT:

Bil Mar Restaurant, 1223 Harbor Drive; 616-842-5920. This is the place in Grand Haven for lake view dining. Located on the beach south of the state park, Bil Mar has a great view of the water, the lighthouses and the often-spectacular sunsets.

West Beach at Indiana Dunes National Lakeshore.

The menu is primarily seafood and meat, with perch a specialty. Other entrees include frog legs, duck, rack of lamb and chicken Kiev. There's a nice wine list, including a good selection of Michigan wines. Get there early or have a reservation; this is a popular place. Outdoor dining is available. Open for lunch and dinner.

Snug Harbor, 311 S. Harbor Drive; 616-846-8400. A casual place overlooking the river on the downtown waterfront, Snug Harbor leans toward Mexican food with items like burritos, enchiladas and nachos. But for those with other tastes, there's plenty to choose from — sandwiches, burgers, salads, steak, chicken, seafood and pasta. The heated outdoor deck is open through October, and the restaurant itself is open seven days a week all year, serving lunch and dinner.

For more information contact the Grand Haven/Spring Lake Visitors Bureau, 1 South Harbor Drive, PO Box 509, Grand Haven, MI 49417; 800-303-4096 or 616-842-4910.
Internet: http://www.grandhavenchamber.org

Natural Attractions

INDIANA DUNES NATIONAL LAKESHORE

Just north of Gary, Indiana, begin the Lake Michigan sand dunes that extend all the way up the coast of the Michigan's Lower Peninsula, making them the largest collection of fresh water sand dunes in the world. The southern portion of the dunes, within the reach of Gary's smokestacks, has been saved from being engulfed by industry through the efforts of conservationists and concerned politicians. Indiana Dunes National Lakeshore is a natural haven at the edge of urban sprawl.

In 1916 the director of the newly formed National Park Service, Stephen T. Mather, launched an effort to establish Sand Dunes National Park. He was unsuccessful, but a toehold was gained with the establishment of Indiana Dunes State Park in 1923. During the war years, when steel was a vital to the war effort, steel mills sprang up in the dunes area. Later conservationist Dorothy Buell, joined by Illinois Senator Paul H. Douglas, mounted a crusade to save the dunes from further encroachment. In 1966 Congress authorized the establishment of Indiana Dunes National Lakeshore, one of two national parks on Lake Michigan. (The other is Sleeping Bear Dunes National Lakeshore in the northern Lower Peninsula.)

Today both the state park and the steel mills remain, surrounded by the pristine dunes of the national park, with its 15 miles of shoreline and approximately 15,000 acres of land. Facilities and recreational opportunities at the park are many and varied, and include swimming, camping and hiking. There are also a number of historical sites in the park.

For those interested in nature, Indiana Dunes offers some amazing discoveries. The park is rated fourth in plant diversity among American national parks, with such unusual plant species as prickly pear cactus and three types of carnivorous plants. The third-largest population of the endangered Karner blue butterfly lives in the park, attracted by the profusion of lupine plants.

Begin your visit at the **Dorothy Buell Memorial Visitor Center**. There you can obtain park maps and information. The center also has a theater where visitors can watch a slide show overview of the park and a bookstore that sells materials about the park and natural history.

If it's a beach you're after, there are several choices. Farthest to the west is **West Beach**, the park's most popular beach and the only one that is lifeguarded. There is a fee for parking (the only fee incurred in the park, unless you go into the state park). The beach has a bathhouse, picnic area and food concession, and several hiking trails nearby. To the east, beyond the steel mills and municipal land, is **Porter Beach**, with bathhouse and concession nearby. **Kemil Beach** and **Central Beach**, both farther east, have rest rooms.

Hikers will find approximately 40 miles of trails in the park, through varied terrain and habitats. The mile-long **West Beach Succession Trail** winds from the beach inland, through dunes, past an intradunal pond, into a pine grove, past a sand blowout

A WORD OF CAUTION...

All up and down the shore of Lake Michigan are piers and breakwalls leading out into the lake, often to picturesque lighthouses. These can be wonderful places for walking, but some common sense is called for. Many breakwalls have rough surfaces that can make for tricky walking. All can be slippery when wet. Some are simply rocks piled to form a line, and these shouldn't be negotiated at all. Even smooth concrete piers should not be walked when waves are high or winds are strong. People have been washed from piers and in some cases have drowned as a result. Unseen hazards like currents, cables, rocks or concrete pilings can spell disaster if you should happen to slip or fall off a pier. If conditions aren't calm, save your pier walk for another day. And even under the calmest conditions, exercise caution.

and through an oak forest. The succession, a process by which a group of plants and animals living in a particular place is gradually replaced by different species, was first studied here in the Indiana dunes. In the early 1900s University of Chicago professor Henry Chandler Cowles used the area as a natural laboratory for his work with plant succession, gaining recognition for both his theory and the dunes themselves. The area became known as the birthplace of modern ecology. Today's visitor can trace some of Cowles' work along this trail.

Much can be learned about dune vegetation and trees along the **Calumet Dune Trail** near the Dorothy Buell Memorial Visitor Center. This half-mile trail leads through open sand, forest, meadow and wetlands. A interpretive guide is available at the center.

For those who want to experience dunes in the most exhausting way possible, there's the short but excruciatingly steep **Mt. Baldy Trail**, leading to the top of the park's largest living dune. From the top there's a spectacular view of the dunes, the beach and the lake. Mt. Baldy and the dunes on the West Beach Succession Trail are the only dunes in the park where climbing is allowed. Visitors are asked to stay off the other dunes because their fragile nature makes them easily damaged by trampling.

If history is your interest, don't miss the **Bailly/Chellberg Trail** near the center of the park. The first of the historical sites is the **Bailly Homestead** established in 1822 by a French Canadian fur trader and his wife. Bailly traded with the Ottawa and Potawatomi Indians who brought him beaver, mink and muskrat skins in return for blankets, threads and other goods. When fur trading declined, Bailly sought to plan a town nearby, but died before his efforts were complete. What was slated to be Baillytown is now occupied by Bethlehem Steel. Buildings remaining at the homestead site include a cabin, kitchen/chapel and two houses, all built by the original Bailly's descendants. The cemetery where the Baillys are buried is at the end of a spur off the main trail.

Farther along the trail is the **Chellberg Farm**, established by
Swedish immigrants Anders and Johanna Kjellberg in 1872.
The Kjellbergs were part of a small Swedish community that
once flourished here. Many of the original farm buildings
remain, including the main house, a maple sugar house, the
barn and the chicken house. It's still a working farm to some
extent. Small plots of crops are planted, as well as a garden.
Farm animals are housed and raised here, much to the delight
of the urban students who often visit.

There are many other park trails; full information is available
from the park office or at the visitor center. Horses may be ridden only on the **Ly-co-ki-we Trail.** Cyclists can use the
Calumet Bike Trail, which follows a flat route for about 10
miles alongside the Chicago South Shore and South Bend
Railroad Tracks. During the winter there are several trails open
to cross-country skiers but no snowmobiles are permitted.

A fascinating historical site is accessible by car at **Beverly
Shores** on Lakeshore Drive in the east end of the park. Most of
this exclusive residential area bordering the lake is private, but
there are several homes that belong to the National Park
Service. (These are nonetheless occupied and are off-limits to
visitors except to view from the road.) These unusual structures
were built for the 1933 World's Fair in Chicago. Architects
from around the country sought to follow the fair's theme of "A
Century of Progress" by showcasing designs for the future. Six
homes were later moved to their present location to lure buyers
for a new real estate development. One is a porcelain-finished
steel frame house built with economy in mind. Another, the
House of Tomorrow, was equipped with such modern novelties
as central air conditioning, a dishwasher, and electric garage
door opener. The garage was built to house what were assumed
to be the everyday vehicles of the future — both a car and private airplane. Over the years the houses have taken something
of a beating from the climate but are now gradually being
restored.

Dunewood Campground is located about a mile and a half
from Lake Michigan and about two miles east of the visitor

Van Buren State Park.

center. There are 79 campsites, 54 of them conventional drive-in sites and the rest walk-in sites. There are rest rooms and showers but no electrical hookups.

Picnic facilities are spread throughout the park. Fishing is permitted, though a Indiana fishing license is required. There are no boat launches in the park, but there are several in nearby communities.

For more information contact Indiana Dunes National Lakeshore, 1100 North Mineral Springs Road, Porter, IN 46304-1299; 219-926-7561.

WARREN DUNES STATE PARK

Visit Warren Dunes on a windy day in spring or fall and you're likely to have a surprise — colorful hang gliders drifting from the top of 240-foot-high Tower Hill. This is the only park in the Michigan state system that allows hang gliding. For its combination of lake winds and high dunes, it's considered to be the best place for the sport in the Midwest.

It's the dunes that give the place its drama. They stretch along the length of the park, framing the 2.5 miles of sandy beach, several of them rising more than 200 feet. It is possible to climb the towering dunes near the beach area, an activity especially enjoyed by children and teens.

The beach is quite large and quite popular. Three bathhouses and stores accommodate the many summer visitors who come to enjoy the vast expanse of sand. Nearby is a shaded picnic area with shelters.

Hikers will find more than five miles of maintained trails throughout the 1,952-acre park, though the most popular is probably the mile-long **Warren Dunes Nature Trail**. This loop passes through dunes and forest, and gives hikers the opportunity to climb Mt. Randall for a spectacular view of the lake. A brochure, available at the park entrance, gives information on 10 points of interest along the trail.

There is one campground in the park, set back from the lake in a wooded dune area, with 180 modern sites with electricity. There are also three mini-cabins, with electricity, that can sleep four people each.

Those wishing to hang glide at the park must be certified and must purchase a permit. For more information contact the park office.

Winter activities at Warren Dunes include cross-country skiing along the park's three miles of relatively flat but ungroomed ski trails.

For more information contact Warren Dunes State Park, 12032 Red Arrow Highway, Sawyer, MI 49125; 616-426-4013.

GRAND MERE STATE PARK

This 985-acre undeveloped unit is for day use only. The park consists of dunes, woods, two miles of Lake Michigan shore and three interdunal lakes — North, Middle and South Lakes.

The beach, which has no facilities, is a half-mile walk from the parking lot. There is a half-mile barrier-free nature trail that begins at the South Lake picnic area, which is also near the parking lot. Several other trails wind through the park, but they are not marked or maintained.

Fishing is allowed on North Lake and Middle Lake, but there is no access to South Lake. In the winter, the park is open to cross-country skiers, but the trails are not groomed and there is no concession.

For more information contact Grand Mere State Park, 12032 Red Arrow Highway, Sawyer, MI 49125; 616-426-4013.

VAN BUREN STATE PARK

Located just south of South Haven, this 407-acre park consists of dunes, a mile of sandy Lake Michigan beach and a 220-site campground. The beach, reached by a cement walkway between two large dunes, has a bathhouse and concession. The nearby picnic area is grassy and shaded, and equipped with

Grand Haven State Park.

67

grills and tables.

The campground, which is set back from the beach, has both shaded and open sites, all of them with electrical hookups. There are modern shower and toilet facilities, though these are open only until mid-October. The park stays open to campers until December but the only facilities available are vault toilets, water, and electricity at the sites.

There is no boat launch in the park, nor are there maintained trails.

For more information contact Van Buren State Park, 23960 Ruggles Road, South Haven, MI 48740; 616-637-2788.

SAUGATUCK DUNES STATE PARK

This 1000-acre park north of Saugatuck is for day use only. Its main features are 2.5 miles of Lake Michigan shoreline and 13 miles of hiking and cross-country ski trails. The park is secluded and quiet, the beach even more so since a mile-long hike over dunes is required to get to it from the parking lot. The landscape varies from sand to forested dunes, some rising 200 feet above the lake. The south portion of the park is a 300-acre natural area containing a coastal dune system and several endangered plant species. There is a picnic area with grills and a shelter near the parking lot and trail heads; this is the only developed area in the park.

The network of trails is divided into three sections, all of which are accessed from the parking lot. The **North Trail** has two loops, both leading to a view of the lake. The **Beach Trail** leads to the swimming beach, but also has connecting spurs to the **North Trail** and the **South Trail**. The 5.5-mile South Trail, the park's longest loop, winds through the natural area. Off of it is the **Livingston Trail**, a one-way, mile-long trek to a bluff high over the water. This is considered the park's most difficult trail. Trail maps are available at the park entrance.

During the winter all trails are groomed and open to cross-

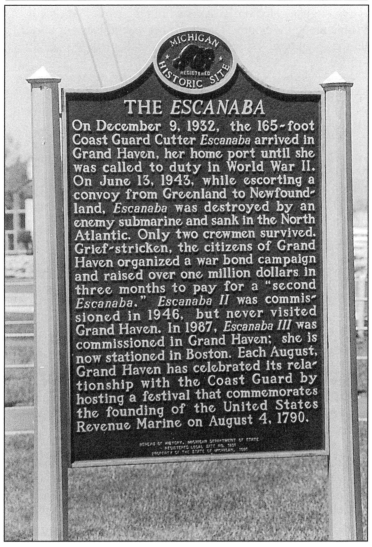

THE *ESCANABA*

On December 9, 1932, the 165-foot Coast Guard Cutter *Escanaba* arrived in Grand Haven, her home port until she was called to duty in World War II. On June 13, 1943, while escorting a convoy from Greenland to Newfoundland, *Escanaba* was destroyed by an enemy submarine and sank in the North Atlantic. Only two crewmen survived. Grief-stricken, the citizens of Grand Haven organized a war bond campaign and raised over one million dollars in three months to pay for a "second *Escanaba*." *Escanaba II* was commissioned in 1946, but never visited Grand Haven. In 1987, *Escanaba III* was commissioned in Grand Haven; she is now stationed in Boston. Each August, Grand Haven has celebrated its relationship with the Coast Guard by hosting a festival that commemorates the founding of the United States Revenue Marine on August 4, 1790.

Historical marker commemorating the Escanaba at Grand Haven.

country skiers, though the steep terrain here makes them most appropriate for advanced skiers.

Michigan Dunes State Correctional Facility, a minimum security prison, is located on 50 acres within the park. Part of it is visible along the South Trail, but otherwise it does not intrude on the serenity of the setting.

For more information contact Saugatuck Dunes State Park, Ottawa Beach Road, Holland, MI 49424; 616-399-9390.

HOLLAND STATE PARK

At 142 acres, Holland State Park is small compared to most Michigan state parks, but it draws an enormous number of visitors in the summer months. Located on the north side of Lake Macatawa and along the channel that leads to Lake Michigan, the park consists almost entirely of a 1,800-foot Lake Michigan beach and two campgrounds.

The wide, sandy beach has the best view available of "Big Red," Holland's famous lighthouse. This active lighthouse is unusual for its large, square lower portion, which once housed giant boilers to heat the steam used to power the fog horn. Its vivid red color stands out brightly from the beach and dunes beyond it, adding to the picturesque quality of this pretty park.

In addition to the beach, the day-use area has picnic tables and grills, children's play equipment, a picnic shelter, bathhouse, beach shelter and concession. Get there early on weekends in the summer, as the parking lot often fills.

Fishing is popular along the channel pier, where anglers often catch perch in the summer or salmon, trout and steelhead in the spring and fall. For fishermen with their own boats, there is a launch on Lake Macatawa, from which there is easy access to Lake Michigan.

The **Lake Macatawa Campground** has 211 sites along the smaller lake, while the **Lake Michigan Campground** has 98 sites set back from the Lake Michigan beach. Much of the Lake Macatawa Campground and all of the Lake Michigan Campground is wide open with no shade. The Lake Michigan campground is asphalt, divided into sites. Both campgrounds have electrical hookups and modern toilet and shower facilities. The Lake Macatawa Campground is open April 1 through October; the Lake Michigan Campground is open from Holland's Tulip Time festival through Labor Day weekend.

For more information contact Holland State Park, Ottawa Beach Road, Holland, MI 49424; phone 616-399-9390.

GRAND HAVEN STATE PARK

This tiny park of only 48 acres is almost entirely beach and campground. Within walking distance from downtown Grand Haven, it is extremely popular, drawing visitors from among the town residents and tourists as well as the campers at the park itself. It is bordered at its north end by the scenic board-walk that leads from the lighthouse pier along the Grand River to the downtown shops and restaurants.

The 2,500 feet of lake frontage attract many swimmers and sunbathers who come to enjoy the fine white sand. Though there is parking for 800 cars, the lot sometimes fills in the summer. There's usually parking available downtown, however, and the tourist trolley will take you to the beach for a nominal fee. The day-use area has picnic facilities, a bathhouse, children's play equipment and a food concession.

For campers there are 174 modern sites on concrete, some just back from the water. There are no trees in the park, and therefore no shade and little privacy. The campground is open from April to November, with electricity and water provided, but rest room facilities are closed in mid-October. The campground is very popular and it is unlikely you will find an open spot in the busy summer months without making prior reservations.

The adjacent lighthouse pier is popular among fishermen, who bring in perch during the summer and salmon, steelhead and trout during the spring and fall. There is no boat launch at the park, but launching is available in the city. Grand Haven is also home port to several fishing charters.

For more information contact Grand Haven State Park, 1001 Harbor Ave., Grand Haven, MI 49417; 231-798-4470.

P.J. HOFFMASTER STATE PARK

The predominant feature of this 1,043-acre park near Muskegon is its dunes. This may be the best place to view a part of Michigan's most unusual natural feature, the world's largest area of fresh water sand dunes. It certainly is the best place to learn about them. The park's **E. Genevieve Gillette Sand Dune Visitor Center**, named for a noted Michigan conservationist, is dedicated to educating the public about the origin and preservation of Great Lakes dunes. Aside from their great beauty, what makes them unique is the rich assortment of natural communities living so close to one another. From the almost sterile desert of sand near the water, to wetlands and shady forest, the dunes change in both appearance and inhabitants as they progress inland. You can see all the dune environments by walking the miles of trails at P.J. Hoffmaster. Each May, when trilliums carpet the wooded dunes, the park hosts its annual **Trillium Festival**, which includes guided hikes, displays and special slide presentations.

From the visitor center, walkers can access the **Dune Climb Stairway**, a 165-step wooden staircase to a viewing platform perched on a dune nearly 200 feet above the lake. There are dunes in every direction, undisturbed by everything but the forces of nature. Ten miles of trails lead through the park's dunes and along 2.5 miles of Lake Michigan beach. All of the park, in fact, is connected by trails, from the designated natural area on the southern side to the wooded picnic areas, the day-use beach and the campground to the north. If you have only a short time to visit the park, stop first at the visitor center, then hike through the dunes down to the lake and back, a trip of about three-quarters of a mile.

Even if you are unable to walk the dune trails, the view from the visitor center is impressive. Tucked down into a valley, the building is dwarfed by the dunes surrounding it; the large windows facing one towering dune offer a stunning sight. There is also a barrier-free trail that leads from the visitor center a short way into the dunes. The focal point of the center is a 82-seat theater where visitors can view multi-image slide shows on dune ecology and the Great Lakes. There is also a gallery displaying art inspired by wildlife and the lake shore. The center's classroom features hands-on exhibits including live specimens of snakes, turtles, frogs and other animals found in the park.

The day-use beach, north of the natural area, has ample parking (though the lot can still fill on a summer weekend), a bathhouse, concession and picnic facilities. There are other picnic areas and a shelter inland from the lake near the visitor center.

The campground is located at the north end of the park in a forested area that offers good shade. There are 293 sites with electrical hookups. Modern toilet/shower facilities are provided. It's about a quarter-mile walk from the campground to the campers' beach.

During the winter three miles of trails are open to cross-country skiing. Hills make these trails best suited to intermediate skiers. Snowmobiles are not permitted in the park. Bicycles are restricted to roadways.

For more information contact P.J. Hoffmaster State Park, 6585 Lake Harbor Road, Muskegon, MI 49441; 616-798-3711.

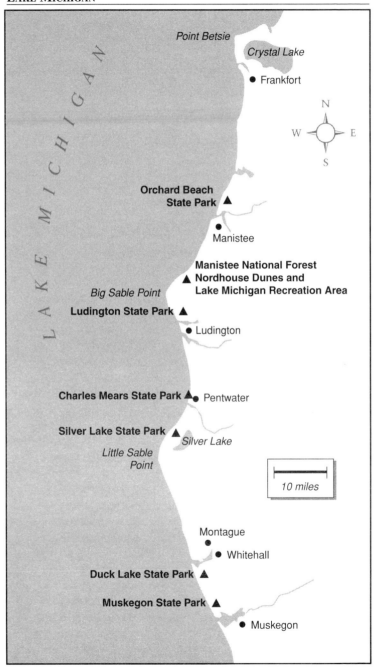

Point Betsie

Crystal Lake

● Frankfort

N
W ← → E
S

Orchard Beach
State Park ▲

●
Manistee

Manistee National Forest
▲ **Nordhouse Dunes and**
Lake Michigan Recreation Area

Big Sable Point

Ludington State Park ▲

● Ludington

Charles Mears State Park ▲● Pentwater

Silver Lake State Park ▲

Silver Lake

Little Sable
Point

10 miles

Montague
●
● Whitehall

Duck Lake State Park ▲

Muskegon State Park ▲

● Muskegon

Chapter

T W O

MICHIGAN'S MIDDLE LOWER PENINSULA

Lumber Barons and Golden Sand

Moving further up the Michigan shoreline the towns begin to take on a different character. Out of the range of Chicagoans looking for a weekend getaway, these are places with less of a tourist atmosphere. In most, there are fewer trendy shops or galleries. The restaurants, beyond the reach of Chicago chic, are far less likely to offer exotic fare, though you'll find plenty of expertly prepared Lake Michigan fish. In general the accommodations, though plentiful and pleasant, are both simpler and less expensive.

This was lumber country, rapidly settled, made wildly prosperous, exploited thoughtlessly, and by the beginning of the 20th century, stripped of both its beauty and its primary resource. The towns, bereft of their main source of income, were forced to look elsewhere. Some turned to industry, others to tourism. Some were more successful than others, whichever path they chose.

Today, the trees are back, though not in the number they once were. Muskegon, Ludington and Manistee depend largely on industry, though all draw tourists as well. Muskegon is by far the largest Michigan town on the lake, larger, in fact, than it was during the lumber industry's heyday. Evidence of the era when Muskegon was the "Lumber Queen" abound, largely through the legacy of lumber baron Charles Hackley. His magnificent home is reason enough to visit the town, though history buffs in particular will find many more sites of interest.

Ludington chose a different tack after the demise of lumber. A railroad terminus with an excellent harbor, Ludington found its niche in trans-lake shipping, serving as home port to a fleet of car ferries that carried cargo across the lake to Wisconsin. But by the mid-20th century, the rise in trucking had put a serious dent in over-water shipping, and the ferries ceased operation. A vestige of this era lives on in Ludington — the last of the car ferries, now converted for passenger use. The S.S. Badger, a 410-foot behemoth, makes daily crossings, carrying passengers across the lake, shaving off 410 miles of driving and offering both modern amenities and a unique historical experience.

Like Muskegon and Ludington, Manistee has also made the transition to modern industry, but with a difference: it is the best preserved of the old lumber towns, a model of the Midwest Victorian era. The entire downtown has been designated an historic area, and the citizens are constantly busy restoring and preserving their beautiful town along the Manistee River.

The smaller towns of Whitehall, Montague, Pentwater and Frankfort are mainly tourist towns, quiet and quaint. All of these places, big and small, tourist areas or not, have beautiful beaches, one after another, all the way up the Michigan shore.

But there is no sand quite like what you'll find between Lake Michigan and Silver Lake in Oceana County — 2,000 acres of rolling dunes, three miles long by more than a mile wide, towering over the two lakes. It is a magical landscape, reflected in shimmering blue water, better suited to the Sahara Desert than the American Midwest. There is no place quite like it anywhere else on the lake.

Don't let the more industrial nature of this part of the shoreline stop you from meandering around here. Mid-Michigan may offer the best of both worlds — fascinating historical sites and mile after mile of gorgeous beaches — all at affordable prices.

Muskegon

With a population of just over 40,000, Muskegon is the largest Michigan town on the lake. It occupies a prominent place in lake history, especially for its brief and meteoric rise to prosperity during the lumber boom.

The town is located on Muskegon Lake, whose short channel empties into Lake Michigan. The smaller lake is the terminus of the Muskegon River, the most important river in the northern part of Michigan's lower peninsula. It was a major travel artery for the Indians who inhabited the area, and with the arrival of Europeans it became an important center for fur trading. For the people who came later, the river's most important attribute was its meandering route through a great forest.

In 1837 the first sawmill was built where the town stands today. By the close of the Civil War, settlers were looking at the vast stands of trees upriver from Muskegon with dollar signs in their eyes, and the forest's wholesale destruction was complete within a single generation. By 1883 there were 47 sawmills around Muskegon Lake and 40 millionaires in town. In 1887 the area produced 665 million feet of lumber, but by 1897 only 25 million were produced. The last sawmill closed shop in 1907. A journalist for the Muskegon Chronicle wrote in 1937: "The finest white pine and hardwood forest in the world is now a man-made desert of fire-blasted stumps and slashings."

The last vestige of the lumber era in Muskegon is a lone paper mill whose odor, unfortunately, is unmistakable. But unlike the other lumber towns, Muskegon made a remarkable transition to other industries, and continues to be primarily an industrial town, producing office furniture, chemicals, automotive parts and other goods.

It therefore has all the appearances of a place dedicated more

Lumber baron Charles Hackley's home, Muskegon.

to industry than to tourists and resorts. (Though the face of things may change considerably when a planned high-speed ferry begins operation between Muskegon and Milwaukee in spring 2001.) That said, there are still many reasons to visit it.

Prominent among these is the legacy left by lumber baron Charles H. Hackley. You can't go far in Muskegon without seeing his name. He was a millionaire with a great civic conscience, and many facets of the townspeople's lives are still enhanced by his efforts.

Hackley built the public library and hospital which bear his name, as well as the Hackley Central School, which is now an administration building. **Hackley Park** in the center of the downtown historic district is an oasis of green in an urban setting. Hackley donated the land and the statuary, which honor the Union soldiers and sailors from the Civil War.

The **Muskegon Museum of Art** (296 W. Webster Ave.; 231-720-2570) was also built with funds donated by Hackley, though he died before its completion. It has an impressive collection — especially for a small city — that includes paintings

by Homer, Whistler and Wyeth, and prints by Durer,
Rembrandt, Picasso and Renoir.

Though Hackley was adept at giving away his money for the
benefit of others, including an endowment which continues to
support the city schools, he wasn't afraid to enjoy the good
things in life himself. This is no more evident than at the
Hackley and Hume Historic Site (Sixth Street and Webster
Ave.; 231-722-0278).

The site contains the homes of Charles Hackley and his partner
Thomas Hume and the carriage barn that was shared by both.
Now being meticulously restored by the Hackley Heritage
Association, the Hackley home is a study in Victorian opu-
lence.

It was built as a showplace, both inside and out. Moorish influence runs strong, especially in the architectural details. Hackley
was an admirer of the exotic, as evidenced in the subjects
depicted in the elaborate wood carvings throughout — animals
and people from all ends of the earth. Appropriately, particularly for a lumber baron, the carvings steal the show, but the
stained glass windows, tiled fireplaces and hand-stenciled wall
designs are also quite impressive.

The Hume home, on the other hand, was built with practicality
and a large family in mind, since Thomas and Margaret Hume
had seven children. Large living spaces and lots of bedrooms
took precedence over showiness, though the exterior of the
house sported 12 different colors, which have now been
restored.

The Hackley and Hume Historical Site is open to the public in
the afternoons, Wednesday through Sunday from late May
through September. There are also limited hours between
Thanksgiving and Christmas.

You can learn more about the area's history at the **Muskegon
County Museum** (430 W. Clay; 231-722-0278), where you'll
find displays about the days when Muskegon was known as the

Lumber Queen. Other exhibits depict lives of Native Americans, factory workers and more recent well-known residents such as Buster Keaton, whose family used to spend summers in Muskegon. There is a natural history gallery as well, with the remains of the "Huls" mastodon, found nearby in 1963.

Also administered by the museum is the **Fire Barn Museum**, located at 510 W. Clay. Though Muskegon fared much better than towns like Manistee in the fires of 1871, the danger of being unprepared was clear. In 1875 the C.H. Hackley Hose Company No. 2 was formed, financed by — who else? — Charles Hackley. As facilities were modernized and opened elsewhere in the city, the fire house was closed. In 1976 the present fire barn was built to resemble the original. Today it houses a museum of fire fighting memorabilia, including a 1923 LaFrance pumper, hose carts, and hooks and ladders. Hours are variable, so call the museum at 231-722-0278 for more information.

Another site of historical interest is the grave of Jonathan Walker in the Evergreen Cemetery at Pine and Irwin Streets. Walker was a sea captain who deplored slavery. For years he transported escaped slaves out of the country to places like Mexico. In 1844 he tried unsuccessfully to run several slaves to the Bahamas and freedom. The slaves were seized and sent back to their owners, and Walker was arrested, tried and convicted. Part of his sentence was to have the letters "SS" (Slave Stealer) branded into the palm of his right hand, a cruel punishment that only fueled the fires of anti-slavery sentiment. He went on to become an abolitionist lecturer and was the subject of John Greenleaf Whittier's 1846 poem "The Branded Hand." After he died near Muskegon in 1877, a group of fellow abolitionists erected the 10-foot monument which still stands over his grave. One verse of Whittier's poem is engraved on part of it; on another is the carving of an open hand with the letters "SS."

A slice of more recent history can be experienced at the **USS Silversides and Maritime Museum** on the south side of the

The USS Silversides at Muskegon.

channel wall near Lake Michigan. The Silversides is a 312-foot World War II submarine built at Mare Island Naval Shipyard in Vallejo, Calif., and launched in August 1941. The ship saw plenty of action in the Pacific, ranking third highest among World War II submarines in ships sunk. Formerly berthed at Navy Pier in Chicago, the submarine was adopted by a preservationist group from Muskegon which has restored it and made it accessible to the public. Visitors can tour the entire vessel, including the engine rooms, torpedo rooms and living quarters. For information call 231-755-1230.

For a different kind of boat experience, you can take a cruise on the **Port City Princess**, a 65-foot steel-hull passenger boat. The boat, which can accommodate 200, takes passengers on

GREAT LAKES CRUISING

Cruise ships aren't just for the ocean. In recent years there's been a new flurry of cruising activity on the Great Lakes, and it took Europeans to do it. In 1997 the MV Columbus was built in Germany exclusively for plying the Great Lakes. This 472-foot boat has all the amenities you'd expect to find on a luxury cruise ship — a restaurant, wine bar, lounges, entertainment, swimming pool with bar, fitness room, sauna, hair salon, photo lab and more, spread out over five passenger decks. It can accommodate 418 passengers and a crew of 170. Though the cruises are sold primarily to Europeans, a few each season are open to North Americans. The Columbus' itineraries change annually, but generally the cruises range from four to ten days; some stay on one of the lakes while others touch on all five. Shore excursions are available, and an on-board historian gives presentations on Great Lakes history. The Columbus offers comfort at an affordable price.

If, on the other hand, money is no obstacle, there's Le Levant, a sleek, new 326-foot ship that offers elegance more commonly seen in another era. There are 45 spacious cabins, all of them with water views, that can accommodate an intimate group of 90 passengers, attended diligently by a crew of 45. There are two dining rooms, a pool and a lounge with dance floor. The French ship sails from Toronto on Lake Ontario along the length of Lake Erie and Lake Huron, with the final docking at Chicago on Lake Michigan. Shore excursions are offered along the way at Saugatuck, Mackinac Island and other locations. This week-long cruise will set you back several thousand dollars, but what a way to see the Great Lakes.

For more information on either ship contact Great Lakes Cruise Company, 3270 Washtenaw Avenue, Ann Arbor, MI 48104; 734-477-6045.

lunch or dinner cruises, scenic tours, sunset cruises and various theme excursions. Though it is designed to sail on Lake Michigan, when the water is rough it turns eastward to Muskegon Lake. For information, rates and to make reservations call 231-728-8387.

Pere Marquette Beach, on the south side of the channel near the USS Silversides, is the municipal Lake Michigan beach. Known for its beach volleyball, the attractive beach also has a children's playground. Adjacent to the park is the conical south pierhead lighthouse, built in 1903 of cast iron and painted a striking red.

On the other side of the channel is **Muskegon State Park** with its sandy beaches and winter sports complex. For more information about the park see "Natural Attractions" at the end of this chapter.

During the summer months you can leave the driving to others if you take the inexpensive city trolleys. The **North Beach Trolley** runs many times a day from Muskegon Mall near the downtown historic district out to Pere Marquette Beach and the USS Silversides, stopping at several shopping and historical areas along the way. The **South Beach Trolley** runs a more southerly route, going all the way to Hoffmaster State Park and the Gillette Visitor Center (see "Natural Attractions" at the end of this chapter). For schedules or information call the Muskegon Trolley Company at 231-724-6420.

If you have kids, you probably won't escape having a little stomach-churning fun when you visit Muskegon. Just north of the town is **Michigan's Adventure Amusement Park** and **Wildwater Adventure**, the largest water park in Michigan (231-766-3377). The amusement park has more than 40 rides, including six roller coasters.

Quieter recreation can be found on the **Musketawa Trail**, a 26-mile recreational trail that leads from the west side of Muskegon to just north of Marne. Only the southeastern half of the trail is paved; the part closest to Muskegon is compacted gravel. It is used for walking, running, biking, horseback riding and in-line skating in the summer, and for cross-country skiing and snowmobiling in the winter. It is wheelchair accessible.

WHERE TO STAY:

Emery House Bed and Breakfast, 446 W. Webster, Muskegon, MI 49440; 231-722-6978. This 1903 brick Georgian Colonial house is in Muskegon's historic district, two blocks from Muskegon Lake. On the second floor are antique-filled guest rooms, some with shared bath, and on the third floor is a ballroom reminiscent of days past. There is also a private suite located in the property's carriage house.

Hackley-Holt House Bed and Breakfast, 423 W. Clay Avenue, Muskegon, MI 49440; 888-271-5609 or 231-725-7303. Located right behind the Hackley and Hume Historic Site, this 1858 Italianate house was built by Joseph Hackley, Charles' father. When Joseph died in 1878, his widow, Catherine, married Henry Holt — thus the name "Hackley-Holt House." The bed and breakfast has four guest rooms, each with a private bath and in-room cable TV. The parlor is particularly beautiful, with its leaded glass windows, Victorian gingerbread details and ornately carved fireplace mantel. Hosts Bill and Nancy Stone's breakfast specialty is Swedish pancakes with deliciously tart imported lingonberry preserves.

Port City Victorian Inn Bed and Breakfast, 1259 Lakeshore Drive, Muskegon, MI 49441; 800-274-3574 or 231-759-0205. This elegant 1877 Queen Anne home overlooks Muskegon Lake near the historic district. There are five guest rooms, each with private bath and air-conditioning. Two are large honeymoon suites with two-person whirlpool tubs. The common areas include a balcony, TV room, sitting room with fireplace, and sun room. Hosts Barbara and Frederick Schossau serve full breakfasts.

WHERE TO EAT:

Rafferty's Dockside, 601 Terrace Point; 231-722-4461.

Located at the marina on Muskegon Lake, Rafferty's offers good food in a pleasant, casual waterfront setting. Specialties include pretzel crumb walleye, perch, pork chops with apple chutney and New York strip steak. The crabcakes are also worth a try, as is the Tuscan salad, a variation on green salad that includes white beans.

Whitehall/Montague

These two small towns lie inland from Lake Michigan along the shores of White Lake, but their history has long been entwined with that of the larger lake. An ideal spot for a protected harbor yet with close proximity to Lake Michigan's shipping routes, the Whitehall/Montague area grew rapidly during the lumbering era.

When the white pine forests were gone, the resort industry began to grow with the help of the Goodrich Steamship Line, which carried vacationing passengers from Chicago. Though the towns support light manufacturing today, they are primarily

The White River Light Station Museum in Whitehall.

resorts.

Aside from its scenic character, there are several reasons to make a stop in the Whitehall/Montague area while touring Lake Michigan.

There is, for example, the **World's Largest Weathervane** in Montague. It stands 48 feet tall along Business Route 31, its 26-foot arrow weighing in at 800 pounds. Above the arrow is a likeness of the Great Lakes schooner Ella Ellenwood, whose home port was Montague until it sank in a storm near Milwaukee in 1901. The following spring the boat's nameplate was found inside the White Lake channel, having mysteriously made its way back home.

On the south side of the channel near Lake Michigan is the **White River Light Station Museum** (231-894-8265). In 1870 the channel between White Lake and Lake Michigan was cut, necessitating a navigational light at its entrance. In 1875 the light station was established and William Robinson was appointed keeper. He and his family lived in the limestone and brick structure with its eight-sided tower, where he remained lightkeeper for 47 years.

Today the lighthouse is a museum dedicated to local maritime history. The original Fourth Order Fresnel lens is on display as well as the fog horn and a number of navigational instruments and nautical artifacts. You can climb the spiral wrought iron staircase to the top of the tower for a bird's eye view of the lake and the surrounding dunes. The museum is open daily Memorial Day through Labor Day and on weekends in September. It is somewhat difficult to find; follow South Shore Road from Whitehall, then look for a series of signs for the museum.

Montague is the location of the southern terminus of the **Hart-Montague Trail State Park**, a 22.5-mile recreational trail that begins in Hart and roughly parallels the coast of Lake Michigan several miles inland. The entire length of the trail is paved with asphalt, making it suitable for just about any type of

The dunes at Silver Lake State Park.

non-motorized bike as well as hikers. The trail meanders along-side fruit orchards and through the small towns of Mears, Shelby, New Era and Rothbury before ending at Montague. There are several cut-offs to the west that lead to Lake Michigan and scenic coastal routes. A trail pass, available from many local businesses or state park offices, is required. For more information call 231-873-3083.

WHERE TO STAY:

Michillinda Beach Lodge, 5207 Scenic Drive, Whitehall, MI 49461; 231-893-1895. While most resorts in the Whitehall/Montague area are on or close to White Lake, the Michillinda Beach Lodge is an exception. Along with its own sandy Lake Michigan beach, this all-inclusive resort offers 49 modern guest rooms of various sizes. They are scattered across the grounds in 10 buildings, most facing the lake. The family-oriented resort has many organized activities such as bingo, variety shows, campfires and children's events. Breakfast and dinner in the resort dining room are included in the rate. Outdoor amenities include a heated swimming pool, wading pool, playground, tennis courts, shuffleboard, basketball, volleyball and mini-golf. On Sunday mornings there is a non-denominational Protestant service.

Riding the dunes at Silver Lake State Park.

For more information contact the White Lake Area Chamber of Commerce, 124 W. Hanson St., Whitehall, MI 49461; 231-893-4585 or 800-879-9702.
Internet: http://www.whitelake.org

Oceana County

The shoreline of this county, which makes a smooth curve out into the lake, is 26 miles of sandy beach. Inland, the county consists of small towns and rural agricultural land where fruit and other types of produce are grown. Known as the "Asparagus Capital of the World," the area hosts the annual Asparagus Festival each June.

There are many beaches accessible to the public, including several township parks, but the most popular place for the sun-and-sand set to gather is **Silver Lake State Park**, about midway along the county's shore line.

Silver Lake, about a mile and a half inland from Lake Michigan, is approximately 2.5 miles long and a half-mile wide. Its sandy beaches and calm, shallow water have made it a popular resort area, and its eastern section, which is not under jurisdiction of the state park, is lined with various tourist attractions, motels and campgrounds. Water skiing, fishing, jet skiing and parasailing are some of the many activities that go on in the area.

But it's what lies in the state park, between Silver Lake and Lake Michigan, that is the real attraction: 2,000 acres of rolling, undulating sand dunes, three miles long and a mile-and-a-half wide. These are "live" dunes, meaning they are in a constant state of change. In appearance they are like a vast desert, unbroken by trees or even by dune grass. Seen from the opposite side of Silver Lake, they seem otherworldly, an exotic landscape unlikely for a Midwest location.

The dunes are divided into three areas. The north section is reserved for off-road vehicles; this is the only place within the Lake Michigan state parks where they are permitted. The middle section is for hikers — sturdy hikers, that is. The dunes are steep and difficult to climb, but the view, both of Silver Lake and Lake Michigan, is spectacular. The south portion of the dunes is occupied by Mac Woods Dune Rides, a commercial operation that has been taking tourists over the dunes since the 1930s. At the extreme southwest corner of the park is the Little Sable Point Light, at 107 feet, the tallest lighthouse on Lake Michigan. (For more information on Silver Lake State Park, see "Natural Attractions" at the end of this chapter.)

The only town in Oceana County that has direct access to Lake Michigan is Pentwater. The town lies along the northwest side of Pentwater Lake and the short channel that leads out to Lake Michigan. Not surprisingly, this location made it a good spot for the lumber industry, since the timber from the Pentwater River watershed could be easily floated down the river to Pentwater Lake where it was loaded onto ships and taken out to Lake Michigan for transport.

Chicagoan Charles Mears was largely responsible for the development of Pentwater during the logging era. In addition to lumbering, Mears engaged in transportation, using his own shipping fleet to carry passengers and goods from Chicago to Pentwater, and to carry lumber the reverse route.

Today this small town of less than 2,000 depends primarily on tourism. There are many shops and casual restaurants in the quaint downtown area near the water. **Charles Mears State Park**, adjacent to the town, has a beautiful 1,500-foot beach.

WHERE TO STAY:

The Candlewyck House B & B, 438 E. Lowell Street, Box 392, Pentwater, MI 49449; 231-869-5967. This 1868 farmhouse is located east of the main shopping area and beaches. There are six guest rooms, each with private bath and cable TV. Common areas include a large family living room with fireplace, a reading room and an attractive outdoor patio with table and chairs. The hosts, John and Mary Jo Neidow, provide guests with bicycles to ride to beaches and shopping. A full breakfast is served.

Historic Nickerson Inn, 262 Lowell Street, Box 986, Pentwater, MI 49449; 800-742-1288 or 231-869-6731. This 1914 inn is situated near Mears State Park and the Lake Michigan beaches. It has been an inn since its initial opening, when it served visitors who arrived by train from Chicago. There are eight guest rooms and three suites, all with private baths and individual heating and air-conditioning. The suites have queen beds, two-person Jacuzzis, gas log fireplaces and balconies. Each room follows a different theme such as nautical, hunting, logging or gardens. Smoking and pets are not allowed; children must be 12 or over. Breakfast in the dining room or on the porch is included. The inn also serves elegant dinners (see "Where to eat").

Pentwater Inn Victorian B & B, 180 E. Lowell Street, PO Box 98, Pentwater, MI 49449; 231-869-5909. Located near village shops and within walking distance to the beach, this 1869 Victorian B & B has five rooms with private baths and air-conditioning. But the main event here may be the three-course breakfast, which hosts Donna and Quintus Renshaw prepare from scratch. Home-baked breads and coffee cakes are accompanied by entrees and homemade jams and fruit sauces made from their own fruit.

WHERE TO EAT:

Historic Nickerson Inn, 262 Lowell Street; 800-742-1288 or 231-869-6731. The emphasis here is on fresh ingredients, local whenever possible, and elegant food prepared to order. Homemade bread is served, some made using 100-year-old sourdough starter. Appetizers include vodka-cured salmon and roasted mushrooms. Entree selections are somewhat limited, but carefully chosen, and include temptations like cumin crusted duck with red pepper apricot chutney or grilled lamb tenderloin with garlic mashed potatoes and apple onion marmalade. No smoking is permitted and guests are asked to leave the beach attire at home.

For more information contact the Oceana County Tourism Bureau, PO Box 168-BR, Hart, MI 49420; 800-874-3982 or 231-873-3982.
Internet: http://www.oceana.net

The S.S. Badger, last of the carferries.

Ludington

This town of 8,500 is largely industrial, though the industry lies outside of the town center. Busy U.S. 10 runs right through the middle of Ludington, coming to an end near the ferry docks where you can catch the boat to Manitowoc, Wis., across the lake. The route is lined with businesses, gas stations, and a number of old lumber baron mansions, several of which are now bed and breakfasts. Unlike the lake towns where tourism is the main economic base, Ludington lacks the kind of quaintness that draws vacationers. It does, however, have one of the most beautiful municipal beaches along the lake. Aside from the ferry, the two things that seem to draw most visitors to Ludington are the excellent fishing and beautiful Ludington State Park just to the north. (See "Natural Attractions" in this chapter.)

Among the first European visitors to the place now known as Ludington was the Jesuit missionary and explorer Jacques Marquette. It is thought that Marquette died and was buried here in 1675 despite efforts to return the ill priest to his mission at St. Ignace. Others dispute this, saying that he was buried further north near Frankfort. In either case, it seems certain that his remains were moved at a later time to St. Ignace, where a small memorial now marks the spot where his body is believed to be. The river that flows into Lake Michigan at Ludington is named for him — the Pere Marquette — as is the small lake formed where the river widens just before reaching the larger lake.

The town was not settled until nearly 200 years later. A small sawmill was built here, an excellent location because of the forests lining the river far upstream and the protected port on Pere Marquette Lake. The mill eventually came into the hands of James Ludington, a prominent Milwaukee businessman. Ludington ran the mill and planned the town, managing to get it named after him. The lumbering business grew, and by 1891 there were eight sawmills at Ludington.

The beach at Stearns Park in Ludington.

When salt was discovered in the area, wells were dug and salt production took a place alongside lumbering. Commercial fishing also played a role, but by the turn of the century catches were dwindling. The lumber story reads like it does everywhere else on the lake: when the wood was gone, so was the prosperity. Salt wasn't enough to sustain things (though the salt industry remains to this day). Hard times hit Ludington.

The bank failed, along with three new factories that had been opened in an effort to attract other kinds of industry. Attempts to spark tourism were not initially successful. Salvation came, eventually, because of the harbor.

In 1874, the Flint and Pere Marquette Railroad reached Ludington. Trains carrying agricultural products ended their route here, where boats awaited the cargo that would be shipped to the other side of the lake. The railroad built a fleet of boats, and the traffic grew. The business became more profitable with the introduction of carferries — ferries that would carry the fully loaded railroad cars, eliminating the need to transfer goods from rail to boat and back again. At its peak, the railroad owned 12 carferries that carried goods from Ludington

Logger's cabin at White Pine Village near Ludington.

to Manitowoc, Milwaukee and Kewaunee.

One of these, the Pere Marquette 18, perished tragically in September 1910. The carferry, which was loaded with 29 freight cars, sailed from Ludington just before midnight, headed for Milwaukee. There were 62 people on board. At 3:00 a.m. one of the crew warned the captain that the boiler room was flooding. No amount of pumping could control the flowing water, so the captain ordered nine of the railroad cars dumped overboard. The ship put out a distress call, and all were relieved to see their sister ship, the Pere Marquette 17, steaming toward them. But suddenly, inexplicably, the foundering ship lurched to starboard and went quickly under the waves. Although 33 people were rescued, the rest lost their lives, including every officer on board. No cause was ever found.

Eventually it was trucking and not the lake's treachery that spelled the demise of the carferries. The only one left in service today is the S.S. Badger, which now carries passengers, not cargo, across the lake to Manitowoc. When it's in port, you'll find the 410-foot boat in the harbor on Pere Marquette Lake.

The biggest attraction in the town itself is the wide, sandy beach at **Stearns Park** on the lakefront. Adjacent to the beach is a grassy, shaded picnic area with tables. There is a food concession nearby, along with mini-golf and shuffleboard. It's a nice walk from here out the old pier to the 1924 lighthouse, an unusual structure shaped somewhat like the bow of a ship.

The other main attraction is **White Pine Village** (231-843-4808), run by the Mason County Historical Society. This complex of 20 historic buildings sits on 23 acres high on a hill overlooking Lake Michigan. Some are original buildings that were brought to the site from elsewhere in the county; others have been reconstructed in period style. Among them are a trapper's log cabin which eventually became the post office, a one-room school house, a hardware store, a chapel and the first Mason County Courthouse, which stands on its original site. The Rose Hawley Museum has exhibits of furniture, clothing, toys and other facets of everyday life, while the maritime museum houses nautical artifacts, including the original Fresnel lens from the Big Sable Point lighthouse at Ludington State Park. The lens, which is six feet tall and eight feet in diameter, cast a light that could be seen from 19 miles away. The village is open mid-April through mid-October.

WHERE TO STAY:

The Ludington House, 501 E. Ludington Avenue, Ludington, MI 49431; 231-845-7769. One of several along busy Ludington Avenue, this large B & B is for those who enjoy Victorian surroundings. Built in 1878, the house is filled with antiques. There are nine rooms, each with private bath and air conditioning. The attractive bridal suite is complete with whirlpool bath. Two rooms can accommodate children. Owner Virginia Boegner prides herself on her hearty home-made breakfasts, which are custom planned according to guests' tastes. The Ludington House participates with other local B & Bs in off-season murder mystery weekends.

Schoenberger House, 409 E. Ludington Avenue, Ludington, MI; 49431; 231-843-4435. This magnificent neoclassical man-

Downtown Manistee.

sion is sure to catch the eye of anyone driving down Ludington Avenue. Built by a lumber baron in 1903, it is full of beautiful woodwork, fireplaces and fine chandeliers. The music room features two grand pianos. The inn has five guest rooms, each with private bath.

Snyder's Shoreline Inn, 903 W. Ludington Avenue, PO Box 667, Ludington, MI 49431-0667; 231-845-1261. Presently this is the accommodation closest to the lake. An inn with country charm but modern amenities, Snyder's faces the water at the public launching ramp area adjacent to the beach. The individually decorated rooms range from standard size to suites; some have wet bars, refrigerators, VCRs and whirlpool tubs. Some rooms have balconies overlooking the lake. There is an outdoor pool. Snyder's is open year round, with discounted rates in the off-season.

Summit Inn, 4711 S. Lakeshore Drive, Ludington, MI 49431; 231-843-4052. Located in a quiet area halfway between Ludington and Pentwater overlooking Lake Michigan, this two-story Cape Cod home was built as a bed and breakfast in 1995.

There are four rooms, all with private bath and individual heating and air conditioning. Balconies overlook the lake for a great view of sunsets. Hosts James and Delphine Evans serve a full breakfast.

WHERE TO EAT:

P.M. Steamers, 502 W. Loomis; 231-843-9555. This is the closest to waterfront dining in Ludington. P.M. Steamers is next to the marina on Pere Marquette Lake, near where the Badger docks. This pleasant, spacious restaurant serves a wide variety of seafood, steaks, chicken and pasta as well as burgers and pizza. It's casual enough for kids, but upscale enough for the two of you to enjoy a nice meal out.

For more information contact the Ludington Area Convention and Visitors Bureau at 5827 West U.S. 10, Ludington, MI 49431; 800-542-4600.
Internet: http://www.ludingtoncvb.com

Manistee

Walking down River Street in Manistee is like taking a step backwards in time. Everyone smiles, no one is in a hurry. People are polite. If it weren't for the cars, you might wonder if you're in a time warp.

This beautiful Victorian city along the Manistee River looks much as it did in the late 1800s when most of the downtown buildings were built. In fact, the entire district is on the National Register of Historic Places.

It wasn't always so genteel. Like the surrounding areas, Manistee was blessed with an abundance of trees that attracted lumbermen and sawmills, and activity sprang up rapidly along the river and Manistee Lake just to the east. It was a hard-drinking, hard-living, rough-and-tumble town whose main occupation on Sundays wasn't church going, but drinking. It was also a man's town, untempered by the presence of women, and fighting was a way of life.

All that changed with a wave of immigrants during the latter part of the century. They brought their faiths with them, and their women, and today this little town of less than 7,000 has 13 churches. And the bars are locked up tight on Sunday mornings.

Manistee hit it big during the lumber boom. The fire that swept the town in 1871 barely put the brakes on long enough to rebuild — this time using brick instead of wood. By the turn of the century more than a dozen lumbermen had elevated themselves to the status of millionaires, and many of their beautiful Victorian, Queen Anne and Italianate homes remain standing.

THE *S.S. BADGER*, THE LAST OF AN ERA

Boats began ferrying passengers and cargo across Lake Michigan as early as 1875, when the Flint and Marquette Railway chartered the steamer John Sherman to make the crossing between Ludington and Sheboygan, Wis. More and more carferries were employed to handle the increasing volume of passengers and freight needing to get from one side to the other. Business boomed through the first half of the 20th century, reaching its height in 1955, when the fleet of boats ferried 205,000 passengers and more than 204,000 railroad cars in nearly 7,000 crossings.

Among those boats was the S.S. Badger, 410 feet of coal-belching, hard working steel. Built in 1953, the Badger and her twin, the S.S. Spartan, were the largest carferries ever built. But by the mid-1970s, the Chesapeake and Ohio Railway System, which then owned the ferries, found it too unprofitable to operate them. The ferries struggled on under new management but service finally ground to a halt in 1990.

In 1881 salt was discovered 2,000 feet underground at Manistee. Wells were drilled, brine was pumped out of them, and wood scraps from the sawmills was used to burn fires to evaporate the water. This new-found source of wealth, coupled with the lumber and ideal port conditions put Manistee even further ahead. Not only did ships arrive to carry away the goods produced, but the railroad soon came through the town.

When the bottom fell out of the lumber industry in Michigan, things took a turn for the worse, though Manistee fared better than many other lumber towns. Although its population today is roughly half of what it was at its height, Manistee kept its hand in industry, which remains at the forefront of the town's economic base.

Today the Badger sails again from Ludington to Manitowoc, Wisconsin, thanks to the vision of Charles Conrad, a Ludington native who didn't want to see the end of an era. Through his efforts the Badger was refurbished, this time for passengers and autos only, to set off across the lake once again.

The daily crossings take four hours and save 450 miles of driving. And this is far more than a boat ride. There are movies, food, beverages, bingo, shopping, a small museum — even staterooms, if you'd rather sleep your way across. You can walk the decks for some refreshing lake air, or on a cool day you can bundle up with a blanket on one of the deck lounge chairs.

This is the last coal-burning passenger vessel operating in America, and the only ferry to cross Lake Michigan (though at the time of writing, another is in the planning stages). It's a great way to experience a bit of Great Lakes history and save some wear and tear on the car. For information and rates contact the Lake Michigan Carferry at 800-841-4243.

Manistee Fire Hall, built in 1888, the oldest continually operating firehouse in Michigan.

Fortunately, Manistee's industrial activity takes place away from historic downtown. Most of the brick buildings built on River Street after the 1871 fire have survived, and in recent years "Project Facelift" has endeavored to restore and enhance them even further. The area on the south side of the Manistee River is a vibrant shopping district with restaurants, a brew pub, a county historical museum and motels. Below street level, along the river, is the town's new **Riverwalk**, a mile-long boardwalk that stretches from the historic commercial district to **Douglas Park** and the **First Street Beach** on Lake Michigan. During the summer, evening concerts are given in the bandshell beside the walkway.

The **Lyman Building**, on River Street, houses one of two county museum buildings in Manistee. The museum is located in what was once a store, built after the 1871 fire. Many of the old fixtures remain, including much apothecary equipment and ingredients. A large collection of dolls, toys, photographs and archival material can also be seen. The **Holly Water Works Building** near the First Street Beach houses the other branch of the museum, which is dedicated primarily to the town's logging, maritime and railroad heritage. For information on the museums call 231-723-5531.

Many buildings of historical interest are scattered around the town. Among these is **Our Saviour's Church**, the oldest Danish American Evangelical Lutheran Church in the United States. Built in 1868, the church miraculously survived the fire shortly thereafter that devastated the rest of the town. Today it is preserved as a museum, but an ecumenical service is held there on Saturday evenings during the summer months. The **First Congregational Church** on Fourth Street is a State and National Historic Site. It was built in the 1890s at a cost of $60,000 — quite a lot of money in those days, but this was, after all, a wealthy town. Among its points of interest are 36 stained glass windows, two of them made by Tiffany.

The ornate **Ramsdell Theater** cost even more — $100,000 — when it was built in 1903. Over the years it has been used for stage performances, silent movie showings and summer stock. Actor James Earl Jones was once a stage carpenter at the theater. Today it is home for the Manistee Civic Players, who present theatrical productions and concerts as well as host art and museum exhibits in the grand old building.

The **Manistee Fire Hall**, on the other hand, cost a relatively paltry $7,500 when it was built in 1888. The oldest continually operating fire house in Michigan, it has changed little structurally throughout the years. The divisions for the old horse stalls are still visible, and the two brass firepoles still gleam. Someone has been on duty 24 hours a day, 365 days a year here for well over a hundred years. If you stop by today, and there's no emergency, someone will be glad to show you around. You can even look at the newest addition — a state-of-the-art fire engine purchased for 53 times what the original building cost, or about $400,000.

On the north side of the river is a residential area and the **Fifth Avenue Beach**, complete with playground, picnic areas, tennis and volleyball courts and bathhouse. The lighthouse pier

stretches along this side of the river out into the lake, ending at
the 39-foot white steel conical tower built in 1927.

Getting around Manistee in the summertime is easy via the
bright red trolley that runs a regular route to the beach, downtown, to shopping and residential areas and out to Orchard
Beach State Park to the north (See "Natural Attractions" at the
end of this chapter). For trolley information call 231-723-6525.

The town hosts several special festivals and events during the
year. The **Manistee National Forest Festival**, over the Fourth
of July holiday, includes a parade, fireworks, a lumberjack
show, a boat parade and many other attractions. The **Manistee
Victorian Port City Festival** celebrates the town's heritage
with musical entertainment, trolley rides, artisan demonstrations and a street art fair. At Christmas time there's an old-fashioned Victorian sleighbell parade with horses and revelers
dressed in period costumes.

WHERE TO STAY:

Harbor Village, 100 Marina Drive, Manistee, MI 49660; 800-
968-0783 or 231-723-0070. This large modern complex borders Lake Michigan on the north side of the Manistee River.
Units range from studio apartments to two-bedroom cottages,
which are rented by the week only during the summer. Some
units have a lake view while others adjoin the marina, which is
just off the river. All have fully equipped kitchens. Other
amenities include private decks and gas fireplaces. There is a
beautiful Lake Michigan beach as well as an outdoor pool.

Lake Shore B & B, 3440 Lake Shore Road, Manistee, MI
49660; 231-723-7644. A new cedar home, the Lake Shore B &
B is located on Lake Michigan about three miles from
Manistee. There are two guest rooms with a shared bath,
though each room has its own deck overlooking the private
beach. Host Willa Berentsen serves homemade cookies every
afternoon. Smoke free.

The Maples, 435 Fifth Street, Manistee, MI 49660; 231-723-

2904. This large 1905 home is located in the historic residential district several blocks from the river. There are three guest rooms: a twin and double that share a bathroom, and a suite with bedroom, private bath and sitting room with fireplace. Continental breakfast is served. This is not a fancy place, but it's clean, economical and comfortable, and owner Carol Krantz is a gracious host.

Riverside Motel, 520 Water Street, Manistee, MI 49660; 231-723-3554. Those most likely to appreciate the Riverside are fishermen, who can enjoy fishing right from the motel dock. Boaters can dock their boats at the motel, and fish cleaning and freezing facilities are available. There's also a heated pool on the premises, as well as a picnic area with grills. The motel also runs fishing charters.

WHERE TO EAT:

Four Forty West, 440 River Street; 231-723-7902. There's nothing fancy here — seafood, steaks and so on — but it's a pleasant place, especially if you can sit outside on the deck and watch the ducks on the river and the people passing by on the Riverwalk.

Lighthouse Brewing Company, 312 River Street; 231-398-BREW (2739). This imaginative menu runs the gamut from burgers to rack of lamb, with unusual offerings like a BBQ duck sandwich and sautéed mussels sofrito. There are also pasta dishes such as ravioli with gorgonzola cream sauce and toasted walnuts. What's even more interesting is that the restaurant brews its own beer: amber, pale, golden and brown ales. Located on River Street with an outdoor deck overlooking the river, this is a perfect place to relax, enjoy a good meal and watch the boats go by.

For more information contact the Manistee Convention and Visitors Bureau, PO Box 13, Manistee, MI 49660; 888-584-9863 or 231-398-9355.
Internet: http://www.manistee.com/~edo/chamber/

Frankfort

The small resort town of Frankfort lies on the north side of the Betsie River where it enters Lake Michigan. Like most other lakeside towns, Frankfort got its start in lumber. But long before that, it is thought that the explorer Father Jacques Marquette visited the area in 1675. Some believe it was here that Marquette was first buried, before his remains were moved north to St. Ignace. A cross marks the spot near the waterfront. (Though it is generally thought that he was buried near Ludington.)

The Betsie watershed lumber stands were depleted by about 1920, but two industries had arisen to save Frankfort from becoming a ghost town. It was a perfect location for iron smelting: there was still enough wood for charcoal and lots of limestone that was essential to the process. The town had a good harbor with easy lake access for receiving ore from the Upper Peninsula and shipping the processed ore out. Salt-making grew in tandem, utilizing sawmill by-products to draw salt from the brine that was hauled up from area wells.

Tourism took hold around the turn of the century when the Toledo, Ann Arbor, and Northern Michigan Railroad began to bring in summer visitors from as far away as Ohio. In 1901 the company opened the Royal Frontenac Hotel, a luxurious destination for the wealthy. It burned down in 1912, and no other local hotel has since replicated its grandeur.

Today the biggest attraction is the natural beauty of the surrounding countryside. Gorgeous, turquoise Crystal Lake, just to the north, is the largest inland lake in the area, offering plenty of opportunities for boating, fishing and swimming.

Farther north is the beautiful Platte River, ideal for kayaking, canoeing or tubing. Boats and tubes can be rented from **Riverside Canoe Trips** (616-325-5622). A gentle trip on the Lower Platte, suitable for young children and adults alike, takes about two hours, terminating at a sandy white Lake Michigan beach. A higher adrenaline trip is the paddle down the Upper

Platte, a three- to four-hour excursion through fast water and tight turns. Reservations are recommended.

Lake Michigan beaches are located at the end of Main Street and at Elberta, on the south side of the Betsie River. The Elberta Beach has a boardwalk leading out to the lighthouse pier.

Lighthouse aficionados will want to drive five miles north to the **Point Betsie** light, one of the most beautiful on the lake. Established in 1858, the light is still active, though now automated. The white brick tower is integrated with the keeper's house, which last served as a residence in 1996. The original Fresnel lens can be seen at the maritime museum at Sleeping Bear Dunes National Lakeshore.

WHERE TO STAY:

Frankfort Land Company B & B Inn, 428 Leelanau Avenue, PO Box 267, Frankfort, MI 49635; 231-352-9267. This 1860 Italianate house is believed to be the oldest in Frankfort. The owners, Ed and Lou Wichert, have taken great care in its restoration. There are two Victorian-style guest rooms, each with queen bed and private bath. The Elvira Room's bath is across the hall, while the Caroline Room's bath is adjoining. Full breakfast is served, including fresh fruit and homemade breads or muffins. Tuesday afternoons are a special time, when the inn hosts Victorian teas. Reservations are required. The inn is within walking distance to shops and the waterfront.

The Hotel Frankfort, Main Street, Frankfort, MI 49635; 231-352-4303; reservations 231-882-9688. Looking for romance? This Victorian hotel specializes in it. A special place for couples, the Hotel Frankfort has 20 individually decorated rooms, some with mirrored canopy waterbeds and spas. There's also a sauna, a steam bath, a tanning solarium, gift shop and wine cellar, where tastings are conducted daily. Guests dine on gourmet fare in the hotel's candlelit dining room. The adventurous can even take a ride in the hotel's hot air balloon. The affordable rates, based on double occupancy, include breakfast and dinner for two.

Little Sable Point Lighthouse in Silver Lake State Park.

WHERE TO EAT:

Cabbage Shed Waterfront Pub, Elberta; 616-352-9843. This casual eatery on Betsie Bay was really a cabbage shed in the 1930s. Today you're not likely to see much in the way of cabbage heads, but you'll find plenty of other good things to eat. Burgers, ribs, chicken wings and broiled whitefish are the fare here, along with live entertainment and dancing.

For more information contact the Frankfort Chamber of Commerce at 616-352-7251.
Internet: http://www.benzie.com/frankfort

Natural Attractions

MUSKEGON STATE PARK

This 1,165-acre park features over two miles of Lake Michigan shoreline and, for winter use, one of only four luge runs in the United States. The park, which is just north of Muskegon, also has a mile-long border on Muskegon Lake.

There are two day-use areas. One is on Lake Michigan, with a bath house, concession and long stretch of sandy beach. The other is on Muskegon Lake, where there are picnic tables, grills, a picnic shelter and a small beach. Nearby Snug Harbor, also on Muskegon Lake, has a boat launch. There is another boat launch at the channel that leads out to Lake Michigan. Fishermen enjoy the area for its perch, bass and walleye.

Three campgrounds offer a total of 278 sites, some modern, others not. The **Lake Michigan Campground** is near but not on the lake, in a wooded area bordered by dunes. Shower and toilet facilities and provided, and the sites have electricity and picnic tables. There are two mini-cabins with electricity and heat, each capable of accommodating four, with bunks and mattresses provided. Across the street from the Lake Michigan campground is the semi-modern **East Campground,** with rest rooms but no electricity. At the south end of the park, adjacent to Muskegon Lake and the channel, is the **Channel Campground**. Like the Lake Michigan Campground, it has electricity and shower/toilet facilities.

There are 12 miles of trails that wind through dunes and wooded areas, some offering scenic views of the surrounding dunes. Another great view can be had from the Blockhouse, a two-story log building that was constructed in 1964 on the site of a similar structure that had burned down. The Blockhouse is located on Scenic Drive south of the Lake Michigan Campground.

Unlike some parks, activity doesn't wane here when the weather turns cold. The **Muskegon Winter Sports Complex** has a variety of activities as well as a heated lodge with food concession. Luge fees include rental of sleds and helmets; instruction is also provided. Proof of health insurance is required. Luge races are held throughout January and February, and are enthusiastically attended by the public. For those who like their winter sports on the tamer side, the complex has an outdoor lighted skating rink and 4.5 miles of lighted cross-country ski trails. Ski rentals are available.

For more information contact Muskegon State Park, 3560 Memorial Drive, Muskegon, MI 49445; 231-744-3480.

REELING IN THE BIG ONES

Ludington is Michigan's hot spot for fishing. According to the Convention and Visitors Bureau, more charters originate, and more trout and salmon are caught out of the port of Ludington each year than any other port in Michigan. A combination of deep water, warm shoals, and access to river mouths add up to make this an ideal place for landing trout, salmon and other sought-after species. If you've got your own boat, the municipal marina has ramps, as well as ample fish cleaning facilities. Or rely on the expertise of the more than 100 charter boat captains that call Ludington home port. The season begins in spring and ends well into the fall. For more information contact the Ludington Area Charterboat Association at 800-927-4370.

Big Sable Point Lighthouse in Ludington State Park.

DUCK LAKE STATE PARK

Located eight miles north of Muskegon, this 728-acre park is for day use only. The dominant feature of the park is its one large sand dune that towers between Lake Michigan and Scenic Drive. Though the park stretches from Lake Michigan across the north side of Duck Lake, the primary recreation area is on the smaller lake. There are picnic tables, grills and a shelter, along with a sandy beach and bathhouse. A boat launch is nearby, and though fishermen enjoy Duck Lake for its bass, crappie and panfish, there is no access into Lake Michigan. There is a paved path that runs along the shore of Duck Lake.

Farther west from the Duck Lake day use area is a parking area that connects with a boardwalk extending to Lake Michigan and a sandy beach.

During the winter the park is closed to vehicles, but open to hikers, cross-country skiers and ice fishermen.

For more information contact Duck Lake State Park, 3560 Memorial Drive, North Muskegon, MI 49445; 231-894-8769.

SILVER LAKE STATE PARK

This 3,000-acre property is located about 10 miles south of
Pentwater on a stretch of land between Lake Michigan and
beautiful Silver Lake. Most of the park consists of dunes,
which are divided into three areas with different purposes.

At the north is the sacrificial lamb of the state parks — the
only dune area in the state park system where off-road vehicles
are permitted. Vehicles must have an ORV registration and dri-
vers are required to follow safety regulations regarding helmets, shoulder straps and one-way directions on the dunes. It's
possible to rent vehicles if you don't have your own. Even if
you can't ride an ORV, it's fun to stand in the pedestrian area
nearby and watch them come careening down the sand.

At the south end of the park is **Mac Wood's Dune Rides** (231-
873-2817) where, mid-May through early October, you can
explore the dunes while someone else does the driving. The
tour winds through several miles of dunes, stopping occasionally to let passengers out to walk and take pictures.

The center area of the dunes — the largest portion — is for
walkers only. Don't be fooled by how close the top of the
dunes look from the parking area. It's a long, hot walk up to
the vantage point that overlooks Silver Lake on one side and
Lake Michigan on the other. The dunes are all but bereft of
vegetation, with a wind-blown look that has often been compared to the Sahara Desert. If you can manage to lug a pack up
to the top, it's a great place for a picnic; the kids can occupy
themselves by running down the steep dunes into Silver Lake
while you relax and enjoy the view.

The park has nearly four miles of Lake Michigan shoreline
unbroken by development. On the south end next to the water
is the **Little Sable Point Lighthouse**, at 107 feet one of the
tallest on the Great Lakes. It's also one of the oldest surviving
brick lighthouses. It is active, its Third Order Fresnel lens still
in place.

The entire western shore of Silver Lake is also park beach, as well as a smaller area by the campgrounds on the southeastern side. There are rest rooms, a picnic shelter and a bathhouse with parking nearby. This beach is popular with families because of the shallow, gently sloping bottom.

There are two campgrounds, one on Silver Lake, the other across the road from it, with a total of 200 modern campsites equipped with electricity. Each campground has a toilet and shower facility.

Boating and fishing, as well as other water sports like jet-skiing and parasailing, are popular on Silver Lake. Fishermen will find walleye, northern pike, crappie and bass, many of which can be caught during winter ice fishing excursions.

For more information contact Silver Lake State Park, 9679 W. State Park Road, Mears, MI 49436; 231-873-3083.

CHARLES MEARS STATE PARK

Located just a few blocks from the business center of Pentwater, this tiny property of only 50 acres is named for lumber baron Charles Mears, who was responsible for much of the development in the area. It consists primarily of a campground and a 1,500-foot Lake Michigan beach.

The campground has 180 sites with electricity and modern shower/toilet facilities. It is tremendously popular, making reservations essential during the prime summer months. The park opens at the beginning of April and remains open through November, though the rest rooms don't open until a couple of weeks later and close a month before the campground does.

There is a short trail up the park's only dune, Mt. Baldy, where an observation platform provides a view out over the lake, the Pentwater channel and surrounding area.

The beach is a beautiful one, attracting many visitors in the summer, who come to swim, picnic or play volleyball on the outdoor courts. There is parking available, but even if the lot fills up, it's not far to park in town and walk to the beach.

For more information contact Charles Mears State Park, PO Box 370, Pentwater, MI 49449; 231-869-2051.

LUDINGTON STATE PARK

At 5,300 acres, this is one of the largest state parks in the lower peninsula. It is also one of the most picturesque and popular. More than five miles of Lake Michigan shoreline and four miles on Hamlin Lake, along with three campgrounds, make it especially busy in the summer months.

Long before there was a state park here, this was the location of Hamlin, a logging village developed by lumber baron Charles Mears. The Sable River was dammed, creating Hamlin Lake, Michigan's largest artificial lake. The lake was used to float logs to the village sawmill. After processing they were transported to the mouth of the Sable River and loaded onto boats bound for Lake Michigan and the cities beyond. Disaster struck in 1888 when the dam broke and swept the entire village down the river and out into Lake Michigan. All that remains is the village cemetery, some parts of the old mill and bits of machinery. The dam has since been rebuilt.

The other site of historical interest in the park is the beautiful **Big Sable Point** lighthouse. The 112-foot tower was built in 1866; both it and the attached keeper's house remain standing though five other outbuildings between them and the lake have since been washed away. In the early 1900s, the brick tower was covered with steel plates to protect it. Then in 1989 a wide black stripe was painted around the center of the otherwise white tower. The light was automated in 1968 and now the original Third Order Fresnel lens is on display at White Pine Village in Ludington. Though the lighthouse suffered during its abandonment, the non-profit Big Sable Point Lighthouse Keepers are now striving to restore the it. Volunteers are on hand daily May through October, and for a small fee you can climb the tower for a great view of the lake and dunes. You have to be somewhat determined, however, since the lighthouse is at the end of a 1.5-mile gravel and sand road accessible only by foot or bicycle.

Hiking is a popular pastime in the park, with its 18 miles of trails. There are 11 separate, marked trails that interconnect, winding through dunes and woods of pine, cedar, hemlock, oak and other varieties. Benches have been placed along the trails, but for longer rests there are four trail shelters where hikers can have snacks or cook meals. For skiers there are 16 miles of Nordic trails; they are groomed, but there is no ski rental facility in the park. Perhaps the most unique trail is the canoe trail that runs for six miles along the shore and into the marshes of Hamlin Lake. The route is marked, and interpretive brochures available at the park office point out highlights along the way.

Two day use areas provide beaches with bathhouses and concessions, one on Lake Michigan, the other on Hamlin Lake. There is a picnic area near the Hamlin Lake beach that has tables and grills. A boat ramp provides access to Hamlin Lake, where fishermen can try their luck for northern pike, bass, walleye and tiger muskie.

The park has 344 modern campsites in three campgrounds, all equipped with electricity and shower/toilet facilities. A camp store is located in the **Cedar Campground**, which is between the two others. The **Pines Campground** is closest to Lake Michigan, while the **Beechwood Campground** is near Hamlin Lake. Each campground has one mini-cabin that can sleep four. They are furnished with tables, chairs, heat, lights, fire circles, grills and picnic tables. The campgrounds are open throughout the year, but the shower/toilet facilities are open only mid-April through October.

Ludington State Park is one of only two state parks on Lake Michigan in the lower peninsula that has a visitor's center. (The other is P.J. Hoffmaster State Park near Grand Haven.) **Ludington's Great Lakes Visitor Center** focuses on the geologic and natural history of the Great Lakes with displays, slide

presentations, videos and live programs. It is open daily
Memorial Day through Labor Day, and on weekends in the
spring and fall.

*For more information contact Ludington State Park, PO Box
709, Ludington, MI 49431; 231-843-8671 or 231-843-2423.*

MANISTEE NATIONAL FOREST

The Manistee National Forest stretches nearly a half-million
acres from Muskegon north to Manistee and inland to Cadillac.
Established in 1938, the forest consists of tracts of pine, spruce
and oak inhabited by deer, foxes, bears, wild turkeys and other
bird and mammal species. Though most of the forest is inland
from Lake Michigan, two areas border the lake between
Ludington and Manistee.

The 3,450-acre **Nordhouse Dunes Wilderness**, just north of
Ludington State Park, is the only federally designated wilderness in Michigan's lower peninsula. The dunes, some as tall as
140 feet, were formed some 3,500 to 4,000 years ago. Junipers,
pines and hemlocks grow here, as well as patches of dune
grass. As its name suggests, Nordhouse Dunes is undeveloped.
Hunting, hiking and camping are the primary recreational
activities.

There is a trail system, though it is limited and not well
marked. Park officials recommend that hikers carry a compass.
No water is available. The beach is wide and sandy, providing a
quiet, uncrowded place for walking or swimming. All vehicles
are restricted to the parking areas; not even bicycles are permitted on the trails. Camping is rustic; no facilities are provided.
Groups are limited to ten or fewer. Camp fires are permitted,
but beach fires are not. A pass is required for entry in the dunes
area. All supplies must be carried in and all refuse packed out.

The **Lake Michigan Recreation Area**, just north of Nordhouse
Dunes, is a popular, developed area devoted to campgrounds,
beach and trails. There are 99 campsites with tables and fire
rings. Water is available, as well as flush and vault toilets.

Three and a half miles of gravel trails are open to hikers and bicyclists. The picnic area includes a playground, and there is a sandy swimming beach. The picnic area and the family campground are barrier-free. Cars must have a vehicle pass, which can be purchased at the ranger station in Manistee.

For more information contact the Manistee Ranger Station, 412 Red Apple Road, Manistee, MI 49660; 616-723-2211.

ORCHARD BEACH STATE PARK

This 201-acre park is located on a bluff overlooking Lake Michigan off M-110 just north of Manistee. To the west of M-110 are the campground, picnic areas and beach, while to the east, the park is primarily woods traversed by trails used for hiking during the summer and cross-country skiing during the winter.

The campground has 176 sites, each with a picnic table, fire pit and electrical hook-up. There is also a mini-cabin that can sleep four people and is equipped with electric lights, heaters, a hot plate, table and chairs, picnic table and fire ring. Though there is no boat launch at the park, the camping area has a fish cleaning station. The picnic area, open to day-use visitors, has tables, grills, a playground, lots of trees and a great view of the lake. There is a picnic shelter that can be rented by the day. Stairs lead down from here and from the campground to the narrow sandy beach.

The half-mile **Beech Hemlock Trail**, a self-guided nature trail, is located across from the park entrance. Ask for a trail guide when you enter the park. There are two miles of other hiking trails, which can be used for skiing in the winter, though there is no ski rental concession at the park.

For more information contact Orchard Beach State Park, 2064 Lakeshore Road, Manistee, MI 49660; 231-723-7422.

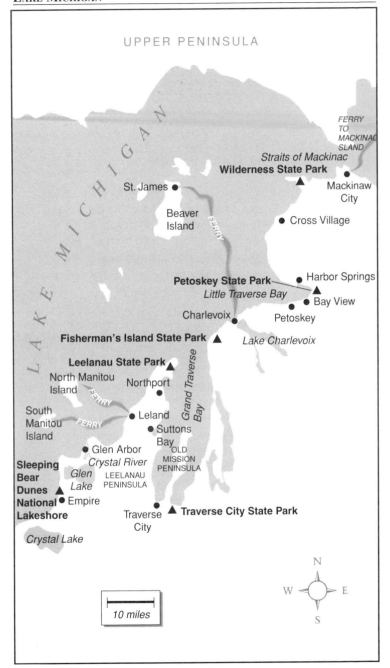

UPPER PENINSULA

LAKE MICHIGAN

FERRY TO MACKINAC ISLAND

Straits of Mackinac

Wilderness State Park

St. James ●

Beaver Island

FERRY

Mackinaw City

● Cross Village

Petoskey State Park
Little Traverse Bay

● Harbor Springs

● Bay View

Charlevoix ●

Petoskey

Fisherman's Island State Park ▲

Lake Charlevoix

Leelanau State Park ▲

North Manitou Island

Northport ●

Grand Traverse Bay

South Manitou Island

FERRY

FERRY

● Leland

● Suttons Bay

● Glen Arbor

Crystal River

OLD MISSION PENINSULA

Sleeping Bear Dunes National Lakeshore ▲

Glen Lake

LEELANAU PENINSULA

● Empire

Traverse City ● ▲ **Traverse City State Park**

Crystal Lake

N
W   E
S

10 miles

Chapter

T H R E E

NORTHERN LOWER PENINSULA

Cherries, Dunes and Old Money

Moving north, the lake shore takes on dramatic change. What has up to this point been a gently rounding shoreline suddenly juts and curves and convolutes itself into peninsulas and inlets, both big and small. This is the land of the Traverse Bays, first named by the French voyageurs who preferred to traverse them — *la petite traverse* and *la grande traverse* — rather than prolong their journey by hugging the shoreline.

The giant dunes of Sleeping Bear National Lakeshore tower over the water, while the inland terrain rises and falls in slopes that bring as many skiers in the winter as the water draws beach goers in the summer. The land is dotted with small lakes the color of a Caribbean lagoon, their warm, calm water a contrast to chilly Lake Michigan. For the first time there are islands, the two Manitou Islands, Beaver Island and a smattering of smaller uninhabited islands.

The northeastern shore is fruit country, where cherry orchards and apricot groves flower against a backdrop of blue. Grapes have more recently found a home here, too, on the Leelanau and Old Mission peninsulas, where they're made into some of the Midwest's finest wines.

An area of stunning beauty and ever-changing vistas, this part of Lake Michigan has long been recognized as a special place. First favored by Native Americans, it later drew French voyageurs, European traders and missionaries. Settlements arose and soon the fishing and logging industries were established. It wasn't long before tourism took hold, and it hasn't let go since.

But there's something a bit different about the tourism here. It's year-round, for one thing, because of the skiing opportunities. But there's something else. It's not quite the beach-ball, dune-buggy, salt-water-taffy tourism found along the southern Michigan shoreline. It's more subdued, more rarefied, more *moneyed*. This is the place wealthy industrialists from Chicago and Detroit chose to vacation over a hundred years ago and it's remained the summer haunt of the well-heeled ever since. Just walk down the streets in Petoskey or Charlevoix, and you'll see shops whose twins hail from places like Palm Beach or Sarasota. Walk into any number of eateries here, and you're likely to have as fine a meal as you'd expect in a top Chicago restaurant.

It's the Midwest version of Palm Springs, Lake Tahoe and Aspen rolled into one, and it's well worth a long meander.

Sleeping Bear Country

Though there are several small, charming towns, a beautiful inland lake called Glen Lake and the exceedingly clear Crystal River, the primary attraction in this area is 70,000-acre Sleeping Bear Dunes National Lakeshore. The park spans 37 miles of lake shore, encompassing beaches, inland lakes, forests and dunes. The most famous of these is Sleeping Bear Dune, whose name originated in a Chippewa legend.

According to the legend, a mother bear and her two cubs were trapped by a raging forest fire on the Wisconsin side of the lake. Forced to flee across the water, they swam until they were exhausted. The mother reached land, but her two cubs had lagged behind. She waited anxiously on shore, but they never

returned, having drowned in the crossing. She, too, finally suc-
cumbed to her weariness, and there she still lies, covered by
sand, facing toward the water and her cubs who were lost for-

CYCLING IN STYLE

If you really want to experience a place — feel the breezes,
taste the air, see the colors — there's nothing quite like
cycling. While it's certainly possible to plan your own itin-
erary, if you want to leave it to the experts, Michigan
Bicycle Touring are your people. In business since 1977,
owners Michael and Libby Robold know what they're
doing.

These guided bicycle trips range from two-day treks based
at a single inn or resort to five-day tours that encompass
several accommodations. All routes are planned for maxi-
mum beauty and minimum traffic. Lodging, breakfasts, dinners and some lunches are arranged and included in the tour
price. Detailed maps are provided, guides ride with the
cyclists, and on the five-day tours baggage is transported by
van. It couldn't be easier. All you have to do is pedal.

While Michigan Bicycle Touring offers tours all over the
state, most of them include at least some mileage along
Lake Michigan. Wind your way along the Leelanau
Peninsula, take a break to wander through Saugatuck's gal-
leries, or pedal the challenging hills of Pierce Stocking
Scenic Drive in Sleeping Bear Dunes National Lakeshore.
Other tours center around Harbor Springs, Pentwater and
Mackinaw Island. Tours run from May to mid-October,
when the fall colors are at their brightest.

Cycling isn't the only possibility. For those who like to get
out on the water the company also offers combination biking and canoeing or biking, hiking and kayaking trips.

For more information contact Michigan Bicycle Touring at
3512 Red School Road, Kingsley, MI 49649; 231-263-5885.

ever. The Great Spirit, known to the Chippewa as Manitou, created two islands in memory of the cubs. Today these are 15,000-acre North Manitou Island and its smaller neighbor, South Manitou Island, both belonging to the park. (For more information about the park, see "Natural Attractions" at the end of this chapter.)

It's possible that French explorers paddled through the area as early as 1622, but it didn't attract permanent white settlers until after 1836. In that year, in the Treaty of Washington, the Indians gave up their claim to the upper western half of the state. The two Manitou islands were the first locations to be settled. Indians had never stayed on the islands, thinking them to be spiritual places, but white settlers soon began to exploit them for their lumber. A lighthouse was built on South Manitou in 1839, making the narrow passage between it and the mainland easier for ships to negotiate.

Lumbering was big business on the mainland also, and as saw mills and trading posts sprang up, so did towns. Among the first of these was Glen Arbor, whose first resident was John Lerue, a trader who in the late 1840s built a log cabin near where the Crystal River empties into Lake Michigan.

The town didn't receive its name until several years later, when John E. Fisher and his wife moved there from Wisconsin. It was Mrs. Fisher who named the town. It must have been a family propensity because John Fisher also named the Crystal River.

By 1867 the township of Glen Arbor had 200 inhabitants, three docks, four stores, two hotels, a blacksmith shop and a handful of other services. Shortly after the turn of the century, however, the lumber that had brought growth to the town had been nearly depleted. Glen Arbor, the dunes, and beautiful turquoise Glen Lake began to attract visitors as a summer resort and the area turned its attention to tourism.

So it is today. Most people come to see the park with its dramatic dunes and lookouts over Lake Michigan, but the small

Kayaking on the Crystal River near Glen Arbor.

towns in the area are also bustling with tourists eagerly browsing at the many galleries and shops.

Though it is surrounded by national park land, the town of Glen Arbor is not a part of the park. It is, however, the closest town to the famous dunes. The commercial area consists of only a few blocks, but they are packed with interesting shops. Among the most unique is the **Cherry Republic**, which capitalizes on the fact that Leelanau County is among the foremost areas for cherry growing anywhere in the world. Here you will find items from plain dried cherries to chocolate covered cherries, cherry salsa and cherry wood bowls. The store also has a bakery and market that sells cherry pies, fresh cherry pastries and just-picked cherries.

For those who decide to rent one of the many cabins in the area, Glen Arbor is presently the best place to pick up food and supplies. The town's large grocery store offers a wide selection, including a variety of fresh local produce. (But don't forget to eat out. Leelanau County has several outstanding restaurants.)

Sports-minded tourists can rent mountain bikes, or kayaks or canoes for runs down the Crystal River. This gently flowing stream offers an ideal experience for children, since it is only inches deep in most places, with a few deeper pockets. Much of the river runs through undeveloped, natural park land. Pack a lunch and pull over to the side for a picnic and a leisurely opportunity to watch fish swimming through the exceptionally clear water.

The arts are also alive and well in Glen Arbor. The **Glen Arbor Art Association**, a non-profit organization, offers a summer music festival, with concerts taking place in Glen Arbor and nearby Leland. The association sponsors a variety of summer art workshops and classes for adults at Lake Street Studios in Glen Arbor. These range from an afternoon to a week and focus on such skills and activities as watercolor painting, print-making, paper marbling and oil painting. Children's "art exploration" classes are also available. For more information contact the Glen Arbor Art Association, PO Box 305, Glen Arbor, MI 49636; 231-334-6112.

The small town of Empire, a few miles southwest of Glen Arbor, is the location of the park headquarters and visitors' center. Like Glen Arbor, it got its start in lumbering. And like Glen Arbor, its first resident was John Lerue, who set up house-keeping there in 1864 when Glen Arbor began to get too crowded for his liking. The town got its name from the schooner that served as a schoolhouse during the winter of 1865 when it was stuck fast in the ice.

During the heyday of the lumber era, the Empire Lumber Company cut 15 to 20 million feet of lumber per year, most of which went to Chicago. It didn't take long to run out. After the mill burned down for the second time, in 1916, it was not rebuilt. Empire never regained the population it lost when the lumberyards closed up and shipped out.

Visitors can learn much about the area's heritage at the **Empire Area Museum**. Consisting of four buildings, the museum contains displays relating to the logging industry and everyday life in an earlier age. The main building features a blacksmith shop, woodworking shop, a covered wagon and the turn-of-the-century Roen Saloon. Behind the main building is the 1911 fire house, which used to be on Empire's Front Street, filled with equipment used from before the turn of the century until 1949. There is also a one-room schoolhouse and a barn with horse-drawn vehicles, including a stagecoach and a hearse.

Though the town is not directly on Lake Michigan, there is a public beach nearby with grills, a picnic area and children's play equipment. Just south of town is the **Empire Bluff Hiking and Ski Trail**. This strenuous trail leads to a 400-foot-high bluff with spectacular views of Lake Michigan, nearby South Bar Lake and the village of Empire.

Canoe and kayak trips are available on the Platt River south of town. There are several options, ranging from calm, "family" trips on gentle water, to more spirited adventures on faster moving water.

WHERE TO STAY:

Bass Lake Cottages, 1042 W. Harbor Hwy., Maple City, MI 49664; 231-334-4825. Phil and Jean Ropp have 12 rental cabins and cottages scattered throughout the area, most of them on or near one of several inland lakes and close to Lake Michigan. Basic, rustic accommodations include equipped kitchens, baths, televisions and phones. There's nothing fancy here, but they do offer a "north woods" feeling. Three of the cottages are within the boundaries of the national park.

Glen Arbor Bed and Breakfast, 6548 M-22, Box 526, Glen Arbor, MI 49636; 231-334-6789. Right in the heart of Glen Arbor, this country-themed bed and breakfast has five guest

A TALL SHIP ADVENTURE

If you've ever looked wistfully at 19th-century engravings of tall-masted schooners plying the Great Lakes and thought how romantic it seemed (though reality was probably not as kind), you might want to experience a bit of that romance yourself on the 114-foot sailing ship Manitou. Modeled after traditional Great Lakes vessels, the Manitou is a two-masted, gaff-rigged topsail schooner capable of carrying 24 passengers for three- to six-day sails on Lakes Michigan and Huron. Though traditional in design, it was built and equipped in 1983 with modern safety in mind.

The Manitou sails June to October from its home port of Northport, at the tip of the Leelanau Peninsula. Destinations may vary according to the weather and conditions, but some of the places visited by the Manitou include Mackinac Island, Beaver Island, Harbor Springs, Grand Traverse Bay or the Manitou Islands. There are several themed trips each season, such as "Fall Color Seeker" or "Music Adventure." Children ages eight and up are welcome on the "Family Sail Aways"; the usual age limit is 16. Those who want an introduction to sailing can opt for the four-day "Sail Trainer."

Guests sleep in double cabins, but those who want to bunk down under the stars on deck can do so. Each cabin has two bunks and electric lights but little else. Showers and toilet facilities are on the main deck. Though quarters are compact and simple, the Manitou is kept meticulously clean.

The Manitou's sister ship, the Malabar, offers day sails out of Traverse City and becomes a floating bed and breakfast after each day's sunset sail. (See the "Traverse City" section.)

For more information about the Manitou or Malabar contact the Traverse Tall Ship Company, 13390 S.W. Bay Shore Dr., Traverse City, MI 49684; 800-678-0383 or 231-941-2000.

rooms, some with private baths, in a 19th-century farmhouse with a large wraparound porch. There's also a cottage on the property that has a fireplace, full kitchen and bath with shower. Bike rentals are available at the B & B; if you're a guest, you get a discount. Those who prefer to get around on foot will find restaurants and shops within easy walking distance. Lake Michigan is just down the road. The B & B is open year round.

The Homestead, Glen Arbor, MI 49636; 231-334-5000 (information), 231-334-5100 (reservations). This is an incredibly beautiful resort on 500 acres with a full mile of beachfront. Many different types of accommodations are available, from hotel rooms to condominiums and vacation homes. Some units face the beach, others are high on a ridge overlooking the lake, and some are in wooded settings. Summer visitors will enjoy the four swimming pools, four tennis courts, stocked fishing pond, boat rentals, fitness trail and nine-hole par-three golf course. The resort's Beach Club has a restaurant, pool and whirlpool overlooking the beach. Eateries range from a deli to a gourmet Italian restaurant. Children's programs are available, and there is even a pre-school center. South Beach, down the road, offers very private accommodations but no amenities on the premises. During the winter there is cross-country and downhill skiing.

Sugar Loaf Resort, 4500 Sugar Loaf Mountain Road, Cedar, MI 49621-9755; 800-952-6390 or 231-228-5461. This large luxury complex is not on Lake Michigan, but in nearby Cedar, about five miles from Sleeping Bear Dunes National Lakeshore. Golfers are attracted by its 18-hole golf course as well as swimming pools, spa, fitness center, restaurant and paved airstrip. Lodging ranges from hotel rooms to four-bedroom suites. During the winter skiing and snowboarding are offered.

The Sylvan Inn, 6680 Western Avenue, PO Box 648, Glen Arbor, MI 49636; 231-334-4333. This historic inn on the outskirts of Glen Arbor's shopping district dates from 1885. There are actually two sections. The historic section has seven rooms, each with in-room sink, and three shared full baths. There is also a suite with bedroom, sitting room, kitchenette and private bath. The other section, which was added in 1987, has six rooms with private baths, seating areas, telephones and TVs. Hosts Jenny and Bill Olson serve continental breakfasts that include fresh baked goods, fruit and juices. Leave the kids at home; this is a quiet, adult atmosphere. The inn is closed in April and November.

WHERE TO EAT:

Good Harbor Grill, 6484 Western Ave., Glen Arbor; 231-334-3555. This is a little piece of heaven for the veggie crowd, with plenty of fresh local produce, home-baked bread and whole grains. Meat-eaters need not shy away, though, because there's also a variety of lean meats and fish. The emphasis is on healthy food, well prepared and reasonably priced. The restaurant is open May to October for breakfast, lunch and dinner, but get there early — it gets crowded. No alcohol is served.

La Bécasse, Burdickville Rd. and South Dunn's Farm Rd.; 231-334-3944. Located in the tiny town of Burdickville, La Bécasse isn't on Lake Michigan, but it's worth the short drive inland to get there. This is French country cooking in an intimate setting. Don't bring the kids; it's on the expensive side and they probably wouldn't appreciate it anyway. Reservations are requested. The restaurant is open for dinner only, Tuesday through Sunday, May to October. Call for winter hours.

Western Avenue Grill, 6410 Western Ave., Glen Arbor; 231-334-3362. This popular spot specializes in pasta, seafood and meat served in a casual atmosphere. There are 10 pasta dishes on the menu as well as pizza. And of course, there's local whitefish. Try it baked with blue cheese — a surprisingly tasty treat. Save room for one of the restaurant's ice cream concoctions.

For more information contact the Glen Lake-Sleeping Bear Chamber of Commerce, PO Box 217, Glen Arbor, MI 49636; 231-334-3238.
Internet: http://www.leelanau.com/glenlake/

Leelanau Peninsula

Fragrant fruit orchards, rolling vineyards and picturesque lake-side towns (with a welcome dearth of fast food franchises) — these are the attractions that await visitors to the far reaches of the Leelanau Peninsula. While the area attracts its share of summer visitors, this beautiful peninsula doesn't yet have the crowds that congregate at Petoskey and Charlevoix farther north.

Like the rest of Leelanau County, the peninsula relied heavily on lumbering in its early years of settlement. Fruit growing also played a major role, and continues to do so. Apples were once an important crop, but they've been replaced by cherries, grown here in abundance. In more recent years, grape growing and winemaking have also seen an upsurge.

Perhaps the town most popular among visitors is Leland, located on Lake Michigan and closely bounded by lovely Lake Leelanau, the two connected by the Leland River. While today's visitors come to shop in exclusive galleries and unique gifts shops, or to dine in the several nautical-themed restaurants, some of the first people to find their way to Leland came to work in the town's iron furnace.

The Leland Lake Superior Iron Company was founded in 1870 by a group of Detroit businessmen. Ore for the furnace came from the Upper Peninsula and was unloaded at the Leland docks. Local farmers provided the limestone needed for the kilns, and workers came from afar — many from Bohemia — to stoke the fires. Some 40 tons of iron were produced each day for shipment to Detroit.

It was a short-lived industry, however, and by the end of the century, the furnace was closed and the town was focused on the lumber business that flourished elsewhere on the peninsula. That too subsided when the seemingly inexhaustible supply of lumber began to dwindle. Things were looking bleak for Leland until it was discovered by summer visitors who found it

MACKINAC ISLAND

Technically, Mackinac Island is in Lake Huron and therefore beyond the scope of this book. But if you've gotten as far as Mackinaw City or St. Ignace, you'll certainly want to take the ferry over to the island for a day, if not for longer.

Mackinac Island has long been known for its quaintness. In the late 1800s the island banned automobiles, and horses have maintained their importance ever since. Taxis are horse powered, deliveries arrive by horse, and local hotels pick up their guests at the ferry docks in horse-drawn carriages. Tourists love it. It's a popular, crowded place in the summer, but there's a secret not many visitors discover.

Mackinac is far more than horse-drawn carriages, fudge shops and the ubiquitous souvenir stands. Get away from the busy downtown area, and it's a different world. In fact, 80% of the island is state park land, where you'll find hiking trails and magnificent natural stone formations. One of the great pleasures of the island is the lack of motorized vehicles, so riding a bike along the park's quiet roads with their backdrop of beautiful scenery is something to be enjoyed by all who are able.

Don't miss Fort Mackinac, also part of the state park (though a separate admission is charged). Construction of the fort began in 1781 when British fur traders and soldiers moved from Fort Michilimackinac in what is now Mackinaw City to the greater protection offered by the island's bluff high over the water. British influence on the island remained strong, and even though it was awarded to the Americans in the peace treaty of 1783, the fort remained in British hands until 1796. It fell to the British again during the War of 1812, and wasn't surrendered until the end of the war. Today, you can witness period reenactments, musket firing demonstrations, canon salutes

Fort Macikinac, Mackinac Island.

and a variety of other special events.

Perhaps the best-known landmark on the island is the graceful Grand Hotel, built in 1887 and billed as the world's largest summer hotel. It is indeed grand, in every sense of the word — size, elegance, service. The 800-foot pillared porch with its splendid view of the water still stands, evocative of the relaxed luxury enjoyed by a privileged few in the 1890s. For information and rates call 800-33-GRAND.

There many smaller places to stay that have no shortage of charm. Among them is the Chippewa Hotel, built in 1902 and recently completely remodeled. Located in the shopping district, the hotel is right on the water, and some rooms have balconies with spectacular views. There is a heated pool, as well as waterfront dining and the Pink Pony Bar and Grill, which features live entertainment. For more information call 800-241-3341 or 906-847-3341.

For more information on the island contact the Mackinac Island Chamber of Commerce, PO Box 451, Mackinac Island, MI 49757; 800-4-LILACS or 906-847-6418.

Leelanau Wine Cellars, one of several wineries on the Leelanau Peninsula.

to be an ideal resort.

Tourism and a modest fishing industry have continued to support the town since the early 1900s. Fishtown, the small dock area on the Leland River where commercial fishing centered, remains the primary attraction. Though the fish shanties are now largely occupied by small shops geared to the tourist trade,

Fishtown in Leland.

commercial fishermen still haul in loads of whitefish daily, which turn up on the visitors' plates as they dine overlooking the water.

On the north side of the river is **Manitou Island Transit**, which operates ferries to the North and South Manitou Islands. (See the section on Sleeping Bear Dunes National Lakeshore in "Natural Attractions" at the end of this chapter.) South of the river is a small public beach on Lake Michigan. Spreading back from the waterfront are several blocks of shops, galleries, fudge stands and restaurants.

To find out more about the peninsula's past, stop in at the **Leelanau Historical Museum and Historical Society** (231-256-7475) located adjacent to the public library. The focus is on local history, including logging, maritime heritage and farming. There is a special emphasis on barn building, an art that has declined along with the number of farms. The museum sponsors occasional day-long guided trips to North Manitou Island, something which is not usually possible since the ferry normally drops passengers off on the island and doesn't return until the following day. Reservations are necessary. The museum is open all year, but off-season hours are limited.

Walkers will enjoy the **Whaleback Conservancy Trail**, located off M22 south of town. The one-mile round trip hike on the trail leads through hardwood forest to a bluff 300 feet above Lake Michigan where a lookout offers a view of the lake and the Manitou Islands.

Traveling north, the next town is Northport, which is actually on the other side of the peninsula, along the considerably calmer water of Grand Traverse Bay. Like Leland, but on a somewhat smaller scale, Northport has shops and restaurants catering to the summer visitor.

Platted in 1852, Northport was one of the first towns on the peninsula to be settled. The first road came through in 1862, an old Indian trail that connected it with Traverse City. Logging was the economic mainstay until, like elsewhere in the area, the trees were depleted. It was then that cherry farming came into its own. In 1912 Cleveland wholesale grocer and canner Frances H. Haserot, along with his partner G.M. Dame, planted 14,000 Montgomery cherry trees, the largest orchard in the area. A canning factory was then built, and by 1948 it was processing four million pounds of cherries a year, even shipping them overseas.

Today, aside from the shops and restaurants, the main attraction is the **Grand Traverse Lighthouse**, located north of town at the tip of the peninsula in Leelanau State Park. One of the oldest on the lake, it was constructed in 1858. Its fourth order Fresnel lens shone light 12 to 17 miles out into the lake until the Coast Guard replaced it with an automatic beacon in 1972. The lighthouse was left to vanquish until 1985, when a local group undertook its renovation and preservation. Today it is a museum open to the public.

The fog signal building, which now houses a gift shop, is located nearby. The lighthouse and fog signal building are open weekends in the spring and fall, daily mid-June through Labor Day. You must pay admission to get into the park, then another small fee to enter the museum.

As M22 curves southward along the western shore of Grand Traverse Bay, it passes through the small town of Peshawbestown. Originally called Eagletown, it was established by a group of Ottawa Indians who came south from Cross Village in 1852. Today the town is a federally recognized reservation and the location of the **Leelanau Sands Casino**, operated by the Grand Traverse Band of Ottawa and Chippewa Indians. There you'll find a multitude of ways to part with your money — or if you're lucky, to go home a bit richer: craps, black jack, Caribbean stud poker and slot machines are just a few. **The Eagle's Ridge** restaurant and **Leelanau Sands Lodge** on the grounds ensure that you won't go hungry or sleepless between rounds. For more information contact the casino at 888-597-2946.

Farther along the east coast of the peninsula is Suttons Bay, previously called Pleasant City, an apt title for such a charming town. In addition to specialty shops, galleries and antiques shops galore, some of the best restaurants on the peninsula can be found here. The protected harbor, which once sheltered ships for the lumber trade, is now the location of a marina for pleasure boaters. Just north of the marina is a sandy public beach with calm water and gently sloping bottom, making it an ideal spot for small children. The boardwalk on the south side of the harbor leads through a small marsh area and along the water, and makes a pleasant place for an early morning walk.

Trails for walking and recreation include the **Leelanau Trail**, which follows an old railroad bed to Traverse City, and 30 miles of trails at **Bahle Park** north of the village. Skiing and sledding are also popular activities at the park.

Suttons Bay is the home of the **Inland Seas Education Association**, a unique non-profit organization dedicated to promoting the study and conservation of the Great Lakes. The association offers one- to two-day classes and educational cruises aboard three schooners: the Manitou and Malabar, owned by the Traverse Tall Ship Company; and the Inland Seas, built specifically as a sailing classroom for the ISEA. The

Inland Seas can often be seen at its berth at the marina in Suttons Bay; the other ships are berthed at Traverse City. Many of the classes are for youths only, though there are also adult seminars and family cruises. The Family Schoolship program is a four-hour cruise during which parents or grandparents and children trawl for fish, collect plankton, take water and bottom samples, hoist the sails and raise the anchor. Registration is required for all programs. For more information and schedules contact the association at 101 Dame Street, PO Box 218, Suttons Bay, MI 49682; phone 231-271-3077.

Aside from these charming towns and pretty beaches, wineries draw a steady flow of visitors. The tempering effect of Lake Michigan and Grand Traverse Bay creates a micro climate suitable not only for cherries, but for wine grapes, which are being seen in increasing numbers on the Leelanau Peninsula. Because the temperature is similar to that of Germany, some of the most successful northern Michigan wines bear some resemblance to their German counterparts, with their subtle fruitiness and delicate flavor. Riesling is one of the best wines found in this region, followed closely by pinot gris. Cherry wines are also made in abundance, though they vary greatly in style and appeal.

There are five wineries scattered over the peninsula and all welcome visitors. Tasting room hours vary, so it's best to call ahead if you're planning a visit.

If there's a signature wine for Leelanau Peninsula, the honor would probably have to go to Fishtown White, produced by **Good Harbor Vineyards**, just south of Leland on M22 (231-256-7165). This pleasant semi-dry blend of seyval and vignoles appears on many area restaurants' wine lists and makes a nice partner for Lake Michigan whitefish. The winery's pinot gris is also quite good, as are the chardonnay and Johannisberg riesling. Winemaker Bruce Simpson's excellent cherry wine is like drinking liquid cherry pie. It just begs for a rich chocolate dessert to accompany it. While at the winery, be sure to stop at the **Manitou Farm Market** on the grounds, a great place to pick up some local produce and fresh bakery goods.

Farther out the peninsula in Omena is **Leelanau Wine Cellars** (231-386-5201). Good wines and friendly people characterize this winery, the area's largest. The most popular offerings include the award-winning "Tall Ship" chardonnay and two "Vis a Vis" wines: the white is a blend of chardonnay and vignoles; the red combines pinot noir and baco noir. The winery also makes a port and a raspberry port, two products unusual for this area.

Boskydel Vineyard (231-256-7272) overlooks Lake Leelanau about midway in the peninsula where owner Bernie Rink has planted 25 acres of French-American hybrid grapes alongside pine groves. The winery's products include varietals such as vignoles and soleil blanc as well as red, white and rose-blends.

L. Mawby Vineyards (231-271-3522) is a bit farther south, between Suttons Bay and Traverse City. Owner Larry Mawby cultivates 12 acres of grapes on his property, from which he produces estate table wines and excellent *methode champenoise* sparkling wines. He often participates in wine events at local restaurants, a good opportunity to sample his wines matched with fine local cuisine.

Shady Lane Cellars (231-947-8865), just north of Traverse City on Shady Lane Road, produces sparkling wines, pinot noir, riesling and chardonnay on a historic 100-acre farm. At the time of writing, the tasting room is open seasonally by appointment only.

WHERE TO STAY:

Falling Waters Lodge, Box 345, Leland, MI 49654; 231-256-9832. This 21-room lodge has a great location on the Leland River near Lake Michigan and overlooking Fishtown. Each type of accommodation is different; there are guest rooms, suites, loft suites and a spacious penthouse with kitchenette, dining area, loft and balcony overlooking the river. All are quite reasonably priced. Guests with rooms on the lower level can fish right from their balconies, and boaters can dock right next to their rooms. There is a deck on the upper level with a grill and a walkway over the water to Fishtown. The public beach is just steps away. Call in the spring for summer bookings — rooms here fill up quickly. The lodge is open in the spring and fall, but closed in the winter.

AND THE WINNER IS...

How it began is impossible to say. But somewhere, sometime, someone said that the drive up M131 from Harbor Springs to Cross Village is the prettiest in Michigan. We know, at least, that the notion was well established by 1944, when historian Milo Quaife wrote his definitive history of Lake Michigan. He called it "the most beautiful driveway in Michigan, bowered in maples and beeches, through which one catches occasional glimpses of the blue waters of Lake Michigan and the distant Beaver Islands." Unlike just about everything else, this is one thing that hasn't changed much since 1944. The narrow, twisting road still winds its way for 31 miles through forests along the edge of a bluff high over the lake. The best times to see the lake will naturally be winter and spring, but don't miss the fall, when driving through the "Tunnel of Trees" in their full colors is truly a memorable experience.

But it's not over when you reach Cross Village. This small town is one of the oldest settlements in the state, having served as a great council center for the Ottawas and the site of a Jesuit mission established in 1740. There's not a lot to betray its distinguished history, nor, for that matter, much to see except for the near-legendary Legs Inn. Built over several decades by Polish immigrant Stanley Smolak, this restaurant and bar features an eclectic decor of driftwood, tree stumps and hand-carved furniture. It's also known far and wide for serving the best Polish food around. So if you're in the mood for golabki or kielbasa, head for an outdoor table with a view of the lake and enjoy. For information call Legs Inn at 231-526-2281. They're open seasonally.

Open Windows Bed & Breakfast, PO Box 698, 613 St. Mary's Avenue, Suttons Bay, MI 49682; 800-520-3722 or 231-271-4300. Don and Norma Bluemenschine had an office supply business in Toledo; when they wanted to get away, they'd drive up to Suttons Bay and stay at a little B & B owned by two sisters. Today they own that B & B, which is called Open Windows. A century home in a quiet residential neighborhood, it is within walking distance to the beach, shopping and restaurants. There are three guest rooms, all with private bath, one with air conditioning. Norma serves full breakfasts with items such as quiche, homemade breads and seasonal fruits. When she's not busy attending to the B & B business, Norma cans her homemade jams and bottles homemade herb vinegars, which she sells. Don crafts Adirondack chairs and matching side tables and foot rests. Guests may place orders for their own furniture. The Bluemenschines host many special events throughout the year, including murder mystery weekends and epicurean feasts in conjunction with Hattie's Restaurant and Mawby Vineyards. Children are welcome at the B & B, but must be under their parents' supervision at all times.

The Riverside Inn, PO Box 1135, 302 River Street, Leland, MI 49654; 888-257-0102 or 231-256-9971. Located on the grassy shores of the Leland River, the Riverside Inn has been hosting guests since the early 1900s. There are eight cozy rooms, four with private baths, on the upper floor of the inn. Half of them have a view of the river. Two pairs of rooms can be rented as suites. The lower level of the inn has a dining room and bar featuring the wines of the peninsula. It's an idyllic spot.

The Stone SchoolHouse Bed & Breakfast, 513 Saint Mary's Avenue, PO Box 156, Suttons Bay, MI 49682; 231-271-2738. You can't miss this B & B while driving down Saint Mary's Avenue — its impressive stone exterior and large size indicate it's not an ordinary house. It was indeed a schoolhouse, built in 1906, and is today a designated historic landmark. The Sheilder family has converted it to a bed and breakfast with two large suites that can accommodate families or two couples traveling together. The Music Room includes a baby grand piano, two queen beds, sofa, love seat, entertainment center and private bath with whirlpool tub. The smaller Art Room, decorated with paintings and prints, has two queen beds, couch, love seat, entertainment center and private bath. Both suites have stained glass windows and plenty of light. The common entertainment area features a 1950s soda fountain and Formica lunch counter where guests can play pool or watch vintage movies on the big screen TV. There's a hot tub down the hall.

WHERE TO EAT:

The Bluebird Restaurant and Bar, 102 E. River Street, Leland; 231-256-9081. The Bluebird is a favorite among the locals — meaning get there early, or you're going to have to wait. It's been in the same family since 1927, so it seems they know what they're doing. This is a casual place that specializes in fresh whitefish, steaks and seafood. It's open daily in the summer for lunch and dinner; during the winter food is served in the bar.

Cafe Bliss, 420 St. Joseph Street, Suttons Bay; 231-271-5000. The chef at Cafe Bliss isn't shy about marrying ingredients in unusual ways. Take, for example, walleye and tuna in a creamy, spicy curry sauce over brown rice and accompanied by sautéed spinach and toasted walnuts. This is just one of the tasty specials that appear at Cafe Bliss, which specializes in vegetarian and ethnic food. The menu is filled with healthy, great tasting food prepared creatively with low fat ingredients. Located in an old house, the restaurant has a quiet, homey atmosphere. Wine and cocktails are available. It's open daily for breakfast, lunch and dinner from Memorial Day to late October; closed in the winter.

The Cove, 111 E. River Street, Leland; 231-256-9834. You couldn't ask for a more picturesque location for dining al fresco in Leland. The Cove is perched along the river overlooking Fishtown, with plenty of outdoor seating available. The restaurant brings in fresh whitefish daily, which it serves in a variety of ways. Be sure to try the excellent fish and chips. Washed down with a glass of Fishtown White wine from Good Harbor Vineyards, it makes a perfect lunch. There's also plenty in the way of sandwiches and burgers. The Cove is open for lunch and dinner mid-May through mid-October.

Hattie's, 111 St. Joseph Street, Suttons Bay; 231-271-6222. Hattie's is a bit on the expensive side, but has excellent food. You'll find appetizers like roasted butternut squash bisque and fettucine with black truffle cream, or entrees such as grilled duck with Traverse City cherries and grilled rack of venison with roasted onions. Go early and ask for the theater menu available 5:30 to 6:30 p.m. (The "theater" is the movie variety — located across the street.) It's a different menu, but a relative bargain. And leave the kids with a sitter — this is food for a sophisticated palate.

White Birch Grill, 1381 S.W. Bayshore Drive, Suttons Bay; 231-271-4100. Don't be fooled by the Plain Jane exterior of the White Birch Grill. Inside you will find such delectables as herb roasted chicken with Michigan cherry sauce or blackened swordfish topped with roasted red pepper salsa. There's also an impressive list of wines by the glass, including a large selection of local wines. And for dessert, you couldn't get any more decadent than Leelanau Mud Pie — mocha ice cream on a chocolate cookie crumb crust topped with chocolate fudge. The restaurant is open year round.

For more information contact the Leelanau County Chamber of Commerce, M204 at the Narrows, PO Box 336, Lake Leelanau, MI 49653; phone 231-256-9895.
Internet: http://www.lelanau.com/chamber

Traverse City

Located on sparkling Grand Traverse Bay, Traverse City is the hub of tourism along this part of the lake shore. Though its population is less than 20,000, the city has a seemingly endless supply of resorts and motels that swell to full capacity in the summertime.

The reasons people go to Traverse City are about as varied as the resorts. For some it's the beaches and swimming here on the bay where the lake is much calmer than elsewhere. For others, it's the nearby golf. There's great boating, sailing, shopping and eating. You can ride a dinner train, go up in a hot air balloon, soar high over the water on a parasail, take a sightseeing plane ride, or go for a sail on a two-masted schooner.

Sleeping Bear Dunes National Lakeshore is less than an hour's drive away. So is the Leelanau Peninsula with its quaint towns, unique shops and beautiful scenery. Interlochen Arts Camp, the site of many concerts and performances, is only 14 miles away. Old Mission Peninsula's wineries are even closer. Truth is, you'll never run out of things to do in and around Traverse City.

The city got its start with lumber in the 1840s. Like other lumbering towns, it had its share of rowdiness, no doubt aided by the 20-some saloons and other hotbeds of immorality. The residents were rough types, sawmill workers and lumberjacks resistant to the tireless efforts of the local churches.

Among the first lumber businesses to open was Hannah, Lay and Company, owned by three wealthy Chicago businessmen, Perry Hannah, Albert T. Lay and James Morgan, who established a mill to supply their Chicago yards. Perry Hannah in particular became very involved in the development of the city, taking part in its planning and later serving as village president and mayor. Hannah's magnificent house still stands, though it is today a funeral home.

Unfortunately, trees couldn't grow as fast as they were cut. With the depletion of the wood supplies, lumbering in the area met its demise shortly after the beginning of the 20th century. The economy shifted gradually to farming, with fruit crops — especially cherries — figuring prominently. The town fathers also began to promote tourism. These efforts shaped the town's future, for it's known today primarily as a resort town and the Cherry Capital of the World.

Fittingly, Traverse City hosts the **National Cherry Festival** each July, as it has for more than 70 years. This eight-day celebration includes air shows, parades, cherry orchard tours, bike tours, races and plenty of cherries. There's a cherry pie eating contest, cherry farm markets, and the crowning of the National Cherry Festival Queen (who used to travel all the way to Washington, D.C., to present a cherry pie to the president).

There is much to see in Traverse City, even if it's not Cherry Festival time. Start at the **Visitor Center** at the corner of Grandview Parkway (U.S. 31) and Union Street. Then head to Front Street, the town's vibrant shopping area, where you'll find galleries, coffee houses, gift shops and restaurants in restored historic buildings. Down the street is the **City Opera House**, currently being restored, which was built in 1891 to seat 1,200 for plays and musicals. If you happen to be in town on a Saturday, head a block or so south where the **Farm Market** takes place along the Boardman River, which winds through the town on its way to the bay.

Two residential neighborhoods nearby are notable for their historic homes. The area around 6th Street, southwest of the Front Street shopping district, is where many lumber executives built their homes in the late 1800s and early 1900s. Perry Hannah's house can be found here at 305 6th Street. The three-story Queen Anne style mansion was built in 1891-93 at a cost of about $35,000 — no small sum in those days. The Boardman Avenue area, southwest of the shopping district, was one of Traverse City's first residential neighborhoods, home to both business leaders and less affluent workers. Nearly 200 of these homes remain.

The waterfront is occupied by a public beach, the municipal marina and **Clinch Park Zoo** (231-922-4904). Children will enjoy this small zoo and its unique collection of Michigan fish and wildlife: otters, beavers, turtles, birds of prey, cougars, lynx, bobcats, bison, deer, elk, American Black Bears and more. The Education Building houses smaller animals such as snakes, salamanders and frogs. The small aquarium features fish common to Lake Michigan.

The zoo complex is also where visitors will find the **Con Foster Museum**, named for Conrad ("Con") Foster, a civic leader in first half of the 20th century. Through his efforts the city's waterfront was cleaned up after the Hannah Mill closed. During the 1930s he organized volunteers to clean the beach and make a waterfront park, which included an aquarium, boathouse and museum.

The museum displays depict the human history of the area. There are exhibits focusing on the native peoples and their customs, including artifacts such as utensils, weapons, clothing and a reconstructed bark wigwam. Community exhibits include doll houses, replicas of Traverse City historic buildings and a diorama of a logging camp.

Small children will enjoy the train ride on the grounds. There is also a refreshment stand with a pleasant outdoor dining area. To get to the zoo and museum you must park across the street and walk through the tunnel underneath busy Grandview Parkway. The zoo and museum are open daily Memorial Day through Labor Day; the museum only is open on weekends in the winter.

If it's in port, don't miss the chance to see the schooner **Madeline**, docked at nearby Clinch Marina. This 92-foot replica of an 1840s commercial sailing vessel was built by volunteers from the Maritime Heritage Alliance, an organization involved with the restoration and replication of historic boats and the promotion of maritime history. The original Madeline served as the first schoolhouse in the region during the winter of 1850-51 and later as a carrier to Beaver Island. The ship tours the Great Lakes, but when it's in its berth at Traverse City, volunteers from the Maritime Heritage Alliance provide evening sails and tours to the public. Contact the Alliance at 231-946-2647 for more information.

If the Madeline isn't available for sails, chances are the **Malabar** is. This 105-foot topsail schooner was built in 1975, modeled on traditional 19th-century vessels. The Malabar can

Sailing on the Malabar, floating bed and breakfast in Traverse City.

accommodate 46 passengers during its excursions around Grand Traverse Bay. It sails daily from the end of May until the beginning of October, offering morning sails, noon picnic sails, afternoon sails and sunset picnics. After its final sail of the day, the Malabar becomes a floating bed and breakfast for up to 21 guests (see "Where to stay"). Though children are welcome on the excursions, keep in mind that restless youngsters may get squirmy. For more information call 800-678-0383 or 231-941-2000.

Walkers, cyclists and in-line skaters will enjoy the **TART Trail** (Traverse Area Recreational Trail), an 11-mile paved path that runs from M72 on West Arm Grand Traverse Bay to Acme on East Arm Grand Traverse Bay. It passes along the waterfront, through downtown, then along the Chesapeake and Ohio railroad tracks, past Traverse City State Park, ending at the small town of Acme.

A bit removed from the waterfront and shopping district, but worth the effort, is the **Dennos Museum Center** (231-922-1055 or 800-748-0566) on the campus of Northwestern Michigan College. This center for visual and performing arts has several galleries, some for changing exhibits and one for the museum's permanent collection of sculpture, drawings and prints by Inuit artists of the Canadian Arctic.

While in Traverse City take the time to drive north a few miles along the eastern side of the bay on M31 to the small town of Acme, where you'll find the **Music House** (231-938-9300). In 1983 a group of private collectors got together, combined their collections and opened this museum of authentically restored rare antique automated instruments on the grounds of an old farmstead. Hour-long tours are led by knowledgeable guides who demonstrate the instruments and give commentary on their history and how they fit into the social fabric of the times. Music boxes, nickelodeons, player pianos and other instruments are displayed in turn-of-the-century settings. The musical highlight is a Weber Duo-Art grand reproducing piano which, as its name suggests, is capable of reproducing performances rendered by such famous artists as George Gershwin or Sergei Rachmaninoff. Visitors will hear an example of these — if they're lucky, part of Gershwin's "Rhapsody in Blue" as played by the composer. Visually, the star of the show is a 1922 Belgian Mortier dance organ that takes up an entire upper portion of the museum. The

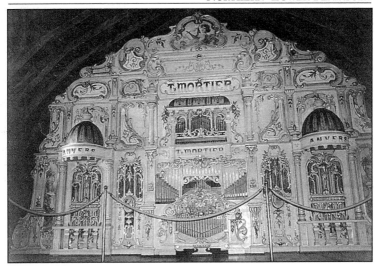

1922 dance organ at the Music House museum near Traverse City.

museum is open May 1 through October 31 and holiday weekends in winter. It's well worth the drive.

WHERE TO STAY:

There are many places to stay in and around Traverse City. What follows is, of necessity, only a small sampler of what can be found. Families with children may be happiest in one of the resorts that line the waterfront. Couples who want a quiet place might prefer to stay on Old Mission Peninsula, only a few miles north but close enough for an easy drive into the city for activities. (See next section for listings on Old Mission Peninsula.)

Bayshore Resort, 833 East Front Street, Traverse City, MI 49686-2703; 800-634-4401 or 231-935-4400. This is one of the prettiest among the many resorts and motels on Front Street. It's right in town, a short distance from the airport (free shuttle available), yet it doesn't feel crowded. The resort has a beautiful sandy beach, indoor pool, whirlpool, fitness center and game room. Most of the rooms and suites have a view of the water; all are nicely decorated in Victorian style. Each suite has a fireplace, spa, wet bar and refrigerator. Continental breakfast is included. There is no restaurant at the resort, but many are within walking distance. Bayshore is open all year; consider visiting in the spring, fall or winter when off season rates apply. It is a smoke-free facility.

Tall Ship Malabar, Traverse Tall Ship Co., 13390 S. West-Bay Shore Dr., Traverse City, MI 49684; 231-941-2000. Got a little of the old salt in your blood? A night on the Malabar might be just the thing. This two-masted traditional schooner takes groups out for sails during the day and serves as a bed and breakfast at night. Overnight guests are treated to a sunset sail with picnic dinner before bedding down in the eight staterooms or, if preferred, under the stars on the open deck. There's a hearty breakfast in the morning. The staterooms can accommodate 21 guests (minimum age is eight). They are simple but clean and comfortable. Each room has bunks, lights and a wash basin. The shared toilet facilities on board are small, but modern rest rooms and showers are available on shore. The boat is moored overnight at the company's private dock.

The Victoriana 1898 Bed and Breakfast, 622 Washington Street, Traverse City, MI 49684; 231-929-1009. Nearly everything about this bed and breakfast is perfect, from its fine antiques to its gingerbread trim. Hosts Flo and Bob Schermerhorn have completely renovated this turn-of-the-century Victorian gem (built in 1898 for an incredible $2,800). There are four bright rooms decorated with family heirlooms, though only three at a time are rented. Each occupied guest room has a roomy private bath. The Betsy Nelson Berg Room has a fireplace and private porch. Guests can enjoy the parlor with fireplace or the outdoor gazebo that was once the bell tower for the Traverse City Central School. The bed and breakfast is located in a quiet historic residential neighborhood. Expect a full breakfast — Flo has 40 different entrees in her repertoire. Leave the kids at home; this is an adult atmosphere.

WHERE TO EAT:

Mackinaw Brewing Company, 161 E. Front Street; 231-933-

1100. Located in the heart of the downtown shopping district, this micro brewery is a popular spot for a casual meal. In addition to the hand-crafted beers, diners will find sandwiches, salads, burgers, pasta and more substantial meals of chicken, seafood or beef. Genuine smokehouse pork, beef, turkey and ham are featured sandwich stuffers.

Sleder's Family Restaurant and Saloon, 717 Randolph Street; 231-947-9213. People have been gathering at Sleder's, Michigan's oldest continuously operating tavern, for more than a hundred years. The attraction here is a casual atmosphere combined with hearty food (and a very large moose guests are invited to kiss). Prices are wallet-friendly. Ever had a buffalo burger? You can get one here. Less adventurous eaters will find Mexican selections, sandwiches, ribs, fish, salads. Sleder's is open for lunch and dinner. There's a children's menu available.

Windows, 7677 West Bay Shore Drive; 231-941-0100. Its location outside of town overlooking Grand Traverse Bay and its elegant food make this a perfect place for a romantic dinner. The specialty here is French-American cuisine with a Cajun bent and an emphasis on seafood, a natural for Chef Philip Murray who came to Michigan from New Orleans. Chocoholics will swoon over the desserts, and wine enthusiasts will be pleased with the wine list that has won national recognition. Windows is open for dinner only.

For more information contact the Traverse City Convention and Visitors Bureau, 101 W. Grandview Parkway, Traverse City, MI 49684; 800-872-8377 or 231-947-1120.
Internet: http://www.traversecity.com

Old Mission Peninsula

Old Mission Peninsula, just north of Traverse City, juts 18 miles into Grand Traverse Bay, dividing it neatly in half. The drive out M37 on the peninsula offers one of the most gorgeous scenes — any time of year — on Lake Michigan. Though only a few miles from the city, the peninsula feels far removed from the bustle of tourism encountered there. The road passes along the top of a high ridge down the center of the peninsula, with views of water, orchards and vineyards everywhere you look. In the spring it's the cherry blossoms that steal the scene; in the fall, the palette of changing colors against the deep blue of the bay.

There are few commercial establishments on the peninsula; it is primarily farmland and wineries, with a handful of restaurants and bed and breakfasts. There are no hotels or motels, nothing to mar the atmosphere which is harmonious to the land itself. The couple of "towns" are little more than small clusters of buildings, the largest being Bowers Harbor, on the shores of a bay with the same name.

Among the first white people to live on the peninsula was Reverend Peter Dougherty, a Presbyterian missionary sent in 1838 to work with the local Chippewas. His house, which is still standing today on Mission Road near the end of M37, was the first frame building in the area. Also on Mission Road is a replica of a log house Dougherty built in 1840 to use as a church and school. It was a short-lived endeavor, however; the

Lighthouse Park on Old Mission Peninsula.

Indians were forced to leave when the peninsula was opened to white settlers.

The settlers began to arrive in the 1850s. Among them were Joe and Mary Hessler, whose log home, built in 1854-56, has been restored. Though it once stood in the southern part of the peninsula, it has been moved to the extreme end at Old Mission Point on the grounds of **Lighthouse Park**. Visitors cannot enter the building, but can see the period furnishings through glassed in areas at the rear of the cabin.

Just next to the cabin is the **Old Mission Lighthouse**, established in 1870 after a large ship sank on the adjacent reef in the 1860s. The 30-foot tower is incorporated into a frame building that was the lightkeeper's house until the light was decommissioned in 1933. Today the light is owned by the township and occupied by caretakers. It is off limits to visitors, but you can still get a nice photograph of the tower and grounds with the lake in the background. The lighthouse is located on the 45th parallel, exactly halfway between the North Pole and the Equator.

The adjacent beach, which is part of the park, is particularly nice for kids because it stays shallow a long way out. There are also marked hiking trails in the park.

Another nice public beach is **Haserot Beach** in the town of Old Mission on East Traverse Bay. There is a children's play area and a lifeguard on duty during the summer months.

Most people, however, don't go to the peninsula for the beaches; they go for the wineries. Like the Leelanau Peninsula, Old Mission has an ideal climate for grape growing. There are four wineries on the peninsula, and a tour of them makes a nice afternoon's activity. (Hours vary; it's best to call ahead to check when the tasting rooms will be open.)

Heading north on M37, the first one is **Peninsula Cellars** (231-223-4310), a small winery with some very nice wines. Though they make dry wines such as chardonnay, it is the fruity wines that are so unusual. Currently, this is the only winery on the peninsula that makes a white cherry wine. Also especially notable is their Mélange, a blend of wine made from Black Ulster sweet cherries and grape brandy, reminiscent of port.

Next comes **Chateau Grand Traverse** (231-223-7355), also on M37, located at the highest point of the peninsula. "Grand" is not an inappropriate term, both for the size of the winery and the quantity and quality of its output. In 1974 Founder Edward O'Keefe set out to establish a world-class winery and to prove that European grape varieties could be grown successfully in Michigan. The result is an extensive offering of award-winning wines. Known primarily for its riesling, for which it has won much recognition, the winery also produces chardonnay, pinot noir and cabernet franc. The large tasting room is open all year; during the summer there are guided winery tours several times daily.

The third winery is **Bowers Harbor Vineyards** (231-223-7615), on Bowers Harbor Road about midway out the peninsula. (Take M37 to Seven Hills Road, turn left, then left again on Bowers Harbor Road. The winery is on the left.) This small winery is a very pleasant place to stop. The cozy tasting room is reached by walking under a vine-covered arbor. Then you'll probably be greeted by a member of the friendly Stegenga family, owners of the winery. Though they produce less and fewer types of wines than some other wineries, they do them quite well. Among the best are the excellent pinot grigio and semi-dry riesling, both grapes that grow well in this cool climate. Perhaps because it's a bit off the beaten path, the winery has a quiet, amiable atmosphere. It is open daily during the summer and weekends during the winter.

The final winery is **Chateau Chantal** (231-223-4110), on M37 about three-quarters of the way to the point. This is a gorgeous setting for the imposing winery and the elegant bed and breakfast that is also on the grounds (see "Where to stay"). Owner Bob Begin has succeeded in creating the "Old World" ambiance he desired when he entered the wine business on the peninsula in 1983. The winery produces wines that range from a dry pinot gris to sweet sparkling cherry wine.

WHERE TO STAY:

Bowers Harbor Bed & Breakfast, 13972 Peninsula Drive, Traverse City, MI 49686; 231-223-7869. This charming bed and breakfast occupies a 1870 farmhouse on the waterfront at Bowers Harbor. There are three guest rooms, each with private bath and each with a different view. (If you want a view of the bay, ask for room #1.) The rooms are nicely decorated and comfortable, complete with down pillows. The large wrap-around porch is a wonderful spot to watch the sunset or curl up with a book. In the winter, the living room with its stone fire-place is a favorite gathering spot. Hosts Gary and Mary Ann Verbanic serve homemade breakfasts that include fresh muffins and fruit. There is a private sandy beach just across the street, and the marina and two restaurants are within walking distance. This is a quiet spot best enjoyed by adults.

Chateau Chantal Bed & Breakfast, 15900 Rue du Vin, Old Mission Peninsula, Traverse City, MI 49686; 800-969-4009 or 231-223-4110. You could hardly ask for a more stunning view than the one from Chateau Chantal, a working winery. This ele-gant B & B, which is in the same building as the tasting room, sits high on a hill overlooking vineyards and the bay in the dis-tance. A brick patio with tables and umbrellas makes a pleasant place to sample one of the winery's products while admiring the scenery. There are three rooms; two are suites and the other a double. The suites can accommodate up to four people (though rates are for double occupancy; there is a charge for all extra people over three years of age). The suites each have a bedroom, sitting room and French doors leading to the patio. The Merlot Suite is fully handicapped accessible. All rooms have private baths and air conditioning. A full home-cooked breakfast is served in an alcove of the tasting room. Chateau Chantal is open year round.

Field of Dreams Bed & Breakfast, 15627 Center Road, Traverse City, MI 49686; 231-223-7686. This country B & B is located on the main road overlooking vineyards. There are three bright, airy rooms, two upstairs and one downstairs. The Chardonnay Room, downstairs, has a semi-private bath and a private entrance from the spacious outdoor deck. The Beaujolais Room and Concord Room, both upstairs, have private baths. Owners Dennis and Sue Field serve full breakfasts. Guests may use the indoor hot tub and the family room stocked with board games and a TV. Children over 10 are welcome. Field of Dreams is within close driving distance to several restaurants, wineries and beaches. It is open year round.

Neahtawanta Inn, 1308 Neahtawanta Road, Traverse City, MI 49686; 231-223-7315. If rest and relaxation in a quiet setting is your goal, this may be your place. The inn has a beautiful location on the small outcropping that forms the bay at Bowers Harbor, across the water from the town. The turn-of-the-century building has five accommodations: a first-floor handicapped-accessible room with private bath; three second-floor rooms with shared bath; and a third-floor family suite with two bedrooms, bath, living room, private entrance and deck. Hosts Sally Van Vleck and Bob Russell serve vegetarian breakfasts. Common areas include a living/dining room with sunken firepit, a library, a wood-burning sauna and 325 feet of beach. Sally also teaches yoga classes on the premises. The inn is open year round.

WHERE TO EAT:

Boathouse Blue Water Bistro, 14039 Peninsula Dr.; 231-223-4030. Located on the waterfront at Bower's Harbor, this small restaurant offers some of the area's most creative cuisine. Try entrees like grilled tenderloin of beef served over a marinated portabella mushroom and topped with gorgonzola and caramelized onions, or lake trout and shrimp with sweet pepper pesto. Vegetarians will find treats like baked stuffed eggplant or stuffed peppers with sweet basil sun-dried tomato cream. Kudos to this restaurant for supporting the local wineries by offering many of their selections by the glass. There's outdoor dining on the deck or indoor dining with piano entertainment. Go at sunset for nature's show over the water — but make reservations; this place fills up. It's open year round, but only for dinner. Ready for dessert? How does chocolate paté with Creme Anglaise and caramel spider web sound?

Bowers Harbor Inn, 13512 Peninsula Drive; 231-223-4222. Stately Bowers Harbor Inn overlooks the water from a hill surrounded by tall pines. The elegant menu is heavy on meat and seafood, but there are a couple of vegetarian dishes. Entrees include temptations like filet mignon with Alaskan king crab and bearnaise sauce, or duck breast with a raspberry-merlot demi-glace. For those who prefer a more casual setting and lower prices, the Bowery, located at the back of the inn, is a good choice (though you sacrifice the view). Whichever restaurant you choose for dining, be sure to arrive in time to have a drink and appetizer on the lovely deck while watching the sunset over the water. Reservations are suggested. Oh, and be forewarned — the place is rumored to be haunted by the ghost of the late lady of the house, a wronged woman who hanged herself in the elevator shaft.

Old Mission Tavern and the Bella Galleria, 17015 Center Road; 231-223-7280. This restaurant, a favorite among the locals, is not located near the water but is on the main road that runs down the middle of the peninsula. Lunch items include sandwiches and burgers; dinners are more substantial, with a balanced menu featuring beef, lamb, liver, chicken, fish and several pasta dishes. The Bella Galleria, located at the restaurant, showcases the work of more than 50 local artists.

For more information contact the Traverse City Convention and Visitors Bureau, 101 W. Grandview Parkway, Traverse City, MI 49684; 800-872-8377 or 231-947-1120.
Internet: http://www.traversecity.com

Charlevoix

Petunias are the trademark of the pretty town of Charlevoix. Every spring, volunteers gather for "Operation Petunia," in which they plant some 50,000 of the colorful flowers along approximately four miles of roadside.

Situated along the Pine River Channel and tiny Round Lake, which connect Lake Michigan and Lake Charlevoix (one of Michigan's largest interior lakes), Charlevoix is quite a busy little town. Its year-round population of about 8,500 swells to 30,000 every summer. Additionally, U.S. 31 runs right through the middle of town, causing even more congestion. When traffic is stopped for the raising of the bascule bridge over the channel, there's plenty of time to admire the petunias.

A better idea is to park the car and explore the town by foot. Along Bridge Street, otherwise known as U.S. 31, is shopping that rivals many towns twice the size of Charlevoix. Specialty shops with second addresses in places like Naples and Sarasota are found here.

It wasn't always so sophisticated. The first European settlers arrived in the 1850s and began to farm the land and fish the waters around the area known then as Pine River. Among the fishermen were Irishmen who had been chased away from their

homes on nearby Beaver Island by the renegade Mormon leader King James Strang and his followers, who had split from Brigham Young and the rest of the Mormon Church.

There was bad blood from the beginning between the fishermen and the Mormons, who controlled the law in the area during that time. They began to enforce legislation that forbade the trading of alcohol to the local Indians. The fishermen ignored it and swore to kill any Mormon who landed on their shores with the intention of interfering.

When Sheriff Miller and 14 men from the Beaver Island Mormon settlement landed their boats at Pine River one day in 1853, the fishermen opened fire. Six Mormons were shot, though not fatally, and all fled to their boats. The fishermen followed in pursuit, chasing them 10 miles into the lake, opening fire again. The Mormons were rescued by a passing ship, and the skirmish became known as the Battle of Pine River, reportedly the only battle in the Great Lakes that was fought on

Lake Michigan beach and lighthouse at Charlevoix.

both land and water.

Thirteen years after the Battle of Pine River, the town was christened Charlevoix in honor of Pierre François Xavier de Charlevoix, a Jesuit explorer and historian who was sent in the early 1700s by King Louis XV to report on the French colonies in North America.

In addition to fishing, which flourished well into the 20th century, the town relied on logging and limestone for its living. The best harbor at Charlevoix was on diminutive Round Lake, but the Pine River connecting it to Lake Michigan was only a few feet deep. So the Pine River Channel was dredged, first in 1873, then in 1882, making it possible for large ships to enter the harbor and take on loads of lumber. The town's harbor remains on Round Lake.

By the early 1900s the timber had been depleted, and Charlevoix was forced to look elsewhere for its economic base. The natural beauty of the area attracted tourists, and large summer homes and resorts began to spring up. Tourism remains the mainstay of income for Charlevoix.

In the 1920s one of these summer visitors became involved with a crime that was thought at the time to be the most heinous of the century. Richard Loeb, son of local landowner and Sears Roebuck Company executive Albert Loeb, and his friend Nathan Leopold were wealthy college students who were both extremely bright, sometimes described as near-geniuses. Instead of putting their brilliance to work on their studies, however, they used it to plan what they hoped would be the perfect crime. They planned to kidnap a young victim and demand a ransom from his family.

They chose 14-year-old Bobby Franks, son of a Chicago millionaire. In May 1924 they carried out the act and demanded $10,000. Things went wrong, however, and before they could claim the ransom, Bobby Franks' body was found. A tell-tale pair of glasses left at the scene traced the crime to Loeb and Leopold. Their defense attorney was the famous lawyer Clarence Darrow, but even he couldn't save them from prison. Loeb himself was later brutally murdered by another inmate. Leopold was eventually released and has since died. The old Loeb estate, Castle Farms, still stands on Lake Charlevoix.

Another source of fame, though considerably happier, is the area's connection with writer Ernest Hemingway. He spent most of his early childhood summers in nearby Horton Bay and married his first wife in the Methodist church there. His experiences in northern Michigan seemed to have made a great impression on the young Hemingway, forming the backdrop for many of his stories, including the Nick Adams stories. The Hemingway cottage still stands, on private property owned by Hemingway's relatives.

The first stop for visitors should be the **Chamber of Commerce** office, located on U.S. 31 at the south end of Bridge Street. In addition to free information, the office sells a small book of historical walking and driving tours of the area published by the Charlevoix Historical Society. (The booklet is also available at the Society's museum, the Harsha House.)

Walking is definitely the preferred mode of transportation in Charlevoix. The town is small enough to be covered easily on foot. Though Bridge Street abounds in interesting stores, don't spend all your time shopping. A stroll on the paved walkway along the Pine River Channel is a great way to watch the boats coming and going into Round Lake. If you time it right, you'll get to see the Beaver Island ferries that make the 32-mile trip from their berths in Charlevoix daily during the warm months. It is possible to walk out the south pier all the way to the lighthouse, an attractive steel structure erected in 1948.

The focal point of interest in the center of town is the 1949 Charlevoix Memorial Bridge over the Pine River Channel. A double bascule bridge, it has two halves that raise, each weighted to facilitate operation. It's a far cry from the original span over the river built in 1869 — a four-foot-wide foot bridge whose wooden planks were removed by hand every time a ship needed to pass.

Just east of the bridge on Round Lake is the City Dock, where the Beaver Island Boat Company docks its ferries. The other major tenant of the dock is the U.S. Coast Guard, which has berthed a cutter there since 1960. The current resident is the U.S.S. Acacia, a buoy tender and ice breaker that is sometimes open to the public for tours.

If old homes are your interest, walk along Michigan Avenue, north of the bridge. It was here, on a bluff overlooking Lake Michigan, that wealthy summer residents built their homes around the turn of the century. They came from places like Chicago and St. Louis. One such summer visitor was the poet Sara Teasdale. Though some of the original homes no longer exist, the street has maintained its air of elegance.

Another pleasant walk is on Belvedere Avenue along the south shore of Round Lake, where there are many stately old homes perched on the hill overlooking the lake. On the opposite side of the street next to the water is John Cross Fisheries, the last vestige of Charlevoix's once-thriving fishing industry. John

Cross came to the town from Benton Harbor farther south and opened a fishery for restaurant sales in 1940. The fishery owned by the Cross family is still there, supplied today by Native American fishermen.

The **Harsha House**, at 103 State Street (231-547-0373), is the place to learn about earlier times in Charlevoix. One of the oldest buildings in the town, it is the home of the Charlevoix Historical Society. The house was built in 1891 for civic leader Horace Harsha and his wife, who raised their five children there. Though the house stayed in the family following the deaths of the older Harshas, it was converted into summer rental units and eventually into year-round apartments until its acquisition by the historical society in 1978. More than $100,000 went into renovation on the building. The lower floor houses a museum. Included are a restored 1890 parlor, a working 1917 player piano and photo displays of local history. The museum is open limited hours.

While walking around Charlevoix, it's impossible not to notice the unusual stone houses that are common throughout the town. Charlevoix resident Earl Young is responsible for these. A realtor and designer, Young began building houses made of local

stone in the 1920s. Over the next 30 or so years Young constructed similar buildings, each designed to harmonize with its setting and location. Some feature cedar slag roofs, giving them a European look. With their fanciful shapes and flowing roof lines, the smaller cottages in particular have a fairy tale appearance. Many of Young's homes are concentrated in an area called Boulder Park on the west side of town. Young also designed larger buildings, two of which are the Weathervane Terrace Hotel and the Weathervane Restaurant. The Chamber of Commerce has maps available that show the locations of Young's fascinating buildings. Earl Young died in 1975, but several family members remain in Charlevoix.

Charlevoix has four public beaches. The closest to the center of town is the **Lake Michigan Beach** on the south side of the Pine River Channel near the lighthouse. This small beach has nice sand, a concession stand, rest rooms and children's play equipment.

The beach at **Mt. McSauba Recreation Area** is far more extensive, but you have to drive just north of town to get there. This is a primitive beach with no lifeguards or facilities, but it is very beautiful, much of it with fine powdery sand. This is also a good spot to look for Petoskey stones, the fossilized coral that is Michigan's state stone. Behind the beach are dunes that rise 165 feet above the lake. Beyond them are woods where hikers can walk the maintained trails. (Insect repellent is a must during warm months.) In the winter, Mt. McSauba recreation area functions as a municipal downhill ski facility, one of only a few in Michigan.

In addition to these two Lake Michigan beaches, there are two on Lake Charlevoix, where the water is generally warmer and calmer than Lake Michigan. **Depot Beach**, north of the Pine River Channel and Round Lake, has lifeguards, a playground, rest rooms and picnic facilities. The **Ferry Avenue Beach** is located south of the channel on Ferry Avenue.

A mile-long beach with limited facilities is also located at **Fisherman's Island State Park** about seven miles southwest of the town.
Hikers and bird watchers will enjoy the **North Point Nature Preserve**, just north of Mt. McSauba Recreation Area. This 27-acre-property has dunes, hiking trails and a half-mile of sandy and rocky lake shore. Three rare plant species can be found at the preserve: Pumpell's Bromegrass, Pitcher's Thistle and Lake Huron Tansy.

Cyclists and hikers can obtain a map of suggested scenic routes from the Chamber of Commerce. The map details four routes, ranging from 3.8 miles to 7.8 miles. These include a downtown tour, an excursion to Mt. McSauba Recreation Area, a trip to nearby Fisherman's Island State Park and a tour along Round Lake and part of Lake Charlevoix.

Charlevoix has many annual events and festivals, the most

famous of which is the **Venetian Festival** that takes place each July. It includes carnival rides, food booths, music and fireworks, but perhaps its most impressive component is the Venetian Boat Parade which takes place on Saturday night of the four-day festival. For more than a half-century this dusk parade has featured boats ornately decorated with lights as they circle Round Lake.

The town's **Apple Festival** takes place the second week of October every fall when local apple farmers sell some 40 varieties of apples along Bridge Street.

WHERE TO STAY:

Charlevoix Country Inn, 106 West Dixon Avenue, Charlevoix, MI 49720; 231-547-5134. This inn, built in 1896 as a summer cottage, has a spectacular location at the end of a street in a residential neighborhood high over Lake Michigan. It's far enough from the bustle to be quiet but close enough for walking to shops and restaurants. A stairway just a few feet from the front door leads down to the lake. There are wonderful views from the front porch, the indoor breakfast and social area, and select guest rooms. The eight rooms and two suites, all with private bath, are decorated in a country motif. The suites also have kitchens. Continental breakfast is served each morning and a wine and cheese social is enjoyed every afternoon. The inn is open seasonally, Memorial Day weekend through mid-October.

The Inn at Grey Gables, 306 Belvedere Avenue, Charlevoix, MI 49720; 800-280-4667 or 231-547-2251. This bed and breakfast was built in 1887 as a cottage in the summer colony called Belvedere Club. Overlooking Round Lake, it is in a quiet residential neighborhood of impressive old homes, but within walking distance to shops and restaurants. Since proprietors Gary and Kay Anderson also own the elegant restaurant next door, they can accommodate guests with a romantic in-room dinner. (They ask that this be pre-arranged.) There are five rooms and two suites, each with private bath. Breakfast and evening snack are included. No smoking.

The Weathervane Restaurant in Charlevoix, one of Earl Young's
famous stone buildings.

Weathervane Terrace Hotel, 111 Pine River Lane,
Charlevoix, MI 49720; 800-552-0025 or 231-547-9955. With
its stone walls, leaded glass and copper-topped towers, the
Weathervane is reminiscent of a medieval castle. This is one of
several commercial buildings designed and built by Earl Young.
(New sections have been built more recently, so not all of the
hotel is Young's original design.) The hotel has a great location
off Bridge Street overlooking Lake Michigan and the Pine
River Channel. There are many types of accommodations —
some suites and others rooms — but all have microwaves and
refrigerators. Some have balconies, kitchenettes, Jacuzzi tubs
or wet bars. Not all rooms have views of the water, so if this is
important to you, ask. This may be a good choice for families
with children, who will enjoy the outdoor pool. Continental
breakfast is included. The hotel offers golf packages for nearby
Charlevoix Country Club. The Weathervane is open year round
— and at less than half the high season rate, off season is a
bargain.

WHERE TO EAT:

The Acorn Cafe, 103 Park Avenue; 231-547-1835. Just a block
away from the bustle of Bridge Street, The Acorn Cafe offers a

WHAT'S DOWN THERE?

Shipwrecks. Lots of them. And many are protected as part of Michigan's system of underwater preserves. The state's eleven preserves encompass over 2000 square miles of Lakes Michigan, Huron and Superior. These are enormously popular with divers because the cold water helps preserve the old ships, making them an ideal window into the maritime history of the Great Lakes. There are three preserves in Lake Michigan.

The Manitou Underwater Preserve is located offshore from Sleeping Bear Dunes National Lakeshore, which encompasses the Manitou Islands. Long a busy shipping channel, this area has snagged its share of ships over the years — more than 50 recorded between 1835 and 1960. In addition, many of the old docks from the logging days have been preserved underwater. Divers often see artifacts and pieces of shipwrecks in these areas, along with the large schools of fish attracted to the pilings.

The most popular of the preserve's wrecks is probably the Francisco Morazan, a freighter that ran aground just offshore from South Manitou Island in 1960. Much of the wreck is above water, and the rest is only 15 feet down, making it a good dive for novices. The Walter L. Frost, a wooden steamer that sank in 1905, lies nearby.

Area dive shops run charter boats to the preserve, or you can haul your own equipment to the islands via the national park's ferry service. (See the section on Sleeping Bear Dunes National Lakeshore in "Natural Attractions.") For information on charters contact Scuba North in Traverse City at 888-692-3483 or 231-947-2520.

Farther north, Lake Michigan shares a preserve with Lake Huron at the Straits of Mackinac. This crossroads of the Great Lakes has served as a marine highway for a couple of centuries, meaning that it's literally littered with ship-wrecks. In addition to the narrowness of the passage itself, ships have had to battle fog, heavy boat traffic, dangerous shoals and the occasional nasty storm. At least 100 didn't make it.

One of the most interesting and popular of these is the Sandusky, a 110-foot two-masted schooner that sank in 1856 and now sits upright in 90 feet of water. It is one of the few shipwrecks in the Great Lakes that has a figure-head, but it is unfortunately a replica that was added after vandals tried to steal the original.

To find out about dive charters in the Straits contact Straits Scuba Center in St. Ignace at 906-643-7009 or 810-558-9922.

The newest preserve, established in November 1999, is the Southwest Michigan Underwater Preserve that stretches from just north of Holland nearly to the Michigan/Indiana border, an area of approximately 350 square miles. The preserve is thought to contain more than 40 shipwrecks, a dozen historic pier structures and important geological sites. Yet to be found, but presumed to be within the pre-serve, is the 210-foot steamer Chicora, lost in 1895 with all passengers and crew.

For information on dive charters in the preserve contact Watermark Scuba of Holland at 616-393-9171.

A cautionary note: don't be tempted to go home with a "souvenir." In Michigan it is illegal to remove any artifacts from the state's underwater preserves. Those caught doing so get more than a slap on the hand; punishment may include heavy fines, imprisonment and confiscation of boats and dive equipment.

The Emerald Isle ferry that runs from Charlevoix to Beaver Island.

tasty variety of breakfast food, salads and sandwiches. Got a craving for an omelet? You don't have to settle for plain cheese (though you can, if you want). Try yours with smoked white-fish and onion with mustard dill sauce, or prosciutto and asparagus. Sandwiches include beef and cheddar on sourdough and grilled chicken Caesar on pita.

Grey Gables Inn, 308 Belvedere Avenue; 231-547-9261. Located next door to the Inn at Grey Gables, this is one of Charlevoix's most popular restaurants for fine dining. Established in 1936, it's also one of the oldest. Evenings in sea-son will find this place very busy, but because it's located in an old house it doesn't feel crowded. (Though it can be somewhat noisy.) Entrees include such items as pan roasted Norwegian salmon on a bed of cherry couscous or cider-and whiskey-mari-nated chicken with whipped potatoes and crisp bacon sauce.

Stafford's Weathervane, Bridge Street at the Bridge; 231-547-4311. The attraction here is the view. Perched above the beauti-ful aqua-colored Pine River Channel, the Weathervane is a great place to watch boats come and go from Lake Michigan. This is another of Earl Young's designs and is distinguished by the stone fireplace in the main dining room, with its nine-ton keystone. The atmosphere is casual, whether on the small outdoor patio or in the larger indoor dining area. The emphasis is on seafood, especially Great Lakes fish. The lamps outside the restaurant once lit streets in Copenhagen, Denmark.

Whitney's of Charlevoix, 305 Bridge Street; 231-547-0818. This oyster bar/seafood house has made a remarkable recovery from a fire that destroyed it in 1997. The new restaurant, on Bridge Street overlooking Round Lake, features lunch and dinner in a casual East Coast-style atmosphere. In addition to Maryland crabcakes, oysters and peel-and-eat shrimp, Whitney's also offers a selection of things that would never appear on an East Coast menu, such as whitefish paté and whitefish sausage. The open-air Whitney's Topside, on the building's top story, has similar food but a different menu.

For more information contact the Charlevoix Convention and Visitors Bureau, 408 Bridge Street, Charlevoix, MI 49720; phone 800-367-8557 or 231-547-2101.
Internet: http://www.charlevoix.org

Beaver Island

Eighteen miles off the mainland lies Beaver Island, the largest of 15 islands known collectively as the Beaver Archipelago. At approximately 58 square miles, Beaver Island, sometimes called Big Beaver, it is also Lake Michigan's largest island. People have lived on Beaver Island throughout known history, from the native and European fishermen who harvested the rich waters surrounding it, to sailors who used the fine natural harbor as a stopover, to today's visitor seeking a quiet place of beauty.

Few of the island's visitors, however, have left a stranger legacy than James Jesse Strang, who came in 1847 and departed in 1856. Strang, a lawyer, teacher and newspaper editor, was a follower of the Mormon faith. When founder Joseph Smith was killed by a mob, Strang made a strong case for being declared

The harbor at Beaver Island.

his successor. He claimed he had a letter written by Smith that foretold his own death and appointed Strang to take his place. For extra measure, Strang had a vision that confirmed his rightful place as head of the Mormons.

So while Brigham Young led his followers to Utah, Strang shepherded his to Beaver Island, which appeared to him in another vision. The settlement on the island grew slowly, but by 1849 there were almost 50 Mormon families.

A further revelation established the desirability of polygamy, which Strang immediately took to heart. His first acquisition was a pretty 18-year-old, who was made to swear she wouldn't tell her parents. For several months, dressed as a boy and posing as his nephew Charles, she accompanied Strang while he rounded up converts and funds.

Strang's revelations were coming fast and furious by 1850, culminating in the one that he must have enjoyed the most. He was, he informed his faithful, rightfully the King of the Earth, so on July 8 he had himself crowned.

All of this didn't sit well with the earlier settlers of the island,

Irish fishermen and their families who didn't take kindly to having fingers wagged at them. (Alcohol, it seems, was an issue.) When Strang became a state legislator, he was successful in having most of them driven from the island. Scattered back on the mainland, the fishermen kept their hatred stoked. The Mormons had nothing good to say about the fishermen, either: Strang's newspaper declared them to be "little else than a band of vagabonds and thieves."

The fishermen struck back in 1853 when the sheriff from Beaver Island and 14 of his men set out for the mainland to summon several of them to court. As the officials neared land, the fishermen opened fire, wounding six of the Mormons. The sheriff and his men retreated, but the fishermen followed in hot pursuit, continuing to fire. Ten miles into the lake the Mormons were rescued, and no one died in what has come to be known as the Battle of Pine River.

The settlement on the island reached about 2,600, though things were by no means rosy. King James held absolute control, which caused resentment in the ranks. His reign came to an end in 1856 when two of his followers ambushed and shot him. He was moved to the Mormon settlement at Voree, Wis., but three weeks later he was dead and his kingdom dissolved. (Today's Mormons, incidentally, lay no claim to James Strang.)

The fishermen returned to Beaver Island, and their numbers grew steadily as they wrote to relatives in Ireland with tales of fruitful waters and land to farm. Famine in Ireland drove many to make the long journey to Michigan to set down roots on the island.

For a time, fishing flourished, and whitefish and trout were shipped to other parts of the Midwest and to the East. But over fishing and the sea lamprey (a parasitic species that invaded the Great Lakes in the early part of the 20th century) combined to decimate the numbers of fish. Logging, too, declined as ships came to depend on fossil fuels rather than wood.

Today the island is a quiet place that subsists largely on income from a modest tourism industry. Though the year-round population hovers at about 500, it swells to 3,000 in the summer. Ferries from Charlevoix on the mainland make the two-hour voyage daily May though September, with limited service in the early spring and late fall.

Don't expect a Mackinac Island. The island's only town, St. James, is nestled inside aptly-named Paradise Bay. It has a handful of shops and restaurants, and there are some nice places to stay on the island, but nothing approaching the grandeur of a resort island. Those most likely to enjoy the island for an extended stay are people looking for a true get-away or those who enjoy outdoor activities such as hiking and mountain biking.

There are more than 100 miles of little-used roads and trails perfect for hikers, mountain bikers or cross-country skiers. (Most roads are not paved, so touring bikes are not a good choice.) The interior is primarily undeveloped forest and marsh, especially in the lower half; visitors are likely to see ducks, loons, herons, wild turkeys, rabbits, foxes and beavers. Hikers are cautioned to come equipped with food, water and compass; warm-weather cyclists and hikers alike should carry insect repellent to ward off mosquitoes and blackflies. Beach hikers may encounter sand flies, but sticking to the windward side of the island may help avoid these pesky insects.

The island has eight inland lakes, two of which are large enough to be explored by kayak. Experienced kayakers can also use Beaver Island as a base from which to explore the other smaller islands in the archipelago; the closest, Garden Island, is only two miles away.

There is a small public beach on the outskirts of St. James and two more at the south end of the island.

Several boat charters will take visitors on fishing excursions or to other islands in the archipelago.

It's not surprising that Beaver Island has attractions of historical interest. Prime among these is the **Mormon Print Shop and Museum** (231-448-2254), located one block south of the ferry dock in St. James. It is the original 1848 building in which King James Strang printed his newspaper, *Northern Islander*, the first daily paper north of Grand Rapids. Among the artifacts housed at the museum is an imposing portrait of Strang that glares down at visitors from its perch on the wall. There is also a room dedicated to Dr. Feodar Protar, one of the island's most beloved residents. A refugee from Russia, Dr. Protar came to Beaver Island in 1894 and stayed until his death 30 years later. During that time he saw to the islanders' medical needs without asking for payment. After he died, local fishermen built a tomb near the cabin where he had lived and included a bronze plaque on which is inscribed: "To our heaven-sent friend in need, Feodar Protar, who never failed us, in imperishable gratitude, his people of Beaver Island." Dr. Protar's house and grave are under the care of the island's historical society and are sometimes open to the public. Ask at the museum.

The historical society also runs the **Marine Museum**, located about a half mile north of the ferry dock in an old net shed that has been restored. The museum's displays deal primarily with the history of fishing around the island, but there is also a lifeboat from the Carl D. Bradley, an ore freighter that sank in a storm near the island in 1958. Only two of the crew of 35 survived the tragedy.

Admission is charged jointly for both museums, which are open seasonally, daily during the summer and on weekends in late spring and early fall.

The island has two historical lighthouses, one of which is still functioning. The **Beaver Harbor Light** is located at Whiskey Point on Paradise Bay, about a mile from the ferry dock. The 41-foot brick tower was constructed in 1870. Its blinking red light is visible to ferry passengers entering the harbor on foggy mornings. Next to the lighthouse is a stone memorial to the islanders who have lost their lives on the Great Lakes.

The **Beaver Head Light**, just east of Iron Ore Bay at the south end of the island, was built in 1858. It no longer serves as navigational aid, having been replaced by a metal tower. The lightkeeper's house and grounds are used by the Charlevoix Public Schools as an environmental education facility, but the tower is often open to the public. It is possible to climb the narrow, winding steps to get a bird's eye view of the lake and nearby beaches.

Getting to the island is easy via the ferry from Charlevoix, 32 miles away. The trip takes about two hours. The Beaver Island Boat Company has recently added a new ferry to their fleet, the large and comfortable Emerald Isle. Although it is possible to take cars to the island on the ferry (reservations required), it is expensive and the island roads are hard on vehicles. There are several places near the ferry dock that rent vehicles. The best bet, if you're up to it, is to plan to get around the island by mountain or hybrid bike. Bicycle and kayak rentals are available in St. James.

The **Beaver Island Chamber of Commerce** is located half a block south of the ferry dock. The staff can provide a business directory, schedule of events and other information. Public restrooms are located just north of the ferry dock.

The ferry company conducts guided driving tours of the island. The hour-and-a-half tour covers the basics around St. James, while the extensive three-hour tour takes visitors around the entire island. Both include lunch at an island restaurant and admission to the two museums. Tour participants must be on the first ferry of the morning. Reservations are recommended for the extended tour. For information, a ferry schedule or reservations call Beaver Island Boat Company at 888-446-4095 or 231-547-2311.

It is possible to fly to Beaver Island from Charlevoix anytime of the year, weather permitting. For schedules and rates contact Island Airways at 800-524-6895.

WHERE TO STAY:

Beaver Island Lodge, Box 215, Beaver Island, MI 49782;

231-448-2396. Beaver Island Lodge is beautifully situated on private shoreline outside the town of St. James. This is a perfect place for a quiet getaway. The 14 rooms are nicely decorated and equipped with microwaves, refrigerators and wet bars. Each unit has a private bath, dining area and sitting area. Most have balconies overlooking the water. Deluxe units have a bedroom and living room with skylights. The lodge has its own private beach on the premises. Now completely renovated, the lodge has been in business since 1950.

Laurain Lodge, 38085 Beaver Lodge Road, Beaver Island, MI 49782; 231-448-2099. The Laurain family owns and manages 10 modern housekeeping units near the Beaver Island Lodge just outside St. James. Though there is no private beachfront, there are public beaches nearby, and the lodge has a playground, making it a great place for families with children. Each unit has a fully equipped kitchen, living room, bathroom with shower, and television. One- or two-bedroom units are available. There are also picnic tables, grills and a deck area.

WHERE TO EAT:

Baileys' Restaurant and Lounge, At the Beaver Island Lodge; 231-448-2396. Baileys' is the island choice for a fine dinner overlooking the water. Located at Beaver Island Lodge, just outside St. James, Baileys' has a full menu that includes local specialties such as whitefish. The adjacent lounge is a great place for a drink or a glass of wine before a quiet meal.

Shamrock Bar and Grill, Main Street; 231-448-2278. Located near the ferry dock, the Shamrock Bar and Grill serves as a social gathering spot for islanders. The atmosphere is casual; there is an outdoor deck overlooking the harbor. Menu selections include burgers, salads, gyros, whitefish and homemade soups. The Shamrock is open year-round for breakfast, lunch and dinner.

For more information contact the Beaver Island Chamber of Commerce, P.O. Box 5, Beaver Island, MI 49782; 231-448-2505.
Internet: http://www.beaverisland.org

Petoskey

No less a luminary than Mark Twain was smitten by Petoskey and its location on Little Traverse Bay, commenting at the opening of the Petoskey Opera House in 1895 that "there is no finer summer resort in the world."

Nine miles long and six miles wide, Little Traverse Bay, like its larger neighbor Grand Traverse Bay, was named by the French voyageurs who preferred to traverse its head rather than round its perimeter in their search for the Indian trade.

The early pursuits of trading and later, logging, have gone the way of horse-drawn wagons. Tourism has taken their place. The bay towns of Petoskey, Bay View and Harbor Springs draw summer visitors like moths to a porch light, attracted by the stellar shopping, fine restaurants, calm water and spectacular sunsets.

Petoskey, located on a bluff on the southern shore of the bay, is the largest and busiest of the three towns, but has by no means lost its charm. This is due in large part to the Gaslight District which rises above the lake shore. Here you'll find gift shops, antiques stores, galleries, boutiques and restaurants with nary a fast food joint or souvenir shop in sight. Petoskey, like Bay View and Harbor Springs, rates an absolute zero on the tackiness index.

What is today a posh resort community was first known as Bear River, a settlement of Ottawas and Chippewas frequented by fur traders. In 1836 a reservation was established here, and the missionaries moved in. Andrew Porter established his Presbyterian school in 1852, and in 1859 the St. Francis Solanus Mission was founded by Father Frederic Baraga, a Catholic missionary. The original mission is still there, tucked away between two houses on quiet West Lake Street overlooking the water.

In the 1870s the area was opened to homesteaders and the vil-

The St. Francis Solanus Mission in Petoskey, founded in 1859.

lage of Petoskey was established. It was named for Ignatius Petosegay, a prominent Chippewa who lived there. The family name somehow evolved to "Petoskey" which, roughly translated, means "sun shining through," though today it is more immediately associated with the Michigan state stone, the Petoskey stone, a fossilized coral that is found here.

The beauty of Little Traverse Bay did little to make life easy for the homesteaders. Most available land was deep in the forest and there were few roads. The settlers were generally inexperienced in the ways of the woods, and had an especially tough time during the harsh winter of 1876-77. They were dubbed "Mossbacks" for the temporary shelters they dug in the ground, then covered with moss.

With the coming of the homesteaders and a rail line, lumbering and other industry took off. So did tourism. The Chautauqua camp at nearby Bay View was established in 1875, and in 1882 the Western Hay Fever Association chose Petoskey as its headquarters, citing it as the best resort town for those suffering from an excess of sneezes and runny noses.

One of the families that made its way to Little Traverse Bay each summer during this era was to give rise to a famous off-spring. From their winter home in Oak Park, Illinois, the Hemingway family journeyed two days to get to their summer cottage at Walloon Lake, south of Petoskey. Nearly every summer of young Ernest's life was spent at either Walloon Lake or Petoskey. Both figured prominently in many of the writer's novels and short stories, including "Ten Indians" and "The Torrents of Spring." He shared his honeymoon in 1921 with his first wife at the family cottage, and returned to Petoskey a final time for one night in 1947.

You can learn more about Hemingway's Michigan youth at the **Little Traverse Bay History Museum** (231-347-2620) on the waterfront. You must cross through the pedestrian tunnel under busy US 31 to arrive at the museum, housed in a 1882 train depot. In addition to the Hemingway exhibit, there are displays and exhibits on Indian artifacts, logging, shipping, and the summer camp at Bay View. Civil War historian Bruce Catton, who was born in the area, also rates a display.

Near the museum and marina is **Bayfront Park**. The most imposing sight at the park is the 62-foot clock tower and bell. Built for the 1902 Buffalo Exposition, the clock and bell, modeled after the Liberty Bell, were bought by a Petoskey resident and shipped to the town. The clock graced the municipal headquarters building until 1965, then the historical museum. At 13 tons, it proved too heavy for the museum building, so it was removed and finally found its current home at the park. Each of the four clock faces weighs 800 pounds. The bell tolls the hours.

In the bay adjacent to the park is an underwater shrine dedicated to scuba divers, both living and deceased. A submerged marble and black walnut crucifix marks the spot, which was blessed by a Catholic priest and Protestant minister, both on scuba, at its dedication.

A four-mile paved bike path leads through the park and on through Bay View and into Harbor Springs.

Bayfront Park in Petoskey, with its bell tower build in 1902 for the Buffalo Exposition.

Though the waterfront park is a pleasant place for a walk, a bike ride or a picnic, there is no beach here. For that you must go to **Magnus City Park**, west of the downtown area. The park also has camping facilities, picnic tables, a playground and rest rooms.

WHERE TO STAY:

Montgomery Place Bed and Breakfast, 618 E. Lake Street, Petoskey, MI 49770; 231-347-1338. This elegant Victorian home was built in 1879 as the Ozark Hotel. There are four guest rooms, each with private bath and sitting area. The master suite has a cathedral ceiling, stained glass window, roof-top porch, a view of the bay, sunken tub and a king-sized bed. The game room is equipped with TV, VCR and videos as well as board games. Innkeepers Diane Gillette and Ruth Bellissimo serve wine and snacks each evening on the 80-foot veranda or in the living room in front of the beautiful marble fireplace. Full breakfast is included. No smoking is permitted, and the B & B is not suitable for small children. Montgomery Place is open year round.

Stafford's Perry Hotel, Bay and Lewis Streets, Petoskey, MI 49770; 800-456-1917 or 231-347-4000. Located in the historic gaslight district, the Perry Hotel is just as impressive outside as it is inside. The pastel brick building, built in 1899, sits on a hill with a magnificent view of the bay. Everything about it

Stafford's Perry Hotel, Petoskey, built in 1899.

spells elegance, from the white-pillared exterior to the Victorian lobby. There are several categories of rooms, from the "basic" Cushman rooms to the larger Arlington rooms, which have balconies overlooking the water. All rooms have telephones, cable TV and private baths. The hotel's H.O. Rose Room serves three meals daily, year round. The hotel offers several different packages, including an Island Hopper to Mackinac Island, a golf package and ski package. For a place this beautiful the Perry Hotel has quite reasonable rates.

WHERE TO EAT:

Andante, 321 Bay Street; 231-348-3321. Another spectacular view can be had at Andante, just down the street from Stafford's Perry Hotel. There's nothing pedestrian about the food, either. The meat and potatoes crowd may want to look elsewhere, but those with epicurean tastes will probably be delighted. Try, for example, the pineapple gravlax appetizer: pepper-cured salmon flavored with allspice, coriander and cognac served over grilled pineapple with mustard dill sauce. Or how about the medallions of quail entree — marinated and chargrilled, served with sweet and sour raspberry glaze, roasted garlic-red pepper couscous and Vidalia onion relish. Expect the unexpected and you'll still be happily surprised.

H.O. Rose Room, Stafford's Perry Hotel, Bay at Lewis; 231-347-4000. The H.O. Rose Room is the main dining room at Stafford's Perry Hotel. The restaurant offers fine dining and elegant service with a stunning view of Little Traverse Bay. You'll find chilled cherry soup on the menu, along with dinner entrees like pistachio crusted whitefish or rack of lamb with a black currant bordelaise sauce. There is an extensive wine list. The Rose room is open for breakfast, lunch and dinner year round, with a champagne brunch on Sundays. This is the perfect place for a romantic dinner. Leave the beach wear at home; the Rose Room isn't stuffy, but you'll feel more comfortable wearing something nice. Reservations are suggested.

For more information contact the Petoskey-Harbor Springs-Boyne Country Visitors Bureau, 401 E. Mitchell St., Petoskey,

MI 49770; 800-845-2828 or 231-348-2755
Internet: http://www.petoskey.com

Bay View

Just north of Petoskey is the resort community of Bay View.
The two are so close together that the only real clue that you're
in Bay View is the sudden proliferation of Victorian gingerbread. There are 440 cottages in all, scattered over a hillside
overlooking the lake and surrounded by beautiful green lawns.
The entire community is designated as a National Historic
Landmark.

Bay View was founded in 1875 by a group of Methodists who
set up a summer tent community. Their purpose was the pursuit
of "intellectual and scientific culture and to promote the cause of
religion and morality." Soon tents gave way to cottages designed
on Victorian models, though many of these are very large and
hardly fit today's concept of a cottage. In 1885 the Bay View
Association initiated a Chautauqua series modeled on the well-
known New York program, and this continues to this day.

Every summer, June through August, the Bay View Association
offers lectures, worship services, concerts, musicals, plays and
recreation programs that are open to both summer residents and
day visitors. Youth programs include swimming and sailing
lessons. Bay View's Conservatory of Music draws students from
around the country, who come to study and perform. For information about summer programs contact the Bay View
Association at PO Box 583, Petoskey, MI 49770; 231-347-6225.

WHERE TO STAY:

Stafford's Bay View Inn, PO Box 3, 2011 Woodland Avenue,
Petoskey, MI 49770; 800-258-1886 or 231-347-2771. This was
the original of the "Stafford's" properties, which also includes
restaurants and inns in Charlevoix, Harbor Springs, Petoskey and
Boyne City. The Victorian-style inn is in a beautiful location on
the waterfront at Little Traverse Bay. Guest rooms are elegantly

decorated and range from simple to larger suites, to the "spa" rooms, which have whirlpool bathtubs and sitting areas with fireplaces. The larger rooms are somewhat pricey in the high season, but during off season the rates drop by more than half. There's a gorgeous view of the bay from the restaurant, which is open for three meals a day during the summer. Breakfast extends spring through fall, and dinner has a varied schedule except during the summer, when it is served every night. The food is quite good, and the restaurant is known for its Sunday brunch (late June to mid-October) No alcohol is served, though guests staying at the inn may bring wine from their rooms to the dining room.

Terrace Inn, 1549 Glendale, PO Box 266, Petoskey, MI 49770; 800-530-9898 or 231-347-2410. This stately Victorian inn was built in 1911 and like the rest of Bay View is a National Historic Landmark. Much of the original oak furniture remains. Located on beautiful grounds two blocks from Lake Michigan, the inn has 44 guest rooms, each with private bath. All have fans and a few are air conditioned. There are no phones or TVs. Continental breakfast is included in the room rates, which are quite reasonable, especially in the off season. Special packages are offered for all seasons, and there are many "themed" weekends, such as murder mystery packages, wine tastings, quilter's getaways, women's only weekends, and winter sleigh rides. Dinner is served in the inn's dining room or on the porch during the warm months. The inn is not permitted to serve alcohol, but guests may bring their own wine. During the summer and fall, dinner is served Tuesday through Saturday, with a buffet brunch on Sundays. In winter the dining room is open on Saturday evenings only.

For more information contact the Petoskey-Harbor Springs-Boyne Country Visitors Bureau, 401 E. Mitchell St., Petoskey, MI 49770; 800-845-2828 or 231-348-2755.
Internet: http://www.boynecountry.com

Harbor Springs

This is a town straight out of a Norman Rockwell painting —

well scrubbed and wholesome, with an air of innocence. No fast food restaurants betray the date, and you'd be hard pressed to find a souvenir coffee cup with "Harbor Springs" emblazoned on it. Nestled into a tiny bay within Little Traverse Bay, it is quiet, charming and picturesque. This is its main attraction, for in the summertime, aside from browsing in the exclusive shops, eating at a handful of restaurants or picnicking at one of the small beaches, there's not a great deal to do in the town itself. Winter brings skiing enthusiasts, who come for the plentiful lake effect snow.

The area that is now Harbor Springs was frequented and lived in by native people and others long before it was established as a town. Ottawa Indians lived here in large numbers, followed by missionaries. Fishermen and traders were frequent visitors. As part of a 1855 treaty Little Traverse, as Harbor Springs was then known, was set aside for the Ottawa and Chippewa people, who could lay claim to land that would be deeded to them after 20 years. What is now Main Street was lined with Indian cabins.

In 1875 the land was opened to white settlement, and things were forever changed. The railroad came through as far as Petoskey, and lumbering began. The town thrived for a time, but by the 1920s the timber was gone. Tourism took roots, though kept in check, for Harbor Springs remains a small, exclusive resort town with little of the trappings of commercial tourism.

One of the town's most interesting buildings is the Ephraim Shay house on the corner of Main and Judd Streets. This hexagonal steel-sided building was the home of Shay, who moved to Harbor Springs from Huron County, Ohio, in 1888. He proved to be the town's inveterate tinkerer and eventually its most famous citizen. In 1881 Shay patented a narrow-gauge locomotive that came to be used for logging and mining throughout the world. Manufactured at Lima, Ohio, the locomotives were known for their great traction and ability to negotiate tight curves. Though none of these locomotives has survived, you can see photos of them at the Little Traverse Bay History Museum in Petoskey.

WHERE TO STAY:

Harborside Inn, 266 E. Main Street, PO Box 666, Harbor Springs, MI 49740; 800-526-6238. This modern hotel near the waterfront is a good option for families with children. Each of the 24 suites includes a kitchenette, TV, telephone and whirlpool tub, and can accommodate four people. Balconies overlook the bay or downtown. A rooftop deck offers a pleasant view of the harbor.

Veranda Bed & Breakfast, 403 E. Main Street, Harbor Springs, MI 49740; 231-526-7782. This charming little piece of gingerbread is right in the heart of Harbor Springs. Owners Doug and Lydia Yoder also own the Brigadoon B & B in Mackinaw City. There are four guest rooms, each with private bath. Full gourmet breakfasts are served daily, including freshly-baked pastries. Adults are preferred. The Veranda is open year round.

Windy Ridge Bed & Breakfast, 6281 South Lakeshore Drive, Harbor Springs, MI 49740-9785; 1-800-409-4095 or 231-526-7650. You couldn't ask for a more spectacular view than the one from this modern country B & B. It's perched high on a ridge over looking the lake about four and a half miles north of Harbor Springs on M199. There's no crowding here — the property sits on 23 acres of rolling hills. There's an outdoor hot tub overlooking the water and mowed paths throughout the grounds. Four spacious guest rooms are available, two of them with private bath. The Bay View Suite has a stunning view and a private sun deck. This makes an ideal place for a quiet getaway; better to leave the kids at home. Owners Lauri and Tom Rowe serve a full breakfast.

WHERE TO EAT:

Stafford's Pier, 102 Bay Street; 231-526-6201. There are several different dining areas here, indoor and out, each with a different menu. It's right on the waterfront, giving it the best view in town. There's casual dining on the deck, with entrees like citrus chicken and broiled whitefish. Slightly more formal dining is offered in the Pointer Room, with selections such as rack of lamb with cherry-gooseberry sauce or wild mushroom shrimp. The room is named for the Pointer, a taxi boat that ran between Harbor Point and Harbor Springs from 1930 until 1962. The restored boat is on display at the restaurant. Lunch and dinner are available.

For more information contact the Petoskey-Harbor Springs-Boyne Country Visitors Bureau, 401 E. Mitchell St., Petoskey, MI 49770; 800-845-2828 or 231-348-2755; or the Harbor Springs Chamber of Commerce, PO Box 37 (205 State Street), Harbor Springs, MI 49740; 231-526-7999.
Internet: http://www.boynecountry.com

Mackinaw City

Mackinaw City is perhaps best known as the place to catch the ferry to Mackinac Island. The view of the town, which is the gateway to the Upper Peninsula, is dominated by two things: water — in almost every direction — and the longest suspension bridge in North America. But before going much further in exploring the town, some advice is in order.

First, pronunciation and spelling: There's Mackinaw City, Mackinac Island and the whole area, known historically as Michilimackinac. To make matters even more complicated, it was known to the early native inhabitants as "Michinnimakinong." What's the story here?

Like many such word evolutions, the variations had much to do with the combination of nationalities that are a part of the area's history and their different ways of perceiving and spelling words that were part of a spoken, not written, language. Suffice it to say that the British pronunciation won out, even where the French spelling remains. Therefore, whether it ends with "ac" or "aw," it's always pronounced "aw." Both "Mackinaw" and "Mackinac" are shorter versions of the original "Michilimackinac."

Second, some general advice: If you've just driven from the

Carved statue of Indian hero Wawatam on the waterfront in
Mackinaw City.

blue-blood haunts of Petoskey and Harbor Springs, the perva-
sive air of saltwater taffy tourism in Mackinaw City may come
as a shock, and the temptation to high-tail it immediately to
Mackinac Island may be irresistible. Don't do it.

Yes, there's plenty of asphalt in Mackinaw, along with tour
buses and souvenir

shops. (The Chamber of Commerce lists "tourism" and "fudge production" as the two main industries for this town of 800). But Mackinaw City is so steeped in Great Lakes history that volumes have been written about it, and if you stay and dig around a bit, you'll see and learn some fascinating things.

The present-day town is situated at the northern tip of the Lower Peninsula on the Straits of Mackinac, the narrow passage of water that flows between Lake Michigan and Lake Huron. Lake Superior is only a short distance north. Its location meant that Michilimackinac has been at the crossroads of travel on the Great Lakes since long before Europeans arrived in the area.

The first white person to travel through the Straits was the French explorer Jean Nicolet, who paddled his birch bark canoe from Lake Huron into Lake Michigan in 1634. In the following years, a French fur trading settlement and Jesuit mission were established in the area. It was from here that Father Jacques Marquette and Louis Jolliet embarked on their historic journey in search of the legendary Mississippi River.

Archeological excavation at Fort Michilimackinac.

Historic renactment at Colonial Michilimackinac State Park.

In 1712 the French government sent a commander to Michilimackinac in order to stabilize relations with the Indians and to stave off intrusions by the British. A fort was built at the site of what is now Mackinaw City, probably in 1715. It became an important trading center and point of departure for military raids against contentious tribes, but its tenure as a French post was short lived.

The fort was one of the many spoils of war garnered by

England during the French and Indian War. In 1760 it was evacuated by the French commander and turned over to the British. Slowly, they trickled in. Among them was the first British trader, Alexander Henry, who arrived disguised as a French-Canadian. The people of Michilimackinac didn't take kindly to the British newcomers, who seemed intent on alienating everyone as best they could. They decreased the amount of gifts given to the Indians and drove hard bargains for furs and other desirables. Unlike the French, who adapted many Indian ways and showed some understanding of Indian customs, the British remained apart and aloof.

The situation continued to worsen until, on King George III's birthday in June 1763, the lid blew. Alexander Henry was there to see it happen, later detailing it in sensational terms in his *Travels and Adventures in Canada and the Indian Territories Between the Years 1760 and 1776*, published in 1809.

The scene appeared innocent enough, wrote Henry. A group of Chippewas and Sacs (another tribe) were engaged in a game of *baggitiway*, better known today as *lacrosse*, just outside the fort. Henry was in his room nearby, writing letters and preparing for a trip to Montreal. Suddenly he heard cries. From his window he saw Indians inside the fort, killing and scalping the surprised British. They had apparently hidden weapons under blankets, and when the *lacrosse* ball was pitched over the side of the fort wall, they rushed inside, pausing only to grab their weapons.

Henry fled for cover to one of the houses owned by one of the French-Canadians, who remained neutral throughout the melee. From there he watched as the attack continued. Henry was soon discovered, and though he was spared, he and other captured Englishmen were put into a canoe headed for the Beaver Islands. They were intercepted by a group of Ottawa, however, and for a time it appeared they would be saved. In an unfortunate twist, the Ottawa changed their minds, and Henry found himself back in the hands of the Chippewas in Mackinaw City.

Enter Wawatam, an Indian who had befriended Henry a year

Lake Michigan Overlook on Pierce Stocking Scenic Drive in Sleeping Bear Dunes National Lakeshore.

before. The two had become blood brothers at Wawatam's request, brought about by a dream in which he adopted an Englishman as son and brother. After Wawatam made an emotional appeal to spare Henry's life, the Chippewa chiefs agreed and Henry was released to Wawatam and his family. For protection against the Indians who held great resentment toward the British, Henry lived with Wawatam for almost a year following his release, once again disguised — this time as an Indian. Wawatam is memorialized today by a statue in the park that bears his name. It was carved from local white pine by craftsman Jerry Prior.

The British eventually returned to the fort, but with the outbreak of the American Revolutionary War, they decided it would be too difficult to defend, and so built a new fort on Mackinac Island. They dismantled parts of the old fort and moved them to the new location, leaving the rest to crumble.

When Mackinaw City was platted in 1857, the land where the fort had stood was set aside for a public park. In 1904 it was given to the state, becoming Michigan's second state park.

Parts of the fort were discovered by park workers in the 1930s, and a full-scale excavation was begun in 1959. At first the work was done by inmates from a nearby prison. Later, students took over. The project continues today, making it the longest ongoing historical archaeology program in the United States.

To date, about half of the fort and its buildings have been excavated. Reconstructed buildings on the site include the soldiers' barracks, traders' houses, the Church of Ste. Anne, the powder magazine and many others. All of these are open to the public as part of **Colonial Michilimackinac State Park**.

If you see nothing else in Mackinaw City, make it a point to visit here; history comes alive as you walk down Rue Dauphine, the fort's main street, or watch re-enactments of voyageur landings or a French colonial wedding and dance. There are many types of demonstrations, such as musket and canon firing, cooking and sewing. Walking tours and children's programs are also available. An added bonus is being able to watch archeology in the making during the summer months when researchers are at work. The fort is open from about mid-May until mid-October. Every Memorial Day weekend the fort is the location of special events commemorating the history of the fort. For more information contact Colonial Michilimackinac at 231-436-5563.

The other primary attraction in the town is the **Mackinac Bridge**, the five-mile span that connects Michigan's Lower Peninsula with the Upper Peninsula. Until the bridge opened in 1957, upper Michigan was effectively cut off from the rest of the state, at the mercy of ferries that plied the Straits. For years, there had been talk of connecting the two portions somehow — with an elaborate system of bridges between the various islands, or even with a type of floating tunnel.

It wasn't until 1950 that the Michigan legislature accepted a plan it thought would work: a 100-million-dollar suspension bridge high over the Straits of Mackinac. Designed by engineer David B. Steinman, it was an ingenious and complicated structure that took more than three years to complete. The project

Mackinac Bridge connecting Michigan's lower and upper peninsulas.

was not without its toll, however; five workers lost their lives during the construction.

The two main towers reach 552 feet above the water, while their bases extend 200 feet underwater. Nearly 12,000 tons of cable were used, employing a total of 42,000 miles of wire. The main cables are more than two feet in diameter. When the wind blows, the bridge swings as much as 20 feet. The towers move also, up to 18 feet, depending on the distribution of weight on the road surface.

Pedestrian traffic isn't ordinarily allowed on the bridge, but if you've got a desire to walk five miles over the Straits, you can do so each Labor Day during the Annual Mackinac Bridge Walk. Cyclists, take note: special arrangements must be made to take your bicycle over the bridge. Call the Bridge Services Supervisor at 906-643-7600 for information.

You can learn just about everything you'd like to know about the bridge by going to the **Mackinac Bridge Museum**, located on the upper level of Mama Mia's Pizza at 231 Central Avenue (231-436-5534). Visitors can watch a video about the building of the bridge while waiting for a table in the restaurant. There are displays of bridge memorabilia such as newspaper articles, photos, and tools used during the construction. The ceiling is lined with hard hats of men who worked on the bridge, among them J.C. Stilwell, the owner of Mama Mia's, who was an ironworker on the bridge. The museum, which is free, is dedicated to the memory of those who died during construction.

While you're there, wander up and down Central Avenue, the main tourist drag, lined with fudge stands and souvenir shops. It's got a bit of a Western feel; in fact, many of the buildings were built in the 1800s. A little of that Wild West rowdiness is evoked, too, by the signs that proclaim: "no snowmobiles on sidewalk."

For state-of-the-art shopping the best place may be **Mackinaw Crossings**, a large, new pseudo-Victorian shopping complex in the middle of town. In addition to restaurants and the usual fudge and souvenir shops, there are several interesting places like the Great Lakes Teddy Bear Factory, where kids of all ages can design their own teddy bear and watch it being made. There's also a theater that stages Hollywood-style productions. Every night during the summer there's a free music and laser show.

The town's waterfront area near the bridge is quite pretty, with a series of small parks and benches that give visitors the opportunity to sit and watch ore boats traveling through the Straits. The Old Mackinac Point lighthouse is here, and though it makes a nice photograph, it is not open to the public; the maritime museum that was once located in the lighthouse has been closed.

As you continue along the waterfront on Lake Huron, you'll arrive at the docks where you can catch a ferry to Mackinac Island. You'll probably also notice the footprints painted on the sidewalks, an indication that you're on the **Historical Pathways Walking Tour** which highlights much of the town's history.

If you're a cyclist, you'll probably enjoy the 15-mile paved bike path along Lake Huron from Mackinaw City to Cheboygan. It runs along both sides of US 23.

Whether traveling by bike or car, a great place to stop on US 23 is 625-acre **Mill Creek State Park**, about four miles outside of town. Like Colonial Michilimackinac, Mill Creek is a historic park, though in addition to the historical attractions there are beautiful tree-lined trails. It was here that Robert Campbell built a watermill to process grain and the lumber used to build the new fort and village on Mackinac Island. The site was discovered in 1972, making it a relatively recent find. Excavation was undertaken, and many of the artifacts found there are on display in the park's visitor center.

The sawmill has been reconstructed and work is underway to build an authentic replica of the millwright's house using methods that would have been used in Campbell's time. Guides in costume give sawpit and mill demonstrations throughout the day.

The trails lead along the top of a bluff, through evergreen and aspen forests, and past several colonies of beaver.

The park is open mid-May to mid-October. It's possible to buy an admission ticket that includes Colonial Michilimackinac and **Fort Mackinac** on Mackinac Island. For more information contact Mackinac State Historic Parks, Box 873, Mackinaw City, MI 49701; phone 231-436-5563 (October - April) or 906-847-3328 (May - September).

WHERE TO STAY:

Mackinaw City is bargain city for families looking for reasonable accommodations. Nearly every motel chain has a facility here. And prices are almost unbelievably low, even for those right on the beach. (Be forewarned, many do not have beach access; if it's important to you, ask.) Here are a couple of independently owned places, each interesting for a different reason.

Brigadoon Bed & Breakfast, 207 Langlade Street, PO Box 810, Mackinaw City, MI 49701; 231-436-8882. The Brigadoon is a first for Mackinaw City. This gracious bed and breakfast — the only one in the town at the time of writing — features eight deluxe suites, each with whirlpool bath, heated floor in the bathroom (for those chilly northern winters), balcony, wet bar, refrigerator, microwave, television with VCR, fireplace and more. Within easy walking distance to the ferry, shopping, restaurants and beaches, the Brigadoon is located on a quiet street away from the motel area. The upper rooms have a nice view of the water. Hot breakfast, including homemade pastries and custom blended coffee, is served in the Tiffany dining room or on the verandah. This is a perfect place for a romantic getaway; leave the kids at home and enjoy the quiet luxury. It's open year round.

Riviera Motel, 520 North Huron Avenue, PO Box 96, Mackinaw City, MI 49701; 231-436-5577. While there are many fancier places in Mackinaw, with its location on the water near the bridge, the Riviera may well have the best view in Mackinaw City. The rooms at this family-owned motel are spacious but not luxurious. There's a heated swimming pool with a fantastic view of the bridge and for those who can brave the cold water there's a public beach in front of the motel. An adjacent park gives the motel a very uncrowded feel in a town that has strings of chain motels just about everywhere else.

WHERE TO EAT:

Fine dining aficionados may have to wait for the ferry to Mackinac Island. However, there are a couple of places in Mackinaw City that provide a substantial, if not gourmet, meal.

The Chippewa Room at Audie's Restaurant, 314 Nicolet Street; 231-436-5744. The Chippewa Room is the slightly more upscale dining room of the two at Audie's Restaurant. (The other is the Family Room.) The emphasis here is on beef, chicken, seafood and pasta, with special attention given to Great Lakes whitefish, served broiled, almondine, Cajun style, herbed, or stuffed with a seafood dressing. The restaurant has full bar service.

Mackinaw Pastie and Cookie Company, 514 South Huron Avenue; 231-436-5113. You know you're getting north when you start seeing signs for pasties (pronounced "past-tees"). These concoctions have their origin in Cornish miners' food so it's not surprising that they fill you up quickly and well. The traditional version consists of chopped beef, potatoes, onions and rutabaga wrapped in dough and then baked. Variations include pasties filled with chicken or vegetables. You can get them topped with gravy, sour cream and chives, or with taco sauce or pizza sauce. The Mackinaw Pastie and Cookie Company has been serving them up since 1964. This is dining at its most casual — you place your order at the counter then wait at one of the tables in the simple dining room. Still hungry? The owners' ice cream parlor is right next door.

For more information contact the Mackinaw Area Tourist Bureau, 708 South Huron Street, PO Box 160, Mackinaw City, MI 49701; 800-666-0160 or 231-436-5664.
Internet: http://www.mackinawcity.com

Natural Attractions

SLEEPING BEAR DUNES NATIONAL LAKESHORE

Some of the most beautiful scenery on Lake Michigan can be found in this 70,000-acre park that stretches along 37 miles of lake shore. Skirting around the towns of Empire and Glen Arbor, it encompasses beaches, inland lakes, rivers, forests, and the two Manitou Islands, but perhaps its most famous feature is the dunes for which the park is named.

Located about midway in the length of the park just south of Sleeping Bear Point, Sleeping Bear Dunes are the result of glacial action and wind. Towering 450 feet over the water at their highest point, they are dramatically pitched at a near-vertical angle.

Climbing the dunes at Sleeping Bear Dunes National Lakeshore.

The dunes were named by the Chippewa Indians who lived in the area. According to their legend, a mother bear and her two cubs were forced to flee the Wisconsin shore of Lake Michigan because of a raging fire. The mother was strong enough to swim to the opposite shore, but the cubs were not. Though she waited anxiously, the cubs never appeared, having drowned in the passage. The Great Spirit, known to the Chippewa as Manitou, created two islands to comfort the mother, who lies on the shoreline, forever waiting for her cubs.

The best way to see the dunes is along 7.4-mile **Pierce Stocking Scenic Drive**, named for the lumberman who first conceived of a road to the top of the dunes. If you're up to it, you can cycle this one-way loop, but be forewarned that parts of it are extremely steep. The drive winds through forest and dunes, with spectacular views of Glen Lake and Lake Michigan. There are two picnic areas on the drive and numerous viewing platforms. One of the most popular is the **Lake Michigan Overlook**. The view from here is dizzying, almost straight down to the water's edge 450 feet below. Take seriously the warning signs that caution against climbing these dunes. Though people persist in doing so, it not only causes erosion to these delicate natural formations, but may cause landslides that result in injury. The return uphill climb is extremely strenuous, and people have suffered heart attacks trying to get back to the top.

You'll have to pay the park entrance fee for access to the scenic drive unless you've already gotten a pass (good for a week) at one of the other checkpoints. Though the park is open year round, Pierce Stocking is closed mid-November until mid-April

Park passes can be purchased at the **Visitors Center** in the small town of Empire. In addition to distributing free information about the park, the center also sells books and other materials relating to the area. A 15-minute slide show runs continuously. Park staff is on hand to answer any questions. The center is open year round, seven days a week, except Christmas and federal holidays, 9:00 to 5:00 in the summer, 9:00 to 4:00 in the winter.

You can climb the dunes at the **Dune Climb**, just north of Pierce Stocking Scenic Drive (or you can just picnic on the grounds at the base of the dunes and watch everyone else do all the work). Though not as high or dramatic as the ones found at the Lake Michigan overlook, these dunes are a safe place to turn the kids loose. The 150-foot dune is the beginning of a hiking trail that leads to the lake, a strenuous 3.5-mile trek that requires three or four hours to complete.

Be sure to stop at **Glen Haven**, tucked into Sleeping Bear Bay at the north of the park. This was once a thriving little town that was a stopover for ships sailing between Chicago and Lake Huron. Like many such towns, the population dwindled and eventually it was abandoned. But unlike other towns that met the same fate, Glen Haven still exists — as a ghost town. The old inn where travelers would eat and sleep still stands. The general store, blacksmith shop and a few woodcutter's cottages have survived time and shifting sand.

For visitors, the main attraction is the old lifesaving station, which is now the **Sleeping Bear Point Maritime Museum**. When the station was built in 1901, it stood farther north, on Sleeping Bear Point. But dunes threatened to bury it, so in 1931 it was moved to a more protected location at Glen Haven. During World War II the station was closed; it stood empty until 1984, when it was refurbished and opened as a museum devoted to Great Lakes maritime history.

Many of the exhibits focus on the U. S. Lifesaving Service (the predecessor of today's Coast Guard), which was once so active in the area. The Manitou Passage, between the mainland and the Manitou islands, has long been dangerous territory for ships. Rocky shoals and storms claimed more than 50 vessels in the years between 1835 and 1960. Sailors who survived a rough encounter often owed their good fortune to the surfmen who risked their own lives to save others.

There is plenty of opportunity for recreation at the park and, understandably, much of this centers around water. Sandy beaches abound, and even in the middle of summer, it's possi-

Grand Traverse Lighthouse in Leelanau State Park.

ble to find solitude here, especially early in the morning. This is a good area in which to find Petoskey stones, the fossilized coral that is the Michigan state stone. For those who want to avoid the cold water of Lake Michigan, there is a public beach and picnic area on Glen Lake, whose impossibly turquoise water looks like it's been dropped out of the sky straight from the Caribbean. Canoes and kayaks can be rented in Glen Arbor for paddling down the Crystal River, or south of Empire for the Platt River. Both rivers are shallow and normally slow moving, making them suitable for families with small children.

Hikers will find more than 50 miles of trails on the mainland and 60 more on the two Manitou Islands. These vary from steep dune trails to meanders through the forest. During the winter, six trails are open to cross-country skiers, the rest to snowshoers. The ski trails are not groomed, but are usually well packed by other skiers. In the warm months, beware of

poison ivy and take bug repellent to ward off mosquitoes. Biting flies can also be pesky, but there's little you can do to foil these annoying insects. The visitors center in Empire has trail guides and maps. Be sure to stay on the trails, since the fragile dunes are easily damaged. Keep away from bluffs, where sand slides and snow avalanches may occur.

The park offers various options for campers. The **D.H. Day Campground** near Glen Haven has 88 rustic sites with vault toilets and pump water. The **Platte River Campground**, which is farther inland from the lake near the park's southern boundary, has more modern facilities, with showers, flush toilets, water and some sites with electricity. There are 149 sites. These are open spring to fall, on a first-come, first-served basis. There is a fee, and camping is limited to 14 days. Backcountry camping is by permit only, available from the visitors center or ranger stations. There are campgrounds on both Manitou Islands, but visitors should come prepared to be self-sufficient. No supplies are available on either island; only drinking water is provided. Backcountry camping on the islands is also by permit only.

Even if you don't plan to camp, make a point to spend a day at

South Manitou Island. (If you visit North Manitou you must camp overnight, since the ferry departs immediately after arrival and doesn't return until the following day.) Today no one lives on the 5,260-acre island except park rangers during the summer, but it was once home for a hardy bunch of settlers who established farms here in the mid-1800s. In 1840 a lighthouse was built, and many ships took refuge in the island's harbor, establishing trade with the island residents. Life on the island proved too difficult, however, and the pioneer village eventually faded out.

But there is still much to remind today's visitors of these past residents. Farm buildings, the schoolhouse and the cemetery remain. What was once farmland, though becoming overgrown with brush, is evident by the lack of large old trees. You can learn more about the human and natural history of the island by taking the guided tours offered by the ferry company, Manitou Island Transit. These hour-and-a-half- to two-hour tours are conducted by vehicle, and will allow you to see more of the island in one day than is possible by foot.

There is a small visitors center near the ranger station by the dock. Here you'll find artifacts and displays about the island's history. Just beyond is the 100-foot lighthouse tower, one of the tallest on the Great Lakes. It was built in 1871 because the original light was often confused with those from the ships in the harbor. At the time, it was considered state-of-the-art, and it remained in service until 1958. Ranger-guided tours are available, and it's a worthwhile though tiring climb to the top, where you'll be rewarded with spectacular views of the island, the surrounding water and — when it's clear — the mainland in the distance.

At the southwest corner of the island is a 50-acre virgin forest and the "Valley of the Giants," a grove of massive old white cedars. Among them is reportedly the largest in the world. The area is accessible by a shaded but very buggy hiking path.

Other paths lead through sand dunes, to the campgrounds and through the old farmlands. Though they are fairly well defined, they are not well marked, and carrying a compass is a good idea. Entering old, decaying buildings is both dangerous and illegal.

Hiking along the beach on South Manitou is particularly pleasant. The fine, white sand is pebbled with beautiful stones, many polished to a luster by the action of the waves. Because the island is part of the park, however, felled trees are left in their natural state, so you may have to climb over them if they have fallen across the beach. Occasionally, they may block the passage entirely.

About seven miles west of the dock, just offshore, is the wreck of the Liberian freighter Francisco Morazon, which ran aground in November 1960. Much of the wreck is above water, making it easy to spot. Visitors are cautioned not to try to swim out to the wreck, however, since currents and very cold water make this treacherous.

Those wanting even more of a wilderness experience will probably enjoy camping and hiking on **North Manitou Island**. At 15,000 acres, it is the larger of the two islands, and like its neighbor it was once active in lumbering and farming. (Many of the old buildings remain, but they are in poor condition and are dangerous to enter.) Today the island is populated instead with deer, and with the rare, endangered piping plover. Fishing is permitted on inland Lake Manitou, though a state fishing license is required.

Visitors should come with all provisions, and should have enough supplies to hold them for two extra days in the event that foul weather prevents the ferry from making its daily run.

There are no docking facilities for private boats at the islands, though a 15-minute stop is permitted. Boaters may anchor offshore in the harbor at South Manitou. There is no harbor at North Manitou, and though boats may anchor offshore, shifting winds and changing weather may make this undesirable. No fuel is available

Visitors to either island are required to pay the entrance fee for the park. The ferry ride is often chilly, so bring a jacket. Be prepared for sudden weather changes. Mosquitoes and poison ivy are plentiful. Don't forget to bring whatever provisions you will need, as nothing but water is available on the islands. Be aware of the ferry schedule or you may find yourself spending an unintentional night in the open. Ferry schedules and information are available from Manitou Island Transit, PO Box 591, Leland, MI 49654; 231-256-9061 or 231-271-4217 (off season). Ferries to the islands leave from the dock at Leland. Reservations are recommended.

For more information contact Sleeping Bear Dunes National Lakeshore, 9922 Front Street, Highway M-72, Empire, MI 49630; 231-326-5134.

LEELANAU STATE PARK

It's easy to drive all the way to the tip of Leelanau Peninsula, to the day use area of the state park, and think you've seen it all. Clustered into this small area are picnic facilities, a playground, campground and the historic **Grand Traverse Lighthouse**, which has been opened as a museum.

But the bulk of this 1,350-acre property lies in an undeveloped area to the south, off Densmore Road. Here you'll find more than six miles of trails and access to a 1.5-mile stretch of beach along Cathead Bay. You'll likely find solitude on this beach, since getting to it involves a hike. The **Lake Michigan Trail**, which has the spur that leads to the beach, loops for a mile and a half through woods and over dunes. The **Manitou Overlook Spur** takes you up stairs to a viewing platform from which it's possible to see the Fox Islands on a clear day. The longer, two-mile **Mud Lake Trail** loop leads through woods and swampy areas and along small Mud Lake. Trailheads are located off the parking lot. In the warm months, insect repellent is advised. The trails are groomed for cross-country skiing in the winter. Though there are no concessions in the park, there are ski rental facilities in Northport, just to the south.

The main attraction in the northern part of the park is the

Kayaking at Petoskey State Park.

restored lighthouse, built in 1852. You can tour the keeper's quarters and climb the tower, but a separate admission fee is charged. (For more information about the lighthouse, see the "Leelanau Peninsula" section.) The picnic area nearby is a pleasant place to spend the afternoon, though there is no swimming here on the rocky beach.

The campground adjacent to the lighthouse has 52 rustic sites, with pit toilets and no electricity, and two mini-cabins, each with two bunk beds, table, fire ring and picnic table. Despite its primitive facilities and lack of a beach, the campground's scenic location overlooking the water makes this a popular spot. Reservations are recommended (800-44-PARKS).

For more information contact Leelanau State Park, 15310 N. Lighthouse Point Road, Northport, MI 49670; 231-922-5270; summer only: 231-386-5422.

TRAVERSE CITY STATE PARK

Located three miles east of downtown Traverse City on US 31, this 45-acre state park has an urban feel. The park has a quarter mile of sandy beach, however, and a grassy picnic area, making it a nice getaway from the city. A large campground is across the road from the water, accessible by a pedestrian overpass above the highway. There are 342 modern campsites, which are usually full in the peak season. The campground is open in the winter, and there are heated rest rooms, electricity and hot water available. This is the only state park on Grand Traverse Bay.

For more information contact Traverse City State Park, 1132 US 31 N, Traverse City, MI 49686; 231-922-5270.

FISHERMAN'S ISLAND STATE PARK

Rumor has it that the small island offshore from this state park was once inhabited by two men who made their living catching and selling fish. No one lives today on the 4.2-acre island, but the name stuck.

At 2,678 acres, this long, narrow park is one of the largest in the state park system. Most of it, especially the southern half, is inaccessible except by foot, though there is a gravel and dirt road that begins at the entrance and runs about 2.5 miles along the lake shore. There are five miles of undeveloped shoreline, including a mile-long beach reached by a rather bumpy drive. Grills and picnic tables are nearby.

The park has 90 rustic campsites, a handful of them right on the beach, in two campgrounds, one located near the park entrance and the other located close to the end of the road. This is a tremendously popular park, so campsite reservations are advised (800-44-PARKS).

For hikers and nature observers, there are several miles of maintained foot trails, beginning near the park entrance. These wind toward the south, passing by the two camping areas and though woods and fields, ending at the parking lot at the end of the gravel road. Visitors are likely to see deer, rabbits, foxes and grouse.

True to its name, Fisherman's Island State Park has some good fishing in the three streams that flow through the park into Lake Michigan.

To reach the park, follow US 31 south from Charlevoix for five miles, then turn right on Bells Bay Road. The entrance is 2.5 miles from US 31.

For more information contact Fisherman's Island State Park, PO Box 456, Bells Bay Road, Charlevoix, MI 49720; 231-547-6641.

PETOSKEY STATE PARK

Tucked into the elbow of Little Traverse Bay, Petoskey State Park attracts day visitors from both Petoskey and Harbor Springs. Much of this 300-acre property was a Petoskey City park until it was sold to the state and opened as a state park in 1970. In addition to the day visitors, others come to set up camp in the park's two campgrounds, which offer 170 modern sites.

The main attraction, though, is the long sandy beach, where hunting for Petoskey stones is a favorite activity. These stones, which are the state stone of Michigan, are actually fossilized coral and are especially plentiful here. Their distinguishing markings are nearly impossible to see when the stones are dry, but are defined almost magically when they are covered by water. Because the bay is often calm, it is possible to spot the stones easily while walking though the water. There is plenty of parking near the beach, along with a bathhouse and a picnic area nearby.

Neither of the campgrounds is directly on the lake, but the water isn't far from either. **Tannery Creek Campground**, at the south end of the park, is the larger of the two. There is also a rustic cabin here. The **Dunes Campground** is located closer to the park entrance in a shady area of shifting dunes. The park is popular among campers, so early reservations are advised.

There are two trails in the park, totaling 3.5 miles. The longer of these is 2.8-mile **Portage Trail**, which winds in a loop from the Dunes Campground to Tannery Creek Campground and back. During the winter, this a popular trail for cross-country skiers.

For more information contact Petoskey State Park, 2475 M-119, Petoskey, MI 49712; 231-347-2311.

WILDERNESS STATE PARK

This park is located eight miles west of Mackinaw City on a sandy strip of land that juts into the lake at the extreme north-west corner of the Lower Peninsula. At its tip is Waugoshance Point, beyond which are several small islands and shoals, right in the path of ships heading through the Straits of Mackinac. In earlier years there were so many shipwrecks that in 1832 the first lightship on the Great Lakes was stationed here. For the next 20 years it guided ships through this dangerous passage until it was replaced by a lighthouse in 1852. The lighthouse was abandoned in the early 20th century, and though it still stands, it is in great disrepair from being used as a bombing target during World War II training.

Wilderness State Park lives up to its name. At 8,286 acres, it's Michigan's second largest state park, and most of it is still wild. At its northern end the park borders Big Stone Bay, from which visitors are treated to a beautiful view of the Straits and Mackinaw Bridge in the distance. On its western edge, the park follows the contour of Sturgeon Bay, lined with miles of sandy beaches. The park has 26 miles of shoreline, 16 miles of hiking trails and 12 miles of cross-country ski trails.

In addition to 250 camp sites, there are six rustic cabins and three bunkhouses that sleep 24 people each. Some of the camp-sites have a great location on the beach at Big Stone Bay. This is a popular place that is often full, so reservations are recom-mended. The six cabins, which sleep four to eight people, have wood stoves, bunks, outhouses and pumps, but no electricity. These often book up a year in advance. Five of the cabins are on the waterfront; the other, Nebo Cabin, is in a wooded area and is accessible only by a two-mile hiking trail. No pets are permitted in the cabins.

There are actually two sections to the park and you can't get from one to the other without going around outside the park boundaries. (Unless you hike the trails.) The entrance for camping and the cabins is on Wilderness Park Drive at the north end of the park. This is also where you'll find the boat launch, a sandy beach and a picnic area.

The southern part, on Sturgeon Bay, is accessed from Lakeview Road. Day visitors looking for beaches will probably want to use this entrance, since the park road that runs south from here is lined with a beautiful beach on one side and dunes on the other. There are many miles of beach to the north along Sturgeon Bay that are accessible only by foot. Parking is available at the end of Lakeview Road.

There are 12 trails in the park, including a 5.5-mile section of the **North Country National Scenic Trail**, which is gradually being developed between North Dakota to New York. The longest trail entirely within the park boundaries is 2.25-mile **Sturgeon Bay Trail**, which connects with several other park trails. Some trails are open to mountains bikes; check at the park office for more information.

Fishing is a popular pastime, especially in the bass spawning grounds on Sturgeon Bay in the spring and early summer. The park stays lively and active in the winter, when cross-country skiers come to use the groomed trails and cold weather enthusiasts fill the cabins. If you opt for a winter stay, be prepared to get to the cabins by ski or snowmobile, as only the park's main road is plowed.

For more information contact Wilderness State Park, 898 Wilderness State Park Drive, Carp Lake, MI 49718; 231-436-5381.

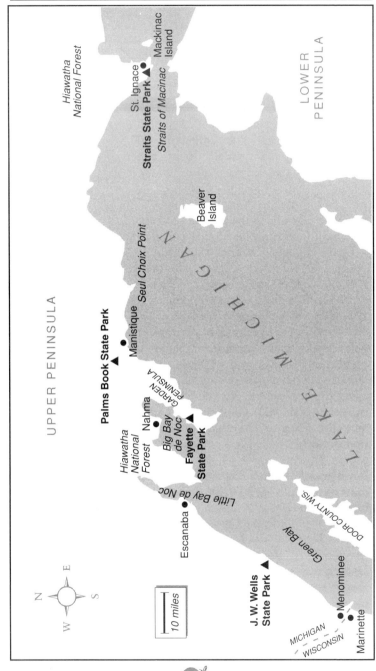

Chapter

FOUR

MICHIGAN'S UPPER PENINSULA

Five Miles and Half a World Away

Across the Straits of Mackinac from Michigan's Lower Peninsula lies the Upper Peninsula, separated by factors greater than just five miles of water. Larger than Massachusetts, Connecticut, Delaware and Rhode Island combined, the U.P. nonetheless has only 4% of Michigan's population. Look at a detailed map and you will see that vast portions of it are public land — forests and lakes with towns few and far between, many of them ghost towns with only a few hundred inhabitants. What separates the Lower Peninsula from the Upper is a way of life.

The Upper Peninsula has supplied Michigan with some of its most important natural resources, but ironically, Michigan didn't even want the U.P. at first. When statehood was being contemplated in the early 1800s, Michigan had its eye on the Toledo Strip, a ten-mile snippet of land on Lake Erie's Maumee Bay. When Michigan was admitted to the Union in 1837, it was awarded instead with the U.P., and the Toledo Strip went to Ohio. As far as most Michigan folks were concerned, they got the booby prize. Few dreamed that there was anything of value up there that would fill lower Michigan coffers. Then copper mines were discovered on Lake Superior and lumbering companies began to mine the peninsula's "green" resource — vast forests of pine and hardwood. Much of that activity has ceased, and the U.P. is now quietly at rest.

Joined physically in 1957 with the opening of the Mackinac Bridge, the two peninsulas remain distinctly different in both appearance and attitude. Instead of the art museums, cultural events, high-priced galleries and sophisticated dining that characterize many of the towns in the Lower Peninsula, the U.P. has space. Lots of it. Filled with forests, some 4,300 inland lakes, 150 waterfalls, 12,000 miles of streams and 1,700 miles of Great Lakes shoreline. Visitors come to the U.P. for the great outdoors, and residents pretty much live their lives for it. Hunting, fishing, camping, mountain biking, snowmobiling and skiing are pursued avidly by visitors and locals alike.

The Lake Michigan shoreline stretches from St. Ignace in the east to Menominee and the Wisconsin border to the west, a distance of almost 200 miles, as the bird flies. In that space there are only four towns with appreciable attractions and populations — St. Ignace, Manistique, Escanaba and Menominee. It's the places in between that count for so much of the Upper Peninsula's appeal: long stretches of pristine beach, quiet bays for fishing, eerily silent ghost towns, and mile after mile of towering forests.

St. Ignace

This is one of the first places in what is now the United States where Europeans have lived continuously since coming to the continent. Even long before that, it was a gathering spot for native peoples. Why this, of all places? There are several reasons. Foremost may be the location, on the Straits of Mackinac at the juncture of Lake Michigan and Lake Huron, with Lake Superior just to the north. In the days when most traveling took place by boat, the Straits area was on the route to just about anywhere. There were also abundant fish, especially whitefish, and game, both for food and furs. For the agricultural Huron, who came here in the 1670s, and the French and English, the land was adequate for growing crops.

Upper Peninsula Beach near St. Ignace.

The town of St. Ignace was founded in 1671 by French missionary and explorer Jacques Marquette, who named it in honor of St. Ignatius, founder of the Jesuit order. Though Marquette soon departed for his explorations and never returned in his lifetime to the mission, fellow missionaries continued their work among the local Indians until 1705.

The French established Fort de Buade at St. Ignace in the 1680s, but its presence was short lived and in 1698 the fort's commander, Antoine Cadillac, moved the garrison south to Detroit.

With the closing of the mission and the removal of the fort, St. Ignace didn't continue to grow but did maintain its importance by virtue of its location at the mouth of the Straits. Lumbering, iron making and fishing each played a part in the town's sustenance until tourism began to make an impact in the early 20th century. This was greatly bolstered by the opening of the Mackinac Bridge in 1957. Today the town's year-round population of 2,600 swells each summer with visitors who come to enjoy its beaches and close proximity to Mackinac Island.

Father Marquette Park and the Museum of Ojibwa Culture, St.
Ignace.

The town is strung along Moran Bay on Lake Huron, the
streets lined with gift shops and fudge stands, and the waterfront dotted with the docks of the various ferry lines that travel
to Mackinac Island. Though less busy than Mackinaw City
across the Straits, St. Ignace gets its share of vacation traffic,
making it difficult to cross the main street, which has no stop
lights and few crosswalks.

For a quieter perspective of historic St. Ignace stop at the
Father Marquette National Memorial and Museum on the
grounds of Straits State Park. Located high over the water west
of town, its atmosphere is a serene contrast to the usual bustle
of a busy summer day. The museum is dedicated to telling the
story of Marquette, one of the greatest explorers of North
America. After establishing the mission at St. Ignace, he left in
1673 for his famous and courageous journey with Joliet which
resulted in the first maps of the Mississippi River and environs.
He died on the return trip in 1675 near Ludington. The grounds
also include a quiet picnic area, trail and scenic overlook. The
museum is open daily Memorial Day through Labor Day, with
limited hours extending into September. For information call

906-643-9394 or 8620.

More about Marquette can be learned at the **Marquette Mission Park and Museum of Ojibwa Culture** (906-643-9161) on State Street in downtown St. Ignace. This site has three parts adjacent to one another. The small Marquette Mission Park, dedicated to Marquette, is located on the site where his mission was established. A memorial marks the place where bones believed to be his are buried.

The museum next to the park is dedicated to interpreting the culture of the Ojibwa people, the original inhabitants of the Upper Great Lakes region. Displays depict the their close ties to nature, their strong family structure and spiritual beliefs. There is an extensive display of beautiful baskets and other woven vessels made from black ash. The museum is open daily Memorial Day to early October.

Behind the museum is the archeological site of a Huron village, occupied for about 35 years from its establishment in 1671.

A SUPERIOR ADVENTURE

As long as you're already so far north, follow the compass a little further and catch a glimpse of Lake Superior. Pictured Rocks National Lakeshore is only about 50 miles north of Manistique. The main attraction here is the rock cliffs that rise as high as 200 feet above the edge of the lake. Elegantly carved by wind and water, the agate-toned cliffs stand in beautiful contrast to the clear aqua water of Lake Superior. The rocks have fanciful names like Miner's Castle, Battleship Rock and Lover's Leap. Only Miner's Castle is accessible by car; visitors must hike to the rest. But the best way to get the full impact of these beautiful formations is by boat. Cruises leave out of Munising daily, Memorial Day into October. For cruise information and a schedule call 906-387-2379. For information on the national lakeshore call the park's visitor center at 906-387-3700.

The lighthouse tender Maple, the oldest coast guard ship built on the Great Lakes.

The Huron and Ottawa people, forced by the Iroquois to abandon their homes in lower Ontario, settled in the protected area on Moran Bay. Archeological excavations have uncovered evidence of longhouses, fire pits and other village features. The site is marked today by a replica Huron longhouse, built of saplings and bark. These impressive structures were large — about 20 feet high by 20 feet wide and 40 to 120 feet long — and built to be permanent homes. Unlike many other tribes, the Huron depended on agriculture and did not move from place to place.

The **Fort de Buade Indian Museum** on State Street is built on the grounds of the original French fort. Open daily from the end of May until October 1, it contains a large collection of Indian artifacts and military items from the early French, English and American periods.

The town is a pleasant one for walking, made all the more so by the mile-long **Lake Huron Boardwalk** that runs parallel to the waterfront. Signs along the way tell the story of St. Ignace and its place in history. At the south end of the boardwalk is the lighthouse tender Maple, the oldest coast guard ship built on the Great Lakes.

Though there are numerous Lake Huron beaches at the hotels in St. Ignace, the most spectacular beaches are along Lake Michigan west of town, stretching for miles in either direction. There are no facilities or lifeguards at these very popular beaches.

St. Ignace hosts several special events each year. In July and August the **French Heritage Days** are celebrated with period reenactments, crafts, music and dance. August brings the **Native American Arts Festival**, while Labor Day weekend is the time for the **Michinemackinong Pow Wow**. On Labor Day itself is the annual **Mackinac Bridge Walk**, the only time pedestrians are allowed on the bridge.

WHERE TO STAY:

The Boardwalk Inn, 316 North State Street, St. Ignace, MI 49781; 906-643-7500. Like Mackinaw City, St. Ignace has a plethora of chain motels strung out along the waterfront, many of them with beaches. But for something unique try this unusual hotel in the heart of downtown across from the boardwalk. Built in 1928, it is the oldest hotel in St. Ignace, somewhat reminiscent of cozy European inns. Completely and carefully renovated by enthusiastic owners Steve and Lanie Sauter, it provides modern convenience in a charming setting. The 15 rooms are individually decorated, each with private bath, air conditioning and cable TV. The Bayview Room and the Vallier Room have views of the harbor. There is no elevator, but if stairs are a problem ask for one of the four guest rooms on the ground level. The hotel's gathering spot is the Fireside Room, which has a phone (there are no phones in guest rooms), microwave, games and ample seating. Continental breakfast is served each morning. Room rates are quite reasonable, and if you stay a week the seventh night is free. This is a non-smoking hotel. It is open mid-May through mid-October, but if you happen to catch the Sauters at home at other times they'll gladly rent you a room if one is available.

WHERE TO EAT:

Dockside Restaurant, 1101 North State Street; 906-643-7911. This is arguably the best dining view in town. Located right on the water overlooking Lake Huron and Mackinac Island, the Dockside is open for breakfast, lunch and dinner. Dinner entrees include filet, prime rib, chicken and Alaskan king crab. The specialty is planked fish — whitefish or walleye baked and served on a maple plank with vegetables and whipped potatoes.

For more information contact the St. Ignace Chamber of Commerce and Convention & Visitor's Bureau, 560 N. State Street, St. Ignace, MI 49781; 800-338-6660 or 906-643-8717. Internet: http://www.stignace.com

Manistique

Route 2 west from St. Ignace to the tiny town of Naubinway gets this writer's vote for the prettiest stretch of road anywhere along Lake Michigan. Just outside of town is the border of the **Hiawatha National Forest**, which stretches all the way north to Lake Superior. (See "Natural Attractions" at the end of this chapter for more information on the park.) The forest's Lake Michigan shoreline is undeveloped, with vast stretches of open beach just south of the road. On sunny days the water here is Gulf-of-Mexico blue (but a lot colder!), sparkling as far as the eye can see.

SOO IMPRESSIVE

The Soo Locks at Sault Ste. Marie boast the two longest locks in the world. Capable of handling superfreighters of 1,000 feet, these locks process 95 million tons of freight every year. Built to provide a passage around the rapids of the St. Marys River, the Soo Locks enable ships to negotiate the 21-foot drop between Lake Superior and Lake Huron. Visitors can view the locks from observation platforms or by taking a boat tour. For more information call the Sault Convention & Visitors Bureau at 800-MI-SAULT. Sault Ste. Marie is about 50 miles northeast of St. Ignace.

About 10 miles west of St. Ignace are the **Lake Michigan Sand Dunes**, a popular place for sunning, swimming and relaxing. Farther west, about 15 miles from St. Ignace, is the **Cut River Bridge**, where an overlook gives visitors a view of the gorge created by the Cut River in its rush to Lake Michigan. There are also nature trails and picnic facilities.

Beyond Naubinway, Route 2 cuts inland and stays away from the water almost until Manistique. But take a detour as you pass through the small town of Gulliver. Turn south on County Road 432, then right on County Road 431. It will eventually turn to gravel, but if you follow it to the end you'll find yourself at one of the most striking lighthouses on Lake Michigan.

Seul Choix Point Lighthouse, built in 1892, stands 79 feet high on a tip of land at the south end of Seul Choix Bay. The bay was named by French sailors who were forced to land here during a fierce storm. They called it Seul Choix (pronounced "Sis Shwa") or "only choice." When the light was built, it offered the only beacon for 100 miles between the Straits of Mackinac and the Garden Peninsula to the west. The light was automated in 1972, but the keeper's house remained. The complex is now maintained by the Gulliver Historical Society,

Seul Choix Lighthouse near Manistique.

whose volunteers have done a commendable job in raising funds and assisting with restoration. Even though this is a working lighthouse, the grounds and buildings are open to the public.

The two-story keeper's quarters are furnished as they might have been when they were occupied, and fortunately the beautiful wood cabinetry in the kitchen remains. Visitors can climb the tower for a magnificent view of the bay and the lake beyond. The old fog signal building has been turned into the Gulliver Historical Museum containing displays on local history. There is a small gift shop in an adjacent building.

If you're curious about things supernatural, ask one of the

216

guides to tell you about the strange goings-on in the lighthouse. There are rumors of silverware moved overnight, of lingering cigar smoke in the mornings, of ghost sightings and sounds of crashing objects.

The museum and tower are open Memorial Day through September 10:00 a.m. to 4:00 p.m., seven days a week.

Manistique is the primary population center along this part of the lake. This small town of fewer than 4,000 got its start with the Chicago Lumbering Company in the 1870s. The company built homes and stores for its employees, creating a company town. It went public, though, in 1912 when the bottom fell out of the lumber business and the company was sold. With the establishment of the Manistique Pulp and Paper Company, owned by the Minneapolis Tribune, paper took the place of lumber at the economic forefront. Paper manufacturing and stone quarrying remain the area's two largest industries, with tourism a close third.

Manistique is very much a working town. Separated from Lake Michigan by U.S. Route 2, it is built up along the Manistique River, which gave the town its name. (The word evolved rather convolutedly from the Indian word "Unamanitigong," which means "red ocher," referring to the river's color.) The lakefront west of the river is beginning to be built up, but the area to the east is, so far, still undeveloped except for a path leading along the water for about two miles from the east breakwall. The surroundings have been left in their natural state, bordered by wildflowers and rocky beach, and if it weren't for the noise of the traffic on the highway, you'd think you were far from any industrial center. A small sandy beach just to the east of the breakwall adds to the pretty scene. This is also a good place to view the striking red lighthouse, built in 1915, at the end of the breakwall.

The town center is busier with its own residents than with tourists, who come mainly for the parks, forests, fishing and other outdoor recreation opportunities in the surrounding area. Nonetheless, there are a couple of interesting attractions in town. One is easily found — just look up. The **Manistique Water Tower** rises 200 feet, well above any other nearby structures. Built of brick in 1922, the tower is an octagonal building unusual for its Roman revival style of architecture, which has earned it a spot on the National Register of Historic Places. No longer used as a water tower, it currently belongs to the local chamber of commerce. Presently it can be admired only from the outside.

Next to the tower is the **Manistique Historical Museum**, housed in the Imogene Herbert home, one of the oldest in Manistique. This tiny museum displays local artifacts such as period clothing and household appliances, lumbering tools, arrowheads, photographs and antique jewelry. The museum is open in the summer only.

Near the museum is the attraction that put the town in "Ripley's Believe It or Not." In the early 1900s the Manistique Pulp and Paper Company built a reinforced concrete flume to channel river water for use by the paper plant. The flume, roughly two-thirds of a mile long, can deliver water at the rate of 8,000 cubic feet per second. But this isn't the "believe it or not" part. When U.S. Route 2 was built along Lake Michigan, the flume presented an engineering problem that was solved by building a bridge that runs four feet below the water level. The 300-foot **Siphon Bridge** gives the strange illusion that you have no right to remain dry while walking across it, attracting the attention of the Ripley's people as well as curious visitors.

Less than an hour's drive north of town is the **Seney National Wildlife Refuge** (906-586-9851), a 96,000-acre refuge established in 1935. More than 200 species of birds live in the reserve, including bald eagles and sand hill cranes. Other animals found here are black bears, otters, foxes, coyotes, bobcats and wolves. Unusual plant species such as carnivorous pitcher plants also thrive in the refuge. Visitors can hike, cycle, canoe and cross-country ski year round. The visitors center, open mid-May through mid-October, offers guided programs. The **Marshland Wildlife Drive**, open daylight hours during the same months, is a seven-mile self-guided auto tour with

Rafting across the spring at Palms Book State Park.

wildlife observation decks.

Perhaps the most well-known — and certainly among the most beautiful — natural attraction in this part of the Upper Peninsula is **Kitch-iti-kipi**, or The Big Spring, in **Palms Book State Park** 12 miles west of Manistique. Michigan's largest spring, Kitch-iti-kipi averages about 200 feet in diameter and 40 feet in depth. More than 10,000 gallons of 45-degree water gush from the limestone bottom of this beautifully clear, emerald-colored spring. Visitors can peer into the depths, watching the water bubble up and the large trout swim lazily, by boarding a hand-powered raft that takes them out to the center.

Many legends surround the spring, though some were the products of the active imagination of John I. Bellaire, the man who first envisioned the spring as a park. In later years he admitted to making up stories about the spring in order to attract visitors. The most well-known legend may be that of the young Indian chief Kitch-iti-kipi. According to the story, he lost his life in the spring during a failed attempt to impress a love interest by paddling out to the center and catching her as she jumped from a branch. Whether there's any truth to the story or whether it was fabricated by Bellaire seems to be anyone's guess.

The lovely park grounds by the spring are perfect for a peaceful picnic. Camping is not available at Palms Book, but nearby **Indian Lake State Park** (906-341-2355) has two campgrounds with over 300 sites combined.

WHERE TO STAY:

Royal Rose Bed & Breakfast, 230 Arbutus Ave., Manistique, MI 49854; 906-341-4886. Located in a residential neighborhood near the center of town, this 1903 home has four guest rooms, a wrap-around deck and two fireplaces. Gracious hosts Gilbert and Rosemary Sablack serve dessert each evening and a full breakfast in their formal dining room every morning. Presently the four guest rooms share two baths, but plans are underway to add another bathroom. This is a quiet place best enjoyed by adults.

Thistledowne at Seul Choix, PO Box 88, Gulliver, MI 49840; 800-522-4649 or 906-283-3559. If you are looking for a place with absolute quiet, isolated from bustle and activity, Thistledowne may be perfect. This elegant modern B & B is located about 10 miles east of Manistique on 60 acres with a private Lake Michigan beach. While many attractions are within an easy day's drive, there are no restaurants or shops nearby. It's so far off the beaten path, in fact, that the last mile to the entrance is an unpaved road. The three guest rooms, all overlooking the water, feature private baths with whirlpool tubs. Two have gas fireplaces and a private deck. Full breakfast is served daily. This is definitely for grown-ups only.

For more information contact the Schoolcraft County Chamber of Commerce, 1000 W. Lakeshore Drive, Manistique, MI 49854: 906-341-5010.
Internet: http://www.manistique.com

Escanaba and Delta County

West of Manistique is Delta County, which, according to the Tourism & Convention Bureau, has over 200 miles of freshwater shoreline, more than any other county in the United States. This is because the coastline snakes and curves around two large bays, the Big Bay de Noc and the Little Bay de Noc, named for the Noquet group of Chippewa Indians who lived in the area. A large portion of the county is undeveloped forest which is part of the Hiawatha National Forest (see "Natural Attractions"); the rest is primarily farmland and countryside. The largest town on the lake here is Escanaba, an important ore port and paper mill town.

White settlers who came to the area in the 1800s named the easternmost of the two peninsulas formed by Big Bay de Noc the Garden Peninsula for its fertile soil. It was soon the site of more than farming when the Jackson Iron Company platted a town 17 miles down the peninsula on the shores of the bay. Named Fayette for Fayette Brown, the company agent who found the site, the town was soon populated with immigrants who came to work in the furnaces and kilns used to turn ore into pig iron, which was then shipped to foundries in Cleveland and Chicago.

Nearly 500 people lived in the town during the 24 years that the blast furnaces operated. When the smelting operation ceased in 1891, the people left, many to pursue farming. What remained was a ghost town. It languished until 1959, when it became part of the state park system. Today this historic site at **Fayette State Park** has more than 20 buildings still standing, including the giant furnaces, the opera house, the company store and the hotel. Many are furnished as they might have been when they were occupied, and others contain displays depicting life in a company town. You can still find bits of slag on the beach and scuba divers often uncover artifacts by the old docks in Snail Shell Harbor. A self-guided walking tour takes visitors through the town and back in history. The site is fairly spread out, so plan to spend at least a half-day here if you want to tour the entire town. (For more information about the park see "Natural Attractions" at the end of this chapter.)

Farther west on the bay is a ghost town that's making a come-back. The tiny town of **Nahma** has fewer than 100 residents. Like Fayette, it was a company town. Nahma belonged to the

Dock ruins at the ghost town of Fayette.

Bay de Noquet Lumber Company, which moved into the area in 1881. They built homes, a school, general store and other community buildings and furnished the residents with utilities and medical care. When they pulled out in the 1950s the whole town went up for sale (for a cool $250,000) and it was soon deserted.

But it won't stay that way if the Groleau family has its way. Three brothers and their wives bought an old company guest house and have turned it into the Nahma Hotel (see "Where to stay and eat"), a truly unique attraction that may spell a renaissance for the town. As for the rest of Nahma, there are a few remains from the company days, such as a large tower near the water that was used to burn waste. Walk along the bay and you'll probably see some of the old machinery. What was once the docking canal is now managed by the Department of Natural Resources and has been turned into a lake access with boat launching ramps. There's a quiet, protected beach and a golf course nearby, but little else to do in the town until evenings, when the Arrow Lounge in the Nahma Hotel starts to hop. The General Store, which is also owned by the Groleau family, is worth a stop. Part store and part museum, it displays some of the original merchandise sold here when it was the company store.

Ghost town of Nahma.

West of Nahma is Hiawatha National Forest property, part of the 879,600 acres that make up this enormous tract. Near the small town of Rapid River is the terminus of the **Bay de Noc-Grand Island Trail**, a 36-mile historic Indian route between Lakes Michigan and Superior that is now used as a recreation trail for hikers, horseback riders and skiers. For information stop at the ranger station in Rapid River or call 906-474-6442.

Just beyond the Bay de Noc-Grand Island Trail, Stonington Peninsula juts south into the lake, making the western edge of Big Bay de Noc and the eastern edge of Little Bay de Noc. **Little Bay de Noc Recreation Area**, also part of the national forest, is about halfway down the peninsula on county road 513. There are 36 campsites, a picnic area with swimming beach, and three hiking trails. If you continue south on the county road to the end of the peninsula you will arrive at **Point Peninsula Light**, maintained by the forest service. Patience and good shock absorbers are required: the last mile and a quarter of road aren't paved, and the final three-quarters is only one lane with sizable potholes. Recreational vehicles are not permitted on this road.

Only the light tower, built in 1866, remains; the keeper's quarters burned in the 1950s. You can still climb the tower, however, for a beautiful view that on clear days stretches to Escanaba in the west, Fayette in the east and the Minneapolis Shoal lighthouse to the south in the vast expanse of blue water. The grounds make a lovely place for a picnic, with water on three sides. Grills and tables, some shaded, are provided. There's no beach, but the rocky shoreline is a pleasant place to walk.

Almost directly opposite from the lighthouse, on the other side of Little Bay de Noc, is the hard-working town of Escanaba. Its perimeter is lined with fast food places, discount stores and ugly signage, making the drive to its center less than promising. The surprise comes when you get to the waterfront, which

Sand Point lighthouse museum at Escanaba.

is beautifully presented in the form of mile-long **Ludington Park**. This wide, green expanse includes tennis courts, picnic areas, a bicycle path and fitness trail. Children will love the big playground with wooden fantasy structures. A bridge leads out to Aronson Island, an artificial island bordered by sandy beach.

The park was named for the Nelson Ludington Company of Marinette, Wis., the lumber company that first put Escanaba on the map. But the town was destined to earn its fame from something other than lumbering: its deep-water, protected harbor made it an ideal shipping port for the massive loads of iron ore mined near the shores of Lake Superior in the 1800s. By 1890, Escanaba declared itself the "iron ore port of the world." Though the town today has other industries, including a large Mead Paper factory, it remains a busy port, shipping millions of tons of ore annually.

Visitors can learn more about the history of Escanaba and the surrounding area at the **Delta County Historical Museum** next to Ludington Park. This small museum has displays on Escanaba's maritime, logging and railroad heritage, as well as the daily lives of settlers and workers. It's open daily June through September. Nearby is **Sand Point Lighthouse**, built in 1867. The lighthouse was decommissioned in 1939 and underwent structural changes as it was used for other purposes, but it has now been restored to its original appearance and is open to the public. Visitors can climb the tower to the lantern room, which was brought to Sand Point from nearby Poverty Island as part of the restoration. The keeper's quarters are decorated much as they might have been in the late 1800s. The lighthouse is open daily June through September.

WHERE TO STAY AND EAT:

House of Ludington, 223 Ludington Street, Escanaba, MI 49829; 906-786-6300. This Victorian hotel, listed on the Register of Historic Places, is located across the street from the water in downtown Escanaba. Built in the 1860s as a boarding house, it has been beautifully restored by new owners Edward and Suzell Eisenberger. The 26 rooms and suites are individual-

ly decorated; three of them have lake views. Continental breakfast is included in the reasonable rates. The hotel offers elegant
dining in its restaurant, open for lunch and dinner Monday
through Saturday.

The Nahma Hotel, 13747 Main Street, Nahma, MI 49864;
906-644-2486. Nahma may be a ghost town, but the hotel is
alive and kicking. Built in the early 1900s by the Bay De
Noquet Lumber Company, it retains the charm of a quiet country inn — until evening. That's when Nahma jolts to life, and
the hotel's Arrow Lounge is at the epicenter. People come from
a 50-mile radius says Ron Groleau, one of the owners. Don't
let it scare you away, unless you're intent on getting to bed by
8:00. This is a comfortable, friendly place — a real find in the
middle of nowhere. There are no phones or televisions in the
rooms. Some have private baths, some share baths. The dining
room serves lunch and dinner daily from a menu that features
seafood, lake fish, steaks and chicken.

Terrace Bay Resort, PO Box 453, Escanaba, MI 49829; 800-
283-4678 or 906-786-7554. What the Terrace Bay Resort lacks
in upscale swank it gains in location. On the lakefront between
Gladstone and Escanaba, the resort has beautiful views from the
restaurant and the lakeside rooms. Built in the 1920s, it has been
through many incarnations and renovations, so it's a bit worn
around the edges. But the rates are reasonable, and the rooms are
spacious and clean, though with vestiges of 1950s and '60s
decor. There are indoor and outdoor pools, a spa, golf course and
tennis courts. The Terrace Bay Restaurant is open for breakfast,
lunch and dinner, serving a variety of meat and seafood dishes.

*For more information contact the Delta County Tourism and
Convention Bureau, 230 Ludington Street, Escanaba, MI
49829; 800-437-7496 or 906-786-2192.*

Menominee

From Escanaba south along the lake, the drive is mostly pine-
lined with a few county parks and J.W. Wells State Park along

the way. The next lake shore town is Menominee, on the shores of Green Bay and across the Menominee River from Marinette, Wis.

The two towns developed along parallel tracks. Menominee, named for the local Indians, and Marinette became centers for fur trading and fishing in the early 1800s. But it was the vast pine forests nearby that determined the towns' future. Literally billions of board feet of lumber were processed at Menominee and Marinette sawmills during the boom years of the late 1800s. Promise of employment brought a flood of workers from Canada, Germany and Scandinavia; by the turn of the

PASTIES — THEY'RE NOT WHAT YOU THINK

How do you feed a hungry miner? The wives of Cornish miners knew. They baked a savory mixture of meat and vegetables inside flaky pastry crusts and rushed them down to the mine shafts to sustain the hard-working miners until supper. When the Cornish workers came to the United States to labor in the copper mines of the North, they brought their tradition of "pasties" with them. Not only did they enjoy them, so did the miners of a dozen or so other nationalities, who discovered that nothing filled stomachs in quite such a satisfying and long-lasting way as these hearty Cornish creations.

This culinary tradition is alive and well on the Upper Peninsula, where sign after sign beckons, promising hot, fresh, homemade pasties.

The traditional pasty filling is a mixture of beef, potatoes, onions, rutabagas and carrots. Today you'll also find them with chicken or turkey, and occasionally vegetables only. But be forewarned: there may not be many miners in this neck of the woods these days, but the pasty is still just as filling as ever. Eat one of these for a snack and you probably won't want dinner.

century nearly half of the residents were immigrants.

Among the prominent lumber barons was Isaac Stephenson, who left a $22,000,000 estate when he died in 1918. Today his name graces public buildings and even an island in the Menominee River. His family's mansions as well as those of other lumber millionaires can still be seen in both towns.

As the timber dwindled, Menominee and Marinette turned to paper making and other industries. More successful at this transition than many other lake towns, the sister cities are still bustling industrial centers, though small — Menominee has a population of about 9,400, while Marinette has about 11,000.

A rarity among former lumber ports, Menominee still has much of its original business district intact. The town's **Historic Waterfront District** along Green Bay includes more than 40 buildings in various stages of restoration. This charming area offers restaurants and cafes, gift shops and galleries, a marina and boat launch, a bed and breakfast and other commercial enterprises. Also in the district, **Great Lakes Memorial Marina Park** has a playground, picnic area and a band shell where concerts are performed in the summertime. The park is the center of activity each August when the town celebrates the **Waterfront Festival** with music, food, a parade and fireworks. Just to the north is **Veterans Memorial Park**, which has a sandy, protected beach.

Visitors with families will also enjoy **John Henes Park** on the north end of town. This 45-acre park has a life guarded beach, bathhouse, playground, picnic facilities, nature trails and a small children's zoo with deer and other local animals.

To learn more about the history of Menominee, visit the **Menominee County Historical Museum** at 904 11th Avenue (906-863-9000). Formerly St. John the Baptist Church, the museum houses displays on the Menominee Indians, early fur traders, the logging industry and everyday life in Menominee. A replica of a trading post, a pioneer kitchen, schoolroom, country store and other rooms offer a glimpse of what life was like during settlement and development. The museum is open daily Memorial Day through Labor Day, Monday through Saturday the rest of the year. Call for hours.

WHERE TO STAY:

Gehrke's Gasthaus, 320 First Street, Menominee, MI 49858; 906-863-2295. Right on Green Bay in the downtown historical district, this 23-room, 1880s mansion has the best possible location in Menominee. Gehrke's Gasthaus consists of a two-bedroom apartment in a former caretaker's quarters as well as three guest rooms with private bath in the main house. Two of the rooms overlook the lake. There is an outdoor hot tub for guests and a private beach. Hosts Nancy and Don Gehrke serve a full breakfast daily.

WHERE TO EAT:

The Landing, 450 First Street; 906-863-8034. With an unobstructed view of the water, this is the place in Menominee for waterfront dining. Housed in a historic building in the downtown waterfront area, The Landing is open for lunch and dinner. Steaks and chops have a high profile on the menu, with entrees such as Jack Daniels Black Jack Steak and filet mignon marinated in cognac. Chicken fans and seafood lovers will also find plenty to choose from.

For more information contact the Menominee Area Chamber of Commerce, PO Box 427, Menominee, MI 49858; 906-863-2679.

Natural Attractions

HIAWATHA NATIONAL FOREST

By the 1920s it was clearly evident that the Upper Peninsula's forests had been ravaged to near destruction. The Hiawatha National Forest was established in 1931 as part of an effort to regenerate the forests that had been carelessly exploited. At 879,600 acres it is the second largest of the four national forests in Michigan (the largest is the Ottawa National Forest, with 927,440 acres). Divided into an eastern section and a western section, the Hiawatha National Forest is the only one to border three of the Great Lakes — Lake Michigan, Lake Superior and Lake Huron. The trees have returned in vast numbers and now support a controlled lumbering industry in the Upper Peninsula that supplies both timber and pulp for paper manufacturing.

What it also supplies, to the delight of the outdoor enthusiast, is wonderful recreation opportunities. There are campgrounds, trails and numerous streams and lakes for canoeing and fishing. The forest also maintains three historic lighthouses: the Point Iroquois Lighthouse on Lake Superior's Whitefish Bay, the Round Island Lighthouse on Lake Huron near Mackinac Island and the Point Peninsula Lighthouse at the tip of Stonington Peninsula on Lake Michigan.

There are two campgrounds directly on Lake Michigan. Just west of St. Ignace is the **Lake Michigan Campground**, with 35 campsites for tents and recreational vehicles. The campground, open from early May through October, has cold running water, vault toilets and some flush toilets. The beach here is beautiful but can be treacherous when the waves run high. Nearby Brevoort Lake has excellent fishing for perch, pike, walleye and other species. Boat and canoe rentals are available. (And there is a campground here as well.) The Lake Michigan Campground is located in the **Lake Michigan Sand Dunes**, where a system of trail loops wind through the dunes. During the summer visitors can hike the trails; during the winter they are used for cross-country skiing.

The other Lake Michigan campground is at the **Little Bay de Noc Recreation Area** about halfway down the western side of Stonington Peninsula. There are 36 single and two group sites, each situated along the water with a path to the beach. The park has a picnic area with grills, an unguarded swimming beach and a boat launch. Three short trails wind along the beach and through the woods, where hikers will find 200-year-old hemlock trees and the ruins of a resort hotel built in the

TWO-WHEELED TOURS

The League of Michigan Bicyclists offers economical and fun week-long trips along Michigan's shorelines each summer. There are several routes to choose from: the West Tour follows the Lake Michigan shore in the lower peninsula from the Grand Haven area up to Mackinaw City. The Circle Tour leads along the Upper Peninsula then across by ferry to Wisconsin's Door County and again by ferry to Ludington. The Northern Exposure is a mountain bike tour over backroads and trails in the Upper Peninsula near Lake Superior. Cyclists camp nightly, usually on school grounds. SAG wagons and most meals are provided, and gear is hauled from stop to stop so cyclists need only carry what they might want during the day. Children are welcome, though for the Northern Exposure ride they must be at least 12 years old. For more information write to the League of Michigan Bicyclists, PO Box 16201, Lansing, MI 48901 or check out their website at *www.lmb.org.*

1800s. All facilities except the campground are open for day use.

Those looking for a longer hike may enjoy 35 miles of the **North Country Trail** that run through the eastern part of the national forest near St. Ignace. The North Country Trail is designated as a National Scenic Trail that, when completed, will stretch 3,200 miles from New York to North Dakota. The portion of the trail in Hiawatha National Forest passes through woodlands and sand dunes, with primitive camping sites and the Brevoort Lake campground along the way. The trail is for hikers only; no horses or vehicles are permitted.

In the western portion of the national forest is the 40-mile **Bay de Noc-Grand Island Trail** that runs from Little Bay de Noc north to Lake Superior following an old Indian route. The trail is open to hikers, horseback riders and cross-country skiers.

For more information contact Hiawatha National Forest, 2727 North Lincoln Road, Escanaba, MI 49829; 906-786-4062.

STRAITS STATE PARK

Perhaps the most striking thing about Straits State Park is its magnificent view of the Mighty Mac Bridge and the straits from the which the park takes its name. Located at St. Ignace, the park is divided into two sections by north-south Interstate 75. On the west side of the park is the **Father Marquette National Memorial and Museum**, while the east side is primarily for camping.

The Marquette historical site commemorates French missionary-explorer Jacques Marquette, who founded a mission at St. Ignace in 1671. (For more information on Marquette, see the "St. Ignace" section in this chapter.) The site consists of two structures: the memorial, a graceful open building in honor of Marquette; and the museum, in which visitors can learn about the life of Marquette and his profound influence on the history of what is now the American Midwest. The museum features displays and a 16-minute film. It is open daily Memorial Day through Labor Day, with limited hours extending into September. Near the memorial and museum is a shaded, quiet picnic ground and an overlook with spectacular views of the straits and bridge from high on a bluff over the water.

The park has two areas of campsites, both east of I-75. The smaller area consists of two wooded loops right on the water. One of these has two mini-cabins that sleep four each. These have electricity, bunk beds with mattresses, fire rings and picnic tables. The other campsites are located inland. All sites have electrical hook-ups, and the rest rooms have flush toilets and modern shower facilities. The campground is not open during the winter, though cross-country skiers can use the campground roads. The park has no swimming beaches or boat launch, but a launch is available nearby in St. Ignace.

For more information contact Straits State Park, 720 Church Street, St. Ignace, MI 49781; 906-643-8620.

Old furnaces of the Jackson Iron Company at Fayette State Park.

FAYETTE STATE PARK

Long before Fayette was the name of a state park, it was a company town, built by the Jackson Iron Company for the purpose of converting Upper Peninsula ore to pig iron before shipping it south to foundries. When the company closed up shop in 1891, the people left, but the buildings remained. In 1959 Fayette became a part of the state park system, which went about preserving the homes, blast furnaces, lime kilns, company store and opera house that were still standing. The historic site, nestled into beautiful, clear Snail Shell Harbor, takes about three hours and a lot of walking to see. A visitors center provides orientation to the site, which can be explored using a 26-station self-guided walking tour. The visitors center and townsite are open daily mid-May through mid-October, though hours vary.

The park also has a 61-site, shady campground with electrical hookups but no flush toilets. Pit toilets and water are available. The campground is connected to the townsite by a half-mile trail.

There is dock space in Snail Shell Harbor for boaters to tie up overnight, though it is very limited. Boaters who trail their boats to the park can launch them from a ramp near the campground on Big Bay de Noc, which has excellent perch, bass, pike and walleye fishing.

Day use areas include a swimming beach and picnic ground with grills, toilets and children's play equipment near the campground. There are five miles of hiking trails that loop through hardwood forest and the townsite, including the 1.5-mile **Overlook Trail**, which provides a panoramic view of the town and the harbor. During the winter the trails are groomed for cross-country skiing.

Scuba diving is permitted in Snail Shell Harbor, though a fee and permit are required. Divers are not allowed to remove any artifacts from the harbor bottom.

For more information contact Fayette State Park, 13700 13.25 Lane, Garden, MI 49835; 906-644-2603.

J.W. WELLS STATE PARK

Named for Menominee lumberman and mayor John Walters Wells, this 678-acre park lies along Green Bay about 30 miles south of Escanaba and 25 miles north of Menominee. It features three miles of shoreline, a modern campground and six rustic cabins facing the water.

The cabins are located in a wooded area at the north end of the park. Each has bunk beds, a wood stove, table and chairs and an outdoor grill. During the winter firewood is provided. Two of the cabins can accommodate 12 people each; the remaining four can accommodate eight people each. There are pit toilets and water near every cabin, though campers must go to the campground for shower facilities. These cabins are popular among cross-country skiers in winter.

The campground is located along the water about midway in the park; some sites are directly on Green Bay. There are 178 sites, most shaded, each with electrical hookup, picnic table and fire pit. Modern rest room facilities include flush toilets and showers. Although the campground is open year round, the rest rooms are open only mid-April through mid-October.

South of the campground is the day use area, with a narrow sandy beach, large shaded picnic area, picnic shelters, playground, rest rooms, volleyball courts and horseshoe courts.

Seven miles of trails wind through the park. The longest is the 2.5-mile **Evergreen Loop** that encompasses parts of other trails at the north end of the park near the cabins. During the winter the park grooms trails for cross-country skiing and stocks trailside warming huts with firewood; however, there is no ski concession in the park. Snowmobiles are permitted in the park only in areas other than the ski trails.

Hunting and fishing are popular activities at Wells. The waters of Green Bay are known for their bass, pike, panfish, trout, salmon and walleye. In the spring anglers try for brown trout near the shore here, said to be one of the best places in Michigan for trout. There is no boat ramp in the park, though nearby Cedar River has several. Hunting is primarily for white-tail deer, which are numerous in the area.

For more information contact J.W. Wells State Park, N7670 Highway M-35, Cedar River, MI 49813-9616; 906-863-9747.

Marinette ●

● Peshtigo

DOOR PENINSULA

Algoma ●

● **Green Bay**

Kewaunee ●

WISCONSIN

Point Beach State Park ▲

Two Rivers ●

Manitowoc ●

LAKE MICHIGAN

Sheboygan ●
Kohler-Andrae State Park ▲

N
W ⊹ E
S

Harrington Beach State Park ▲

Port Washington ●

10 miles

Chapter

F I V E

WISCONSIN

Brats, Beer and Hard-working Industry
Traveling from Michigan's Upper Peninsula into Wisconsin is
more than just crossing a state line. Gone are the long stretches
of empty shoreline, the ghost towns and the vast tracts of forest. Instead there are industrial towns dotting the lakeshore all
the way down to Milwaukee, a string of bustling commerce
largely uninterrupted except for the resorts of Door County,
here given a separate chapter.

Like much of the area surrounding Lake Michigan, the west
shore was settled primarily by those who came to work in the
lumber industry. The predominantly Germanic settlers soon
branched out into other industries: commercial fishing, shipbuilding, furniture-making and agriculture, though these waxed
and waned over time. The fires of 1871 swept through this part
of Wisconsin with a vengeance, destroying much of the lumber; the rest was simply depleted. Commercial fishing, too,
declined as over fishing took its toll, though a few commercial
fisheries still exist. Shipbuilding went north to Sturgeon Bay.
Furniture-making is still alive, but on a very small scale, while
agriculture remains strong. The railroad and carferry lines that
once made these towns important transshipment points are
gone.

What hasn't changed is that these are still very enterprising towns and cities – they're just engaged in different industries than they once were. Like the towns of the central Michigan shore – Ludington, Muskegon and Manistee – these Wisconsin towns went the route of commerce rather than tourism.

But they each have something special for the visitor. Sheboygan, known to many as the "Bratwurst Capital of the World," is perhaps the most attractive, with its boardwalk-lined waterfront, many parks and acre after acre of green public spaces. Manitowoc has the largest marine museum on the lake, and is the Wisconsin port for the S.S. Badger ferry, the last of its kind on the Great Lakes. Port Washington has its breweries, art deco lighthouse and lovely downtown. Algoma and Kewaunee offer great charter fishing and a host of historic buildings. And Two Rivers may have more museums than any other town its size on the lake, including a well-preserved 1800s fishing village.

Lest all this talk of industry give the impression that Wisconsin is all work and no play, rest assured – there are plenty of opportunities for outdoor fun here. Almost every town has a municipal beach, and there are numerous parks and trails. Point Beach State Forest alone has six miles of Lake Michigan beach. Whether your interest is in nature or history, whether it's rainy or sunny, winter or summer, you'll find the Wisconsin shore has something to offer.

Marinette

Just across the Menominee River from Menominee, Mich., and along the shores of Green Bay is the industrial town of Marinette, Wis. With a population of about 11,000, it is large enough to have sprouted a plethora of unattractive commercial businesses — fast food places, strip malls, car dealerships — lined up along the main streets, but small enough so that the remaining historical gems aren't too hard to find.

The town was named for the granddaughter of a Chippewa chief who lived in the area until her death in the 1860s.

Logging museum at Marinette.

Married successively to two white traders, she managed a trading post and became a well-respected citizen. Her reputation as a kind woman who was always willing to help someone in need has followed her throughout the years.

Though in its early years Marinette was a trading center for Indians and French Canadians, like its sister city, Menominee, Marinette later developed into a lumber town. After the Civil War, vast forests of white pine that lined the Menominee River and its tributaries began to supply the lumber companies of Chicago and Milwaukee. Among the lumber barons who prospered during this era, Isaac Stephenson may be the most memorialized today. Along with his brothers, Isaac developed the river for the log runs that would run until the wood dried up in 1917. Isaac accumulated enormous wealth — $22 million by his death in 1918 — which is still evident in the Stephenson Public Library, which was built with funds he donated, as well as in the family mansions on Riverside Avenue along the Menominee River.

Just opposite these mansions lies Stephenson Island, site of the **Marinette County Historical Museum** (715-732-0831), open

STAYING SAFE IN THE WATER

At times equal in ferocity to any ocean, Lake Michigan should be approached with the same caution. The primary dangers come from currents, cold water and heavy surf. Like the ocean, Lake Michigan has currents that can be strong at times. If you are caught in a current, do not attempt to swim against it as this may tire you to exhaustion without getting you anywhere. Instead, swim diagonally across the current, which will allow you to make progress. Rip currents are strong currents that move out from the shore. These tend to be very narrow; if you can swim a short way out of them, not against them, you will likely find yourself free and able to make your way to shore. The most important thing to remember is to stay calm and think clearly about your situation. Panic kills faster than currents.

Many people underestimate the danger of cold water. Parts of Lake Michigan warm to only 50 or 60 degrees Fahrenheit in the summer. Body heat is sucked away 25 times faster in water than in air. A person submerged in 60-degree water without an insulating wet suit can expect to survive for only about two hours before dying of hypothermia, a fatal lowering of the body's core temperature. For this reason, do not attempt a long swim away from shore, even in calm water and even if you are an excellent swimmer. If you will be sailing, canoeing or kayaking in open water, especially in cool weather, consider wearing some kind of thermal protection.

Lake Michigan can go from glassy to churning in short order, so be sure to wear a lifejacket if you are out on the lake in any kind of a small craft. If you should happen to capsize, your chances of survival, even in the cold water, will be greatly improved. Likewise exercise caution even from shore. If waves are crashing over a breakwall, don't go out on it. Countless rescues have had to be carried out to save people who were washed from piers and breakwalls into the water. And in periods of heavy surf, walk along the beach and enjoy the drama, but stay out of the water. It may look like fun, but it can quickly turn deadly.

daily Memorial Day through September. You can't miss the bigger-than-life-size statue of horses pulling a load of lumber in front of the museum. Quite naturally, the lumber heritage figures prominently in the museum displays, which include a miniature logging camp complete with bunkhouse, blacksmith shop and workers. The museum also has artifacts from the local Indian cultures and, from later years, furniture and memorabilia belonging to Isaac Stephenson. On the grounds outside the museum is the Evancheck cabin, a 100-year-old log cabin from the county's farmsteading days. Be sure to ask for a guided tour of the museum and cabin. The grassy park-like setting around the museum is a nice place for a picnic. There is also a children's playground and a boat launch.

The other nearby museum of note is the **Peshtigo Historical Museum and Fire Cemetery** (715-582-4322), a few miles southwest of Marinette. The museum is largely devoted to telling the story of the fire that destroyed the town of Peshtigo in 1871 on the same night as Chicago's Great Fire. It was an extremely dry year, and Peshtigo, surrounded by forests, was a conflagration waiting to happen. Small fires had been smoldering in the brush outside of town for days, but on the evening of October 8 they exploded into an inferno that swept through the streets, destroying Peshtigo and killing more than 800 people in just one hour. The scene depicted in the museum's exhibits is one of sheer terror: men, women, children and livestock trapped in chaos, unable to escape the heat and flames. Behind the museum, which is housed in a former church, is the Fire Cemetery, where many of the fire's victims are buried. A mass grave marks the burial site for 350 people whose bodies were burned beyond recognition.

Marinette County is large — bigger than Rhode Island — though only a very small portion borders Green Bay. And, truth told, this is not the most attractive part of the county. If you have time, travel inland to visit the area's dozen beautiful waterfalls, most of which are in county parks. Or ride your bike through scenic forests and alongside streams and rivers. For a map showing the waterfalls, or a map of suggested bike routes, contact Marinette County Tourism, 1926 Hall Avenue,

Marinette, WI 54143.

WHERE TO STAY:

Lauerman Guest House Inn, 1975 Riverside Avenue, Marinette, WI 54143; 715-732-7800. An imposing and stately mansion, the Lauerman Guest House was built as the home of Marinette businessman Joseph A. J. Lauerman. It is in good company among the lumber baron mansions overlooking the Menominee River and Stephenson Island. The colonial revival style home has been restored to its original elegant appearance, with modern amenities such as whirlpool tubs added. There are five guest rooms, all with private baths, period furniture and 10-foot ceilings. Breakfast, morning newspaper, and transportation from the local airport (Twin County) are provided.

M & M Victorian Inn, 1393 Main Street, Marinette, WI 54143; 715-732-9531. Built in 1890 by lumber baron Augustus Brown, this elegantly restored Queen Anne style mansion is in a residential area close to downtown. It has five guest rooms, each with private bath, air conditioning, telephone and cable TV. All are uniquely decorated with antiques, many of which are for sale by the owners. Beds are fitted with fine linens, including hypo-allergenic down pillows and comforters. Two of the rooms have two-person whirlpool tubs. Full gourmet breakfast is served each morning. Wine, champagne, liquor and specialty beers are available for purchase. The inn is also the location of Pour Vous Too, a boutique of women's clothing, lingerie and skin products.

For more information contact the Marinette Area Chamber of Commerce, PO Box 512, Marinette, WI 54143; 800-236-6681.

Algoma

This small town of about 3,500 went through several name changes before arriving at its present one. It was first known as Wolf Creek, then Ahnapee, and finally Algoma, which meant "park of flowers" in the local Native American language. Like its neighbors, Algoma developed as a lumber town in the

1850s. The lumber business led naturally to boat building, and in its heyday, Algoma launched many sizable lake vessels. Commercial fishing was another economic pursuit; salted whitefish and trout caught and processed by Algoma fisheries found their way to markets in Chicago, Milwaukee and other Midwest cities.

The fires of 1871 dealt a severe blow to Algoma, decimating the supply of raw lumber and forcing the town to turn to other means of support. It became an important marketplace for distribution of produce from the surrounding countryside, an enterprise that was furthered when a railroad line was built from Algoma to Sturgeon Bay, providing access to Green Bay and other points.

Today this lovely little town, nestled into Crescent Beach Bay at the mouth of the Ahnapee River, draws tourists and fishermen who come to try their luck in the "Salmon and Trout Capital of the Midwest." A brand-new Visitors Center and lake front boardwalk are testimony that more and more summer visitors are finding Algoma. Many use it as an economical base from which to explore the resort towns of the Door Peninsula to the north. But there are several reasons to explore Algoma itself.

Among these is the **von Stiehl Winery** on Navarino Street (800-955-5208 or 920-487-5208), the oldest continually operating winery in Wisconsin. Built as a brewery in 1868, it was first owned by Dr. Charles Stiehl, whose hobby was wine-making. He wrapped his special bottles of cherry and apple wine in a distinctive gauze and plaster covering, similar to a cast, in order to protect them from light and temperature variation. Today, a limited number of wines are still wrapped in these unique white casts.

The winery produces wines from apples, cherries, plums, raspberries and other fruit grown nearby. (The growing season on this side of the lake is too short for grapes, though grapes grown elsewhere are used to make some wines.) Visitors can taste the two dozen or so offerings, tour the historic building and browse in the extensive gift shop. The guided tours are offered seven days a week May through October.

Another historic building, also on Navarino Street, is **Netto Palazzo**, a triangular-shaped structure that was built originally as a hotel in 1890. It was never completed, however, and it became in turn a furniture factory and then a net factory. In the 1980s it was abandoned and seemed fated for razing. Through local efforts, though, it was saved, and today it houses a number of retail shops and the rather unlikely **Motorcycles of Italy Museum** (920-487-3356).

Just north of town on Highway "S" is **Renard's Cheese**

THE KOHLER STORY

In 1898, Austrian-born Sheboygan businessman John M. Kohler decided to build a new plant for his iron enamel ware production in a location four miles west of the city. Though he died shortly thereafter, his son Walter took over the project. His idea was to create a planned community with the Kohler Company at its nucleus. Homes resembling English cottages were built, with the surrounding land retaining much of its natural beauty. Over the next decades **Kohler Village** developed as one of the country's first planned communities. It is still growing, and still planned, now under guidelines established by the Frank Lloyd Wright Foundation.

The Kohler Company, too, has grown and is today one of the foremost manufacturers of bathroom and kitchen fixtures, known for its innovative and artistic designs. Visitors can see the cutting edge of such products at the **Kohler Design Center** in the village. Looking at showers and toilets may not sound exciting, but this is one impressive showroom. On the Water Deck, for example, you can see water cascading into 14 bubbling whirlpool baths.

Factory and Outlet Store (920-487-2825), where morning visitors (before 9:00 a.m.) can see the cheese-making process in action. The store next door has plenty of cheese and other edible goodies for sale.

Another unique culinary specialty found in Algoma is Lake Michigan fresh and smoked fish, supplied by local commercial fisheries. Check out **Bearcat's Fish House** and **LaFond's Fish House**, both located downtown.

The **Ahnapee State Trail**, running from Algoma north to Sturgeon Bay and west to Casco, attracts hikers, cyclists, horseback riders, cross-country skiers and snowmobilers. The

Downstairs is a museum with some of Kohler's earliest designs, which will make you wonder how you could ever do without your modern washing machine and dishwasher.

Those who want to see the works in action can take a tour of the factory, though participants must be at least 14 years old. The three-hour guided tour takes visitors through the foundry and other areas. Reservations are required.

If your idea of fun is being pampered, not watching molten iron, Kohler Village has something for you as well. The tony **American Club**, established in 1918, is the Midwest's only Five Diamond resort hotel. There are 236 luxurious rooms and suites, each equipped with a Kohler whirlpool bath. Nearby in the village are restaurants ranging from elegant to casual, a variety of shops and boutiques, and two 18-hole PGA championship golf courses.

For general information on Kohler Village call the Visitor Information Center at 800-923-1138 or check out the web site at *www.kohlerco.com*. To find out about the American Club, contact the hotel directly at 800-344-2838 or 920-457-8000.

30-mile trail has a packed crushed gravel surface eight to 10 feet wide. The flat trail follows an old railroad bed along the Ahnapee River and through farmland and the small towns of Forestville and Maplewood. Parking is available at both Algoma and Sturgeon Bay. There is no fee to use the trail, but donations are accepted. These are used by the Friends of the Ahnapee Trail to support trail maintenance.

WHERE TO STAY:

Algoma Beach Motel and Harborwalk Condominiums, Highway 42, 1500 Lake Street, Algoma, WI 54201; 888-ALGOMA-1 or 920-487-2828. These two facilities are separate, but both on the lake, the condos closer to the center of town. The motel has 32 units, some with kitchenettes. The fully equipped luxury condos feature three bedrooms and three baths, with fireplaces and whirlpool tubs in each unit. Charter fishing and golf packages are available.

Amberwood Inn, N7136 Highway 42, Lakeshore Drive, Algoma, WI 54201; 920-487-3471. Perched at the lake's edge on three acres of grounds just south of Algoma, the Amberwood Inn is a 1920s Cape Cod home furnished with antiques. There are five elegant guest rooms, each with private bath, fireplace, private deck with lake view, cable TV and refrigerator. Some have whirlpool tubs and microwave ovens. The inn has 300 feet of private beach. Hosts Mark and Karen Rittle serve a full breakfast, either in the inn's dining room or in guest rooms, if preferred. This beautiful inn is also reasonably priced.

For more information contact the Algoma Area Chamber of Commerce, 1226 Lake Street, Algoma, WI 54201-1300; 800-498-4888 or 920-487-2041.
Internet: http://www.algoma.org

Kewaunee

About 10 miles south of Algoma is the even smaller town of Kewaunee, population 2,800. It is the proverbial "two-blinker" – two blinks while passing through and you've missed it. Yet it was once an important Lake Michigan town.

Long before it was permanently settled by Europeans,
Kewaunee was inhabited by Potawatomi Indians. The first
Europeans to arrive in the area are thought to be Jacques
Marquette and his party in 1674. As French traders came
through, Kewaunee was established as a trading post.
Permanent white settlement began in the 1830s, and land spec-
ulation underwent an unexpected boom when rumors of gold in
the swamps around the town proliferated.

But lumber, not gold, proved to be the mainstay of Kewaunee,
as logs cut upstream along the Kewaunee River were floated
down to the town at its mouth, where an excellent harbor facili-
tated shipping to Chicago and Milwaukee. By the end of the
19th century, the lumber was disappearing, and the town turned
to other industries, primarily those supporting the surrounding
farms. These included canning facilities and manufacturers of
agricultural machinery and implements.

An economic upswing took place when the railroad came to
town. Shortly thereafter, the Toledo, Ann Arbor and Northern
Michigan railroad began passenger and carferry service
between Kewaunee and Frankfort, Michigan. Though this made
Kewaunee an important shipping port and distribution point for
a time, trucking later supplanted the carferries and service
ended.

The town is far less busy than it once was, but there are several
interesting historical attractions worth a stop. The **Tug
Ludington**, 115 feet of bulldog strength and determination, is
moored at the waterfront. Though it is shiny and clean today, it
has done years of hard, dirty work on two continents.
Originally christened the Major Wilbur Fr. Browder, it was
built in Oyster Bay, New York, in 1943 for service in World
War II. It participated in the D-Day invasion of Normandy,
hauling ammunition across the English Channel to France, then
served the remainder of the war in Cherbourg and Plymouth,
England. It was later used on the East Coast of the U.S. as part
of the Army Transportation Corps. In 1947 it was transferred to

The tug Ludington, which participated in the invasion of Normandy.

Kewaunee, where it was dispatched for work in the Great Lakes, and was renamed the Ludington. The tug is open to visitors May through September.

The **Kewaunee County Historical Museum** (920-388-4410) is housed in the 1876 county jail on Dodge Street. The cell blocks, some of the last of their kind in the United States, are still there. The sheriff's office and living quarters have been converted to a museum highlighting local history. Among the items on display are carvings depicting Marquette's 1674 landing in Kewaunee and a model of the U.S.S. Pueblo, built in Kewaunee in 1944 and captured as an alleged spy vessel by North Korea in 1968. The museum is open Memorial Day through Labor Day.

The **Ship's Wheel Gallery and Nautical Museum** at 224 Ellis Street (920-388-0777) opens a window on the maritime history of Kewaunee, including the area's original nautical explorers, the Native Americans. More recent history is covered in exhibits about the U.S. Army Corps of Engineers, which maintains a station in the town. Other displays depict ships built in Kewaunee but made famous elsewhere, such as the Pueblo, and Wisconsin people involved in maritime tragedies like the sinking of the Titanic. The museum and gallery are open Thursdays through Saturdays, Memorial Day through October.

Make a stop at **Svoboda Industries** on Highway 42 one mile north of town, where you can see what is claimed to be the world's largest grandfather clock. The factory originated with the work of Joseph Svoboda, a Bohemian woodworker and designer who founded the company in 1881. Though the company has made many wood products throughout the years, it is known primarily for its grandfather clocks and clock kits. The area open to the public is primarily a retail shop, but it is also possible to see some artisans at work. Call 800-678-9996 or 920-388-2691 for more information.

WHERE TO STAY:

The Gables Bed and Breakfast, 821 Dodge Street, Kewaunee, WI 54216; 920-388-0220. Located in the Marquette Historic District, a quiet residential area listed in the National Register of Historic Places, the Gables has five guest rooms. Owners Penny and Earl Dunbar are known for their hearty full breakfasts in which Wisconsin products figure prominently. The B & B is about three blocks from Lake Michigan. Bathroom facilities vary, with some rooms having private baths and others with shared baths.

For more information contact the Kewaunee Visitor Center, 308 N. Main Street, Kewaunee, WI 54216; 800-666-8214.

Two Rivers

Just like the name says, this small industrial town is built along two rivers, the West Twin River and the East Twin River, which converge just before emptying into Lake Michigan. The Indians who first inhabited the area called it Neshotah, meaning "twins." The French called it Deux Riviers, from which its English name originated. While generally engaged in the seri-

Historic Rogers Street Fishing Village at Two Rivers.

ous business of manufacturing, Two Rivers has several interesting historical attractions (with many enthusiastic local supporters) and at least one light-hearted claim to fame.

In 1881 a customer asked the owner of a soda fountain in Two Rivers to top a dish of ice cream with chocolate sauce, usually used only for ice cream sodas. The combination became popular, but for some reason was available only on Sundays. The concoction became known as the ice cream sundae, though it eventually was sold any day of the week and with a variety of toppings. This little bit of heritage is well celebrated in Two Rivers, the only town along the lake with a working ice cream parlor in one of its public museums.

Long before it was known for its ice cream sundaes, the area around Two Rivers was acclaimed for its fishing. Native Americans found whitefish to be plentiful, and later so did the Europeans who settled here. Lumbering, tanning and shipbuilding all had their day in Two Rivers, but fishing was at the forefront in the mid to late 1800s. Fisheries sprang up to take advantage of what appeared to be an endless supply of whitefish, attracting French Canadians from their fishing grounds in Quebec. Unlike more recent fishermen, the French Canadians fished from open boats called "mackinaws," which left them exposed to wind, cold and churning Lake Michigan waters. For a time, the fisheries flourished, but as in the lumber industry, shortsightedness resulted in depletion and commercial fishing went into decline, being replaced gradually by manufacturing.

Remnants of the fishing era can be seen today at the **Historic Rogers Street Fishing Village** (920-793-5905), located on the east side of the East Twin River in the downtown area, the original location of a French Canadian fishery established in 1837. This small open-air museum complex includes four historic buildings, the fishing tug "Buddy O" and a tiny, picturesque 1886 lighthouse perched over the river. The adjacent **Great Lakes Coast Guard Museum** commemorates the United States Lifesaving Service Station that was established in Two Rivers in 1877. Displays feature photographs from this predecessor to the Coast Guard and artifacts recovered from local shipwrecks. Both museums are open daily during the summer and fall, with limited hours the rest of the year.

At the **Historic Washington House,** 17th and Jefferson Streets

(920-793-2490), visitors can learn more about local history. Built in 1850 as a rooming house for immigrant workers, the museum contains displays about local breweries, musical endeavors and a variety of other facets in the history of the town. On the second floor are former sleeping rooms turned into period dentist's and doctor's offices, a barber shop and a 1890s hotel room. The second floor also features the old ballroom with murals that have been beautifully restored. But the favorite room for children of all ages is the replica of Ed Berner's ice cream parlor where the ice cream sundae was born. Visitors can enjoy 18 different sundaes here, including the specialty of the house — the red, white and blue Washington House Sundae. In Berner's day, a sundae may have set you back a nickel, but today's Washington House has an even better bargain — the coffee is free. The museum is open every day, year round.

Just down Jefferson is the **Two Rivers History Museum** (920-793-1103), housed in the former St. Luke's Convent. This eclectic assortment of displays includes many of the convent's religious items side by side with artifacts from the town's social and cultural history. Some of the more unusual items are memorabilia from local sports teams (including the Green Bay Packers) and from the Boy and Girl Scouts.

There is yet another museum in town, one that at least a few visitors may find to be the most interesting of all. Across the street from the Washington House is the **Hamilton Wood Type and Printing Museum** (800-228-6416 or 920-793-2490). The Hamilton Manufacturing Company was established in 1881 by James Hamilton, an inventor and woodworker who became well known for his wood type. This fascinating museum, housed in part of the present-day factory, contains machinery — much of it still working — and case after case of wooden type: letters, borders, designs and foreign language characters. Volunteers guide visitors through the process of making the type, as they work the lathes used to cut the letters. The Hamilton Company no longer makes type, but manufactures furniture and equipment for scientific labs. Call the museum for hours.

Two Rivers has a mile-long beach at 50-acre **Neshotah Park**, along Lake Michigan on the north side of town. The park has many facilities including a playground, picnic area with shelters, rest rooms and basketball, beach volleyball, horseshoe and tennis courts.

Farther north of town, about seven miles, is the **Point Beach Energy Center** at the Point Beach Nuclear Power Plant. The visitors center features educational displays focusing on nuclear energy. The center's Lake Walk, which is partially wheelchair accessible, is a quarter mile walk down to the lake where water from the plant is discharged. Call 920-755-6400 for hours and more information.

Just south of town is the **Woodland Dunes Nature Center** (920-793-4007), a small pocket of marshland, swamps, fields, woods and meadows with several short nature trails, two of which are wheelchair accessible. The center is located in what is known as a "tension zone," the division between two areas of differing natural growth. What makes it unusual is that both northern and southern species of plants and birds can be found here. Naturalist and educational programs are offered.

WHERE TO STAY:

Lighthouse Inn, 1515 Memorial Drive, Two Rivers, WI 54241; 800-228-6461 or 920-793-4524. Presently the only accommodation right on the waterfront, the Lighthouse Inn has great views. The 67 rooms are reasonable, modern and comfortable, but the real attraction is the lake, so spend the extra few dollars for a lakeside room. The inn's restaurant, the Water's Edge, has the only lakefront dining in town. The inn sits right at the edge of a breakwall; there is no beach, but there is an indoor swimming pool, a Jacuzzi and a sauna.

Red Forest Bed & Breakfast, 1421 25th Street, Two Rivers, WI 54241; 920-793-1794. This three-story, 1907 home is located in a residential neighborhood on the east side of the East Twin River. Built in 1907, it is now owned by Kay and Alan

Rodewald, whose name translated from German means "Red Forest." There are four guest rooms, all on the second floor, each decorated with antiques. Two of the rooms have private baths; the others share a full bath on the second floor and a half-bath on the first floor. Full breakfast is served. Older children are welcome.

WHERE TO EAT:

Kurtz's, 1410 Washington Street; 920-793-1222. This popular lunch and dinner spot has been in business since 1904. Beer is the beverage of choice in the pub-like restaurant whose walls are lined with posters from the Munich Oktoberfest. Kurtz's serves casual food in a casual atmosphere suitable for families. Sandwiches are meant to fill — meatball subs dripping with sauce and cheese, reubens piled high with corned beef and sauerkraut, or fat bratwursts jammed into a special bun. For those with lighter tastes, there are plenty of salads to choose from. Then treat yourself to a root beer float made with Baumeister draft root beer made in nearby Kewaunee.

Water's Edge, at the Lighthouse Inn, 1515 Memorial Drive; 800-228-6416 or 920-793-4524. The best view in town is at the Water's Edge. Open for breakfast, lunch and dinner, the restaurant offers sandwiches, burgers and salads for lunch and a large variety of seafood and meat entrees for dinner — not gourmet fare, but good food served in a pleasant atmosphere.

For more information contact the Two Rivers Visitor Information Center, 1622 Jefferson Street, Two Rivers, WI 54241; 888-857-3629 or 920-793-2490.

Manitowoc

Built along the Manitowoc River where it flows into Lake Michigan, Manitowoc has been inhabited since long before the arrival of Europeans. The Indians called the place "Munedoo-owk" — "land of the great Spirit." Now largely industrial, with a population of just under 35,000, Manitowoc may be best known among travelers as the Wisconsin port for the carferry S. S. Badger, which now carries passengers and cars instead of railroad cars and freight. Built in 1953, the Badger is the last of the great carferries operating on the Great Lakes. It makes daily runs from Ludington, Mich., to Manitowoc from mid-May until mid-October, saving about nine hours of driving for those who want to get to the other side of the lake. (For more information on the Badger see Chapter 2 or call 800-841-4243.)

But Manitowoc deserves much more than a drive through on the way to somewhere else. This hard-working city has much to offer, with a modern legacy that began with its founding in the 1830s. Like other lake towns, Manitowoc got in on the lumber boom and grew with various industries that accompanied it — tanning, sawmilling, shipping and the production of wood shingles and other products. Commercial fishing also was important for a time. But in one area Manitowoc excelled — shipbuilding.

From 1847, when the first ship built at Manitowoc was launched, the city produced hundreds of schooners, steamers and tugs, earning it the nickname of "The Clipper City." In 1902 the Manitowoc Company was founded, going on to become one of the Great Lakes' most important ship builders. During World War I the company built 33 freighters for government use in the war effort. After the war, it produced car ferries, tankers and a self-unloading freighter. Once again plunged into conflict with the U.S. entry into World War II, the defense department contracted the company to produce landing craft, mine sweepers and submarines. Rosie the Riveter was hard at work here in those days, welding, riveting and performing the electrical work necessary to complete the contracts. The larger of these vessels had to be floated down the Mississippi River on huge dry docks that could manage the shallow water which the ships themselves could not. In the post-war years the company built huge ocean-going container ships.

In the late '60s and early '70s, the Manitowoc Company's shipyards were moved north to Sturgeon Bay. Presently the only boat-building activity in Manitowoc is at the Berger Boat Company, where luxury aluminum yachts are produced. (Aluminum is also the business of one of the city's main industrial employers, Mirro Company, which makes cookware and kitchen accessories.)

Much of Manitowoc's proud maritime history is on view at the **Wisconsin Maritime Museum**, located on the Manitowoc River downtown. The largest museum of its kind in the state, it has many displays about the ships built here, including a full-size replicated cross-section of the schooner Clipper City, built in the town in 1854. A separate gallery houses an extensive collection of model ships, the most impressive of which is the 11-foot, 1,680-pound model of the Hikawa Maru, a passenger ship that once operated between Japan and the west coast of the United States.

The **U.S.S. Cobia**, a World War II submarine, is docked outside the museum. Though the Cobia was not itself built in Manitowoc, it is similar to 28 submarines constructed here. Visitors can tour the entire ship, including the torpedo room, engine room and crew quarters. Organized groups can even arrange to spend the night on the Cobia. The museum is open seven days a week, year round, though it's closed on major holidays. Hours vary by the season, so call 920-684-0218 for more information.

Manitowoc's Lake Michigan waterfront is a great place for walking. It's a long, pleasant jaunt out the breakwall past the marina to the 1918 lighthouse. (Though it can be a bit like a scene from Hitchcock's "The Birds," with thousands of screeching gulls flying around.) Maritime Drive, which stretches along the lake north of the river, is also a scenic spot.

While downtown, take some time to walk around this commercial district which is on the National Register of Historic Places. Restaurants and shops are plentiful in the restored area along 8th Street near the waterfront.

One of the gems along 8th Street is the **Rahr-West Art**

The USS Cobia at dock at the Wisconsin Marine Museum, Manitowoc.

Museum (920-683-4501). The museum consists of two sections. The Rahr mansion, built in 1891, houses a collection of 19th-century paintings and decorative arts. The newer portion, the 1975 West wing, includes changing exhibits and a permanent collection of 20th-century works by artists such as Georgia O'Keefe, Andrew Wyeth, Chagall and Picasso. There's an interesting oddity in the foyer between the two wings: a replica of a piece of Sputnik IV that landed on the street outside the museum, making a three-inch-deep indentation in the pavement. The real piece was returned to the Soviets.

John and Ruth West, who donated both funds and artwork to the museum, owned a little piece of serenity along the lake that is now also open to the public. **West of the Lake Gardens** (920-684-6110), high on a ridge overlooking the lake north of downtown, spreads over six acres of grounds surrounding the West's former home. The house, built in the 1930s, was inspired by the architecture of Frank Lloyd Wright, which earned it the nickname of "Shoebox Estate." Though people may have poked fun at the house, they loved the gardens, tended meticulously by Mrs. West. When Mr. and Mrs. West died, respectively in 1989 and 1990, their gardens were opened to

The grounds of Pinecrest Historical Village, Manitowoc.

the public, as was their wish. With a magnificent panorama of blue Lake Michigan beyond, the grounds bloom with roses, mums, begonias, lilies and a host of other varieties in a series of formal and natural gardens. The gardens are free and are open every day, seasonally.

Lincoln Park Zoo (920-683-4685), on 8th Street north of downtown, is a pleasant surprise. This small, shaded zoo primarily houses animals that are native to northern states: bobcats, timber wolves, bison, bald eagles. But the prairie dogs, which are not Wisconsin natives, steal the show. These antic creatures play, eat, burrow and pose for cameras in their concrete and dirt home near the entrance to the park. There are also walking trails, a playground and picnic areas. The zoo is open year round.

Children will also enjoy the petting area at the **Natural Ovens' Food and Farm Museum** off of I-43 just south of town. Sheep, goats, chickens and rabbits are part of the farm museum that includes an extensive collection of John Deere tractors and other farm machinery. The Natural Ovens bakery is adjacent. Visitors can tour take a tour and watch what it takes to turn out 3,000 loaves of all-natural bread per hour, along with bagels, rolls, cereals and muffins.

Though it's a few miles out of town, don't miss **Pinecrest Historical Village** (920-684-5110 or 920-684-4445). Situated on 60 acres of rolling countryside west of downtown, this open-air museum highlights village and farm life in the county from the 1850s to the early 1900s. The county historical society moved 20 historic buildings from around Manitowoc County to the site, restored them and furnished them with period items. An excellent audio program takes visitors on a self-guided tour of the village, bringing to life settlers' daily chores, struggles and small pleasures. Buildings include a one-room schoolhouse, town hall, fire house, church, law office, shops, cheese factory, saloon and beehouse. There is also a self-guided nature trail. The village sponsors an annual German Fest, Fall Harvest Festival and Christmas at Pinecrest, as well as special programs throughout the year. It is open daily from May 1 to mid-October, though hours change with the seasons. It is open for the special Christmas event on the first weekend in

Saloon at Pinecrest Historical Village, Manitowoc.

December.

Visitors can see a different slice of history at **Zunker's Antique Car Museum** (920-684-4005) on MacArthur Drive just west of downtown. Over 40 restored antique cars are on display here, including a 1917 Studebaker, a 1937 Packard, a

A WORD ABOUT B & B'S...

With a few exceptions, the bed and breakfasts listed in this book are members of statewide B & B organizations in Wisconsin or Michigan. These bed and breakfasts must live up to high standards of cleanliness and safety, and are inspected regularly to ensure compliance. This is not to say that bed and breakfasts that do not belong to these organizations are unsafe or undesirable, but simply that if you choose a member B & B you can be *sure* you are staying in an establishment that cares enough to be inspected and approved.

Not every bed and breakfast in each town covered in this book is listed here. There are simply too many to be comprehensive. The ones included – like other types of accommodations reviewed in this book – have been chosen for their proximity to Lake Michigan or one of its bays, or some other feature that makes them unique.

For complete listings of member bed and breakfasts in the lakeside towns, as well as throughout the states of Michigan and Wisconsin, contact the Wisconsin Bed and Breakfast Association, 108 S. Cleveland Street, Merrill, WI 54452; 715-539-WBBA; and the Michigan Lake to Lake Bed and Breakfast Association, 3143 Logan Valley Road, Traverse City, MI 49684; 616-933-5378. (The Wisconsin member directory is free; there is a fee for the Michigan directory.) Further information is available on the respective web sites: *www.bbonline.com/wi/wbba/* (Wisconsin) and *www.laketolake.com* (Michigan).

1947 Ford Woody Wagon and a 1965 Marlin Fastback.

Avid beachgoers will probably want to drive north to Two
Rivers' **Neshotah Park** or even a bit further to beautiful **Point
Beach State Park** (see "Natural Attractions"), though 26-acre
Red Arrow Park south of town has a beach, picnic area, play-
ground and boat ramp.

WHERE TO STAY:

The Inn at Maritime Bay, 101 Maritime Drive, Manitowoc,
WI 54220; 800-654-5353; 920-682-7000. This modern, 107-
room facility doesn't have much more personality than a big
chain motel, but it's the only show in town if you want a seat
by the water. It's not right by the water's edge, but set back
from the bay, with a pretty expanse of green lawn in front. Be
sure to specify that you want a water view — the alternative is
a somewhat dreary view of the indoor pool. Daily membership
passes to the YMCA next door are available. The inn has a full-
service restaurant and lounge.

WestPort Bed and Breakfast, 635 North 8th Street,
Manitowoc, WI 54220; 888-686-0465 or 920-686-0465.
Located downtown several blocks from the waterfront, the
WestPort is a 1879 Italianate Victorian home with three guest
rooms. Each room has a private bath, though the one for
"Grandma's Room" is unattached. (It does, however, have a gas
fireplace and private sitting room.) Full, formal breakfasts —
including homebaked pastries — are served by candlelight in
the dining room, or guests can request a continental breakfast
delivered to their room.

WHERE TO EAT:

The Breakwater, at the Inn on Maritime Bay, 101 Maritime
Drive; 920-682-7000. Offering the only waterfront dining in
town, The Breakwater has a pleasant view of the bay and lighthouse. The menu features somewhat standard fare such as
steak, chicken and seafood, though the walleye with white wine
sauce is exceptional.

Beerntsen's Confectionary, 108 North 8th Street; 920-684-9616. The smell that greets you is chocolate — rich, velvety, hand-dipped chocolate in dozens of different variations and shapes. There's also homemade ice cream, sandwiches and several hot dishes like creamy mac and cheese. This Manitowoc tradition still has its walnut booths and old fashioned soda fountain. You won't believe how little it will set you back to have lunch here. And don't skip the chocolate.

The Wallstreat Grill, 9th and Buffalo; 920-683-1125. What was once a bar and rooming house is now a very comfortable bar and restaurant with lively, creative food. Even if you can't stay for a meal — though you should — stop by and enjoy a drink in the bar, which has comfy couches and a large coffee table facing the street. The dining room is intimate, with small tables and candles, and the menu has literally dozens of sandwiches, entrees and salads. The dinner choices favor Italian-inspired food like pasta, but there's plenty of meat and seafood, such as grilled tuna with toasted sesame sauce or blackened swordfish. The prices are quite reasonable, and there's a children's menu available.

For more information contact the Manitowoc Visitor & Convention Bureau and Visitor Information Center, PO Box 966, Manitowoc, WI 54221-0966; 800-627-4896 or 920-683-4388. Internet: http://www.manitowoc.org

Sheboygan

With a population just under 50,000, Sheboygan is the largest city covered in this book. And what a city it is. Sheboygan has just about everything – museums, parks, a top-notch arts center, plentiful recreation opportunities, a wide sandy beach, and one of the most beautiful, people-friendly waterfronts anywhere on Lake Michigan. To top it off, people here are friendly, welcoming and rightfully proud of their city and its heritage.

Originally a Native American fishing center and later a fur trading post, Sheboygan was platted in the 1830s, and soon after settlers began arriving from Chicago. Later, German and

Fishing boat docked at the boardwalk in Sheboygan.

other European immigrants poured into the area to work in the many industries that sprang into up in this energetic town.

Like many other lake settlements, Sheboygan sits at the mouth of a river — in this case the Sheboygan River – in the protection of a natural harbor. The town developed into an important shipping point and shipbuilding center, but other kinds of industry quickly found a foothold as well. Tanneries and furniture manufacturers grew in number and size, and by the end of the 19th century a majority of the town's work force was employed in the furniture factories. Also at the this time, Austrian John M. Kohler founded an iron enamelware plant, an establishment that would prove to be of great importance in the town's economic and cultural future.

So Sheboygan grew from a lumbering town to a bustling manufacturing center, supplying the country with chairs, leather goods, enamelware, machinery and other products. Today the town's largest employer is the Kohler Company, whose presence is evident in the impressive arts center that bears its name.

Municipal beach at Sheboygan.

Germanic influence runs strong here in the city whose culinary trademark is bratwurst. In the late 1800s, the work force was primarily German-speaking, and German drama, music, clubs, newspapers and social services predominated. Later, influxes of other cultures helped create the diverse population that characterizes the city today. The first of these were from eastern European countries and Greece; later many Hispanics arrived. The latest are Southeast Asian Hmong, who now number about 3,000. The cement that binds this largely blue collar city seems to be a strong work ethic and family orientation.

Sheboygan's crowning jewel is its waterfront. Get out your walking shoes and take a hike through these beautiful public spaces. All along the river downtown and north along the lake is green parkland, carefully groomed and maintained, dotted with benches and picnic tables. The **Riverfront Boardwalk** along the north side of the Sheboygan River curves past working fish shanties and alongside boutiques, galleries and restaurants. This is also where fishing enthusiasts will find charter boats for Lake Michigan sportfishing excursions.

At the end of the boardwalk, across the 8th Street Bridge, pick up the **Lakefront Promenade**. This leads past **Deland Park** to the **Harbor Centre Marina**. Deland Park is the recreational

264

Remains of the Lottie Cooper at Deland Park in Sheboygan.

hub along the lakeshore, with a beautiful sandy beach, bathhouse, playgrounds, boat launch, tennis and sand volleyball courts, and picnic facilities.

Stop to see the remains of the **Lottie Cooper** on display at the park. This 131-foot white oak schooner was built in 1876 at nearby Manitowoc. Put into service as a lumber schooner, it was while carrying out this duty that the Lottie Cooper sank off Sheboygan on April 9, 1894. It carried a crew of six and a load of 230,000 board feet of lumber. Five of the crewmen were saved, but one perished.

The ship wasn't salvaged, and was largely forgotten until 1990, when the city began construction of the marina. It was then that divers found the wreckage of a wooden schooner that matched the description of the Lottie Cooper. The wreck was excavated, reassembled and put on display at the park. Though much of it is missing, gone forever to the whims of lake storms and winter ice, a large portion remains. It is possible to walk through the center of the ship to see the workmanship employed in its construction and experience the size of these vessels that were once common in Great Lakes waters.

Along the waterfront at Sheboygan.

Beyond the marina, the **North Point Recreation Trail**, an all-purpose paved walkway, continues along the lakefront, a scenic route for walkers, runners, in-line skaters and cyclists.

The 17-mile **Old Plank Road Trail** leading west through farmland and woods to the town of Greenbush can also be accessed from the waterfront at the boardwalk. The asphalt/turf, all-season trail is open for running, walking, cycling, skating, horseback riding and snowmobiling. At Greenbush it connects to the 61.4-mile trail system in the Northern Unit of the Kettle Moraine State Forest and a 33-mile segment of the Ice Age National Scenic Trail. A system of interconnecting trails leads to the historic towns of Kohler Village, Plymouth and Sheboygan Falls.

A unique outdoor attraction is **Indian Mound Park**, Panther and South 9th Street, south of downtown (920-459-3444). This 15-acre park contains 18 Indian burial mounds constructed by the Effigy Mound Indians sometime between 500 and 1000 A.D. These Indians, whose legacy is limited almost exclusively to Wisconsin, made mounds in the shape of birds, reptiles and other animals. In this location there are good examples of deer and panther shapes, as well as round and conical-shaped mounds. One of the mounds is open to show the manner of burial. A self-guided tour leads visitors along a path through the area. There is also a boardwalk nature trail leading through wetlands, where plants rare in this part of Wisconsin can be seen.

As much as there is to do outdoors in Sheboygan, rainy days offer no threat of a visit ruined. There are plenty of interesting indoor attractions. Foremost among them is the impressive **John Michael Kohler Arts Center** at 608 New York Avenue (920-458-6144). Originally housed in Kohler's 1882 Italianate mansion, the center has recently expanded to triple its space. Its focus is contemporary American art, with an emphasis on craft-related forms and the work of self-taught artists. Named for the founder of the Kohler Company, the center, like the company, has a visionary outlook that may surprise visitors expecting small-town traditionalism. Be prepared to be excited and challenged by the cutting edge work you'll find here, including pieces resulting from Kohler's unique Arts/Industry program that teams artists and factory workers. Be sure to check out the rest rooms here, where Kohler bathroom fixtures are complemented with original art. (Also be sure to visit nearby Kohler Village, where you can tour the Kohler factory and browse the display center. For more information see the sidebar elsewhere in this chapter.)

The primary historical attraction in the town is the **Sheboygan County Museum** at 3110 Erie Avenue (920-458-1103). The core portion of the museum is the David Taylor home built on this site in the 1850s. Taylor, a New York attorney, moved to Wisconsin and went on to play a prominent role in local and state politics. The mansion, which sits high on a hill overlooking the Sheboygan River valley, opens a window on the lives of the well-to-do of the era. Though the original floor plan has been lost (the building had many incarnations after the Taylors' residency, including stints as a workhouse for the county insane asylum and as a jail), it is full of period artifacts and its appearance today is typical of similar homes from the second half of the 19th century.

In addition, there are three other historical buildings and an administration center that houses exhibits on the indigenous Indians and the lives of the early European settlers. The Weinhold log cabin, circa 1864, shows how the average immigrant lived – with much less elegance than the Taylors were accustomed to. The Schuchardt barn, also of local German heritage, is filled with early farm implements that highlight the county's rich agricultural history. The Bodenstab Cheese Factory, which was moved from elsewhere to its present site, is one of more than 200 such cheese factories that once existed in the county. The real treat at the museum is seeing the Taylor House and the other historical buildings, which are opened only for those on a guided tour. These fascinating, lively tours are given at different times throughout the day, so be sure to call for the schedule. This is a great place for kids – the staff takes a special interest in making the tours entertaining as well as educational. The museum is open April through October.

Children will also enjoy the **Heritage School**, 1208 S. 8th Street (920-459-3512), a 1876 two-room schoolhouse that has been transformed into a museum dedicated to showing what education was like in the 19th century. Groups can make arrangements to experience first-hand the rules, regulations and curriculum of days gone by. There are also exhibits of artifacts and memorabilia relating to education. The museum is open limited hours, in the summer only, so be sure to call ahead.

For a general hands-on experience, take the kids down the street to the **Above and Beyond Children's Museum** at 902 N. 8th Street (920-458-4263), where interactive exhibits will interest kids of all ages. It's open all year, Tuesday through Sunday except for holidays.

Sheboygan keeps itself busy year round, beginning with the annual **Polar Bear Swim** each New Year's Day, when some 400 hardy swimmers take a plunge into Lake Michigan. If you don't want to participate, just go and watch – it will remind you just how lucky you are to be dry, if not warm. Spring brings **Flapjack Day** in March, when locals gather to celebrate the running of the sap with maple-sugaring demonstrations, entertainment and, of course, flapjacks with maple syrup. July 4th is a big celebration with the usual fireworks, parade and entertainment, but Sheboygan puts a new twist on this traditional holiday with the **Great Cardboard Boat Regatta**, in which personal-powered cardboard boats race for prizes. The **John Michael Kohler Outdoor Arts Festival** takes place on the center's grounds later in July. The first Saturday in August and the Friday preceding it are **Bratwurst Days**, no small event in the Bratwurst Capital of the World. A parade, entertainment, brat-eating contest and flea market are just part of the fun.

WHERE TO STAY:

Brownstone Inn, 1227 N. 7th Street, Sheboygan, WI 53081; 920-451-0644. This elegant 1907 home has five guest rooms, all with private baths and whirlpool tubs. Some rooms also have fireplaces and wet bars. There's a billiard room on the lower level and a spacious ballroom on the third floor that can be used for meetings or gatherings. An expanded continental breakfast is served. An unusual amenity is the inn's sailboat, Wiki Wiki, which can be taken for excursions by experienced sailors. Don't know how to sail? The resident captain will take you for a spin. The Brownstone Inn is not appropriate for children.

English Manor Bed & Breakfast, 632 Michigan Avenue, Sheboygan, WI 53081; 920-208-1952. There are five guest rooms, each with private bath, in this lovely 1908 Tudor home. The Hundley family, owners of the B & B, make guests feel welcome with an afternoon tea, evening wine and cheese, and full English breakfast. This is a relaxed, quiet atmosphere best enjoyed by adults.

Lake View Mansion Bed and Breakfast, 303 St. Claire Avenue, Sheboygan, WI 53081; 920-457-5253. A spectacular home with a spectacular view, the Lake View is perched on a hillside overlooking the lake. The four guest rooms have king size beds, private baths, cable TV and air conditioning. The Lake Michigan Room and the Lake Superior Room each have fireplaces. Gorgeous, elegant common areas include a living room complete with a baby grand piano, a library and a glassed-in dining room with panoramic view. The mansion has eleven fireplaces for cozy conversation on winter evenings. Full breakfast is served. Children will be happier elsewhere.

WHERE TO EAT:

Brisco County Woodgrill, 539 Riverfront Drive; 920-803-6915. Located on the Riverwalk, this casual eatery has outdoor dining on a deck right next to the water. The menu features steaks, chops, ribs and seafood cooked over a wood grill, the specialty being black angus beef. Other offerings include faji-tas, rotisserie chicken and several entrée salads.

The Mucky Duck Shanty, 701 Riverfront Drive; 920-457-5577. Also on the Riverwalk, the Mucky Duck has plenty of seafood items like trout, salmon, crab cakes and orange roughy. Ribs, steaks, fried chicken, a variety of salads, burgers and sandwiches – including the famous Sheboygan bratwurst – are also available. There's a deck for warm-weather waterfront dining.

Riverside City Streets, 712 Riverfront Drive; 920-457-9050. Arguably some of the tastiest food in Sheboygan can be found at Riverside City Streets. This pleasant ocean-themed restaurant is across the street from the Riverwalk, offering a less scenic view than the restaurants directly on the water. But the food is excellent, and though is may take some time once your order is placed, that's because everything is prepared carefully to order. Seasonal specialties include duck confit and pork schnitzel; regular menu items are the traditional meat and seafood dishes like strip steaks, filets, lobster tails and Canadian walleye. A bit more expensive than the town's more casual restaurants, this makes a nice place for a relaxed meal of fine food.

For more information contact the Sheboygan Area Convention and Visitors Bureau, 712 Riverfront Drive, Sheboygan, WI

53081; 800-457-9497 or 920-457-9495.
Internet: http://www.sheboygan.org

Port Washington

Port Washington, first known as Wisconsin City, is a port due
largely to the efforts of man. Not blessed with a natural harbor,
the town boasts the first manmade port in North America. With
the harbor in operation by the late 1860s, Port Washington
grew as a transshipment point for the entire western lakeshore.
Commercial fishing and light industry had a parallel development, but it was perhaps for chair making that Port Washington
was best known. One of the factories, the Wisconsin Chair
Company, founded in 1888, kept the country supplied until it
closed down more than 60 years later.

In the 1800s the town was inhabited mainly by immigrants
from Germany and Luxembourg. They lent a hard-working
backbone to the town and figured largely in its development.
They didn't, however, take kindly to the Civil War or the draft
that came with it. A large group of disgruntled Port
Washingtonians was one of several from the surrounding area
that marched in protest against the situation. A rowdy mob of
1,000 assaulted the local draft commissioner and went on to
cause havoc in the town before a force of 750 armed soldiers
were able to contain them.

Today Port Washington, about 25 miles north of Milwaukee, is
a tidy little town of about 10,000 spread over seven hills that
rise from the lakeshore. The downtown streets are lined with
fine old buildings housing shops and restaurants, though the
skyline is dominated by the smokestacks of the coal-burning
Wisconsin Electric Power plant opposite the harbor.

The best way to explore the waterfront is to take the two-mile
HarborWalk tour that is detailed in a brochure available
from the Chamber of Commerce. This leads through the harbor area, where the Port Washington Chair Factory once
stood, past the charter fishing fleet and marina to Veterans
Memorial Park and the public beach. Looking out toward the

Downtown Port Washington.

lake, you can't help but notice the distinctive 1935 art deco lighthouse that has become a familiar symbol of Port Washington. While it's possible to walk out the north break-wall to the light, the surface is very uneven and narrow at points, making it treacherous on all but the calmest days.

Take some time to browse the downtown area, with its well-kept shops and restaurants. One of the most unusual buildings you'll find there is the **Pebble House** at 126 E. Grand Avenue. Built in 1848 by a blacksmith named Edward Dodge, it is made entirely of Lake Michigan pebbles beautifully arranged by shape, size and color. The 20-inch-thick walls have proved to be remarkably sturdy, having survived intact through more than 150 years and two moves. Built on land acquired by the power company, the house was preserved and used as a gatehouse, but it had to be moved. Later, the power company offered the Pebble House to the city, and it was moved once again. It is now the Visitor Information Center and office for the chamber of commerce. It is open year-round, Monday through Friday, and on weekends during the summer.

Another landmark is **St. Mary's Catholic Church**, built on the highest point in Port Washington, where its graceful spire stands out strikingly against the sky. Built from 1881 to 1884, the Gothic Revival church is worth a visit to see its beautifully decorated interior.

Near the church, on what is known as St. Mary's Hill, is the old **Port Washington Light Station** that was in use before the 1935 tower was built in the harbor. This 1860 brick building is missing its tower and lantern room, which were removed when the newer lighthouse was built. The light station is undergoing restoration that will revert the interior to its pre-1935 appearance.

Restoration has also taken place at the 1872 home of Leopold Eghart, an Austrian immigrant who came to America hoping to lead the life of a gentleman farmer. Instead he was elected judge and lived out the rest of his days in his Victorian home. The **Judge Eghart House**, at 316 Grand Avenue (414-284-2897) has been carefully restored and decorated with period furnishings, including some of the furniture that belonged to the original builder and owner, Louis Teed. It is open on Sundays, Memorial Day through Labor Day.

Port Washington's art deco lighthouse.

True to its German legacy, Port Washington is a beer-drinking town. There are two breweries, one of which is a restaurant (see "Where to eat"). The other, **Harbor City Brewing Company** (414-284-3118), is open to visitors who would like to see the fermentation process at work. Producers of Mile Rock Amber Ale, Main Street Brown Ale and the intriguingly named Transcendental Wheat Beer, Harbor City uses all natural ingredients and no preservatives. The brewery is open for tours on weekends.

Port Washington's main event is the annual **Fish Day**, celebrated the third Sunday of every July. Billed as the "World's Largest One Day Outdoor Fish Fry," Fish Day includes a parade, entertainment, a craft fair and plenty of fish and chips. To combat all that tasty but calorie-filled fare, there's also a run and fun walk/run whose proceeds benefit charity.

WHERE TO STAY:

The Grand Inn Bed and Breakfast, 832 West Grand Avenue, Port Washington, WI 53074; 414-284-6719. There are two guest rooms in this 1903 Victorian home located about six blocks from Lake Michigan. The second-floor guest rooms have private baths and whirlpool tubs. The guest parlor outside the rooms is a cozy place to relax, next to the woodburning stove. Full breakfast is served on weekends, continental breakfast is available during the week.

The Inn at Old Twelve Hundred, 806 West Grand Avenue, Port Washington, WI 53074; 414-268-1200. This restored Queen Anne home is furnished with antiques. There are four guest rooms, each with private bath. Other amenities include fireplaces, whirlpool tubs, private sitting rooms or porches. A guest house on the grounds has two rooms, also with private baths and furnished with antiques. Continental breakfast is served in the main house; no breakfast is served in the guest house. It's a six-block walk to Lake Michigan. The owners specify that the inn is not suitable for children.

Port Washington Inn, 308 West Washington Street, Port Washington, WI 53074; 414-284-5583. Built by brewery owner George Blessing in 1903, the Port Washington Inn sits high atop Sweetcake Hill in a residential area overlooking the town. There are four guest rooms in this large Victorian house, each with private bath and TV. "Dorothy's Room" has a view of the lake, several blocks away. There are several common areas, including a parlor with baby grand piano. Homemade breads and cookies are among the amenities guests enjoy. Full breakfast is served.

WHERE TO EAT:

Smith Bros. Fish Shanty, 100 N. Franklin Street; 414-284-5592. This popular restaurant and brewery is really several things under one roof. On the ground level there's the brew pub and main dining room, which has a view of the water. Upstairs is The Landing, an open-air, screened dining room overlooking the lake. Beer made on premises is served throughout — Porter, Amber, Lager, Hefe Weis and root beer. The food here is excellent, testimony to the fact that the owners have been in the restaurant business for over 40 years. The specialties are Lake Michigan smoked fish (which is also available for carry out from the deli on the lower level), broiled or fried whitefish, walleye or perch. Open for lunch and dinner.

New Port Shores, 407 Jackson Street; 414-284-6838. A favorite of the locals, New Port Shores is a casual, inexpensive place that's great for families. Located right on the water, it's open for lunch and dinner every day except Mondays. The menu is loaded with sandwiches, salads, burgers and seafood specialties like Canadian pike and lake perch.

For more information contact the Port Washington Chamber of Commerce, 126 E. Grand Avenue, PO Box 514, Port Washington, WI 53074; 800-719-4881 or 414-285-0900.

Natural Attractions

POINT BEACH STATE FOREST

For the day visitor, the main attraction at 2,903-acre Point Beach may be the six miles of beautiful sandy beach that stretch along the lake. These unguarded beaches are used by a few hardy swimmers who don't mind braving the cold, but also by beach lovers who simply enjoy long walks along the quiet, scenic shoreline.

Lighthouse aficionados are also drawn to the park to see the

Rawley Point Lighthouse at Point Beach State Park.

Rawley Point Lighthouse, an unusual octagonal skeletal structure that is the only one of its kind on the Great Lakes. Though a light was established here in 1853, the present tower was not in place until 1894, when it was moved and reconstructed from its original location on the Chicago River. It is an active lighthouse, automated since 1980, with a light that can be seen 28 miles away. The keeper's quarters are occupied by Coast Guard personnel, so the entire property is off-limits to the public, but a very good view can be had from the beach.

Prior to the establishment of a light here, this was a treacherous

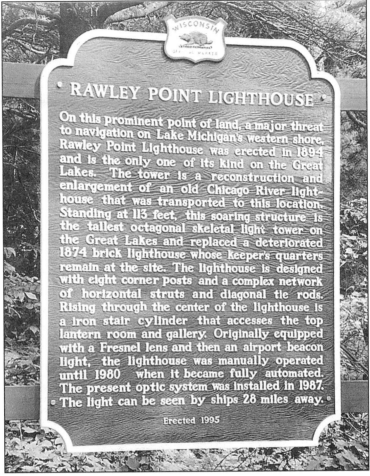

Rawley Point Lighthouse historical marker at Point Beach State Park.

part of the lake, the site of more than 20 shipwrecks including the steamship Vernon, which foundered and sank with an estimated 36 crew and passengers. A list of the ships lost is posted near the contact station.

The park has about 11 miles of hiking trails through woods and dunes, including the half-mile, self-guided **Swales Nature Trail** located at the north end of the park near the nature center.

The 3.1-mile **Red Pine Trail** is open to mountain bikes.

The nature center includes displays and hands-on exhibits about local wildlife, geology and maritime history. Programs such as lectures and naturalist-led hikes are frequently offered through the center.

With 127 sites, the park has one of the larger campgrounds along the Wisconsin shore (though considerably dwarfed by Peninsula State Park in Door County with its 469 sites). Sixty-six of the sites have electrical hookups; all have access to shower and toilet facilities. The campground is in a wooded area; most of the sites are shaded for at least part of the day. There is a concession that sells snacks, ice cream and ice. Campers can also buy firewood in the park. The park is open to winter camping and cross-country skiing. A snowmobile trail runs between the park and the town of Two Rivers just to the south.

For more information contact Point Beach State Forest, 9400 C.T.H. O, Two Rivers, WI 54241-9561; 920-794-7480.

KOHLER-ANDRAE STATE PARK

This 924-acre park, just south of Sheboygan, owes its existence largely to the generosity of two donors. Frank Theodore Andrae bought 92 acres here in 1924, later adding another 30. Mrs. Andrae, who took a special interest in botany, hired forestry experts who helped her reforest the land that had been ravaged by logging. After her husband's death in 1927, Mrs. Andrae donated the 122 acres to the state of Wisconsin, and Terry Andrae State Park was established.

Then, in 1966, 280 adjacent acres were donated by the Kohler Company, manufacturer of plumbing products, in honor of its founder, John Michael Kohler. The state rounded out the parcel by purchasing another 600 acres, bringing the total acreage to about 1,000. Although the parks are still considered separate entities, they are managed as one unit.

Foremost among the attractions is a two-mile beach along Lake Michigan. Though there are no life guards, there is a bath house and concession where beach goers can buy ice cream, soft drinks and other snacks. There's plenty of room to spread out here, so your chances of having a sandy spot to yourself are always good.

Walkers will find two nature trails and two hiking trails to enjoy. The **Creeping Juniper Nature Trail** in the north end of the park loops through gently rolling sand dunes over a wooden cordwalk (boards held together with rope). This half-mile trail offers an easy way to learn about the plants, animals and geological history of the park through interpretive signs posted along the way.

In the south section of the park is the **Woodland Dunes Nature Trail**, a one-mile trail that also has interpretive signage. The trail winds through rolling forested dunes, a quarter-mile of it with a surface of crushed limestone, making it wheelchair accessible.

The **Dunes Cordwalk** has two sections, the half-mile portion north of the Creeping Juniper Trail and the park's nature center, and the 1.5-mile south trail, which runs inland from the nature center parallel to the shoreline. Meandering through rolling dunes, the trail offers good views of the lake and interdunal wetland. The **Black River Trail** is in the most remote section of the park, to the northwest and inland. This 2.5-mile trail, which is mostly flat with a grassy surface, leads through fields and woods. This is the one trail in the park that is open to horses and mountain bikes. Dogs on leashes are permitted on the trail, as well as on the Dunes Cordwalk, but are prohibited on the two nature trails.

Naturalist-led hikes are often offered. Notices of scheduled hikes and other special programs are posted throughout the park.

Walkers and hikers are likely to see at least some of the park's 33 species of mammals that include deer, ground squirrels, fox,

WISCONSIN — WANT TO KNOW MORE?

There's a lot more to Wisconsin than the Lake Michigan shore and Green Bay – 15,000 lakes, for example, and dozens of waterfalls. There are more than 80 state parks, forests, trails and recreation areas that offer skiing, mountain biking, canoeing and even whitewater rafting. The state is rich in history and in Native American culture. And there's another Great Lake along Wisconsin's borders – 156 miles of Lake Superior shoreline, including the 22 islands that make up the Apostle Islands National Lakeshore.

The state tourism department has plenty of free information about these other Wisconsin attractions. In addition to a full-color, magazine-sized general guide to the state, there are a dozen or so specialized guides for cyclists, history buffs, adventure seekers, golfers, campers and more. To order these free guides call 800-432-8747. Visit the Wisconsin tourism web site at *www.travelwisconsin.com.*

muskrats, mink and the occasional river otter or badger. Over 150 species of birds have been spotted here, including migrating hawks and diving ducks. Species that live in the park range from tiny vireos and warblers to herons.

Plant life in the park is also quite diverse, with over 400 known species and 50 different varieties of trees. Many of these plants are unique to the area. They flourish particularly well in the 200-acre **Kohler Company Forest Preserve State Wildlife Refuge** that is adjacent to the park's north boundary.

Even if it's a rainy day, you can learn about the park's animals, birds and plants at the **Sanderling Nature Center**, in the north section of the beach area. In addition to displays on these and other subjects, the center has slide shows, lectures and movies in the facility's auditorium. There is an observation deck on top of the center, accessible via an inside stairway.

Outside the center is a portion of the keel from the Challenge, a schooner built in Manitowoc in 1852. In 1982, 130 years later, the piece washed up on shore at the park.

The campground, which is located at the south end of the park near the beach, has 105 sites, 49 of them with electrical hookup (28 of these are open in winter as well). The area is heavily wooded, ensuring plenty of shade. Showers and flush toilets are provided. The park has one authentic Native American Plains tipi available for rent. On rainy days campers can warm up and stay dry in the enclosed shelter that features a stone fireplace. During the summer months the campground is often full, so it's wise to make reservations ahead of time.

Winter activities at the park include camping, cross-country skiing, sledding, snowshoeing, tobogganing and hiking.

For more information contact Kohler-Andrae State Park, 1520 Old Park Rd., Sheboygan, WI 53081; 920-451-4080.

HARRINGTON BEACH STATE PARK

This 637-acre day use park is about 35 miles north of Milwaukee. It is comprised of a mile-long Lake Michigan beach, a 25-acre quarry lake, lowland forest and upland area with a panoramic view of Lake Michigan. Bird watchers flock here in the spring to see warblers, water birds, raptors and other birds that make the annual trek along the Mississippi Flyway, the highway in the sky that migrating birds follow year after year.

The park was once the site of a quarry where limestone was excavated for roadbeds or to be processed into lime. A company town grew around the quarry, with barracks and homes for the mainly Italian immigrant workers. The quarry machinery included huge stone crushers, a 40-foot kiln, and tracks used by carts ferrying stone to the crushers. The quarry was eventually sold, and most of the houses torn down or moved. Water filled the excavation site, creating a deep, calm lake. In the late 1960s the quarry lake and surrounding land became part of the state park, named for C. L. Harrington, a former superintendent of the Wisconsin Conservation Commission.

Today, **Quarry Lake** makes a scenic spot for a picnic or a walk along the trail that follows it shoreline. It's also a popular spot for fishermen, who try their luck at hooking bluegill, trout, bass and bullheads. In the winter, ice fishing is allowed. Swimming, wading, boating and scuba diving are not permitted on Quarry Lake.

Puckett's Pond, a smaller lake in the center of the park, also has good fishing and a pretty picnic area. It is connected by a path to Quarry Lake. There are several other picnic areas overlooking Lake Michigan.

The Lake Michigan beach is unguarded so caution should be exercised. There is parking nearby, but on weekends and holidays, the lot may be full. A shuttle bus operates from the main parking lot to the beach, which is also connected by a trail to Quarry Lake. Beach facilities include changing stalls, toilets, a concession stand and a sand volleyball court. Nearby is a welcome center with a fireplace that is available for rent, popular in the winter with cross-country skiers.

Harrington Beach has several trails in addition to the one around Quarry Lake. There is a half-mile interpretive nature trail through a white cedar forest, a historical trail that highlights the history of the quarry operation and town, and about two miles of cross-country ski trails.

For more information contact Harrington Beach State Park, 531 Highway D, Belgium, WI 53004; 414-285-3015.

N
W E
S

10 miles

WISCONSIN

Green Bay

Porte de Mortes Strait

Rock Island State Park ▲

Washington Island

Gills Rock ●
Ellison Bay ●
Ephraim ●
Newport State Park ▲
Peninsula State Park ▲
Fish Creek ●
● Cana Island
Egg Harbor ●
Baileys Harbor ●

▲ **Whitefish Dunes State Park**

Potawatomi ▲
State Park
Sturgeon Bay ●

LAKE MICHIGAN

● Algoma

●**Green Bay**

● Kewaunee

Chapter

SIX

DOOR COUNTY

Wisconsin's Vacationland

Seventy-five miles long and only 10 miles wide, Door County offers nearly every conceivable type of leisure or recreational activity you can imagine. This narrow finger of land that juts upward from the Wisconsin shore to make Green Bay is prime vacation territory. With 250 miles of shoreline, five state parks and more lighthouses than any other county in the 48 contiguous states, it's not surprising that Door County draws visitors from all over the Midwest and beyond. In addition to its natural beauty, much of the county has managed to retain its civic beauty as well; the northern resort towns in particular are completely devoid of ugly signage and unattractive commercial buildings, making them an aesthetic delight.

The county is divided here into two sections: the busy ship-building city of Sturgeon Bay, and the small, charming resort towns further north, including rural Washington Island. Those who like a faster pace will probably enjoy staying in Sturgeon Bay and making day trips to the quieter parts of the county. Those who want to immerse themselves in lakeside calm will find what they want in one of the smaller towns on Green Bay or along the mostly rural Lake Michigan shoreline.

There are over 100 places to stay in Door County – from simple hotel rooms to luxury condos, quaint cottages, bed and breakfasts or complete vacation homes. Of necessity, only a handful are listed here, though they cover a range of types so that no matter what your preference, you'll probably find something among them that suits you. Nonetheless, it's well worth contacting the local chambers of commerce for complete listings.

So take the time to smell the cherry blossoms (there are thousands), watch a sunrise over Lake Michigan or a sunset over Green Bay. Go to a fish boil – the Door County culinary feast explained later in this chapter – because you won't find a taste like this anywhere else. Hike, bike, kayak, sail, walk a beach, have a gourmet meal, take a class, see some live theater or go to a concert. Whatever you do, have a great vacation. This is the place.

Sturgeon Bay

The upper portion of Door County is, in effect, an island cut off from the rest of Wisconsin by a narrow shipping channel that runs between Green Bay and Lake Michigan. Sturgeon Bay straddles that channel, both physically and atmospherically. Serving as a gateway to the smaller, quaint lakeside towns to the north, it bulges with tourists during the summer, while still retaining the demeanor of a working town. Huge shipyards lie side-by-side with sophisticated resorts, flashy restaurants and fast food places. It's a busy town, often clogged with traffic trying to squeeze its way across the channel bridge and up north to calmer quarters.

The channel didn't always exist. The town of Sturgeon Bay grew up beside Green Bay at the narrowest spot on the peninsula. Plenty of travelers and traders had been coming through the area for years, taking advantage of the relatively easy portage to Lake Michigan, a far safer route than through the dangerous passage at the northern tip of the peninsula, an often-churning maelstrom known as "Death's Door." Jacques Marquette was among the first Europeans to pass through the place now called Sturgeon Bay, and later, Claude Allouez, who

A shipyard at Sturgeon Bay.

referred to the site as "La Portage des Esturgeons."

Settlers began arriving in the mid-1800s, but growth was slow until town leaders persuaded the federal government to finance the building of a canal between the two bodies of water. It opened for commercial use in 1882, and from that point on the town began to expand and prosper.

Sturgeon Bay became nearly synonymous with shipbuilding. The Sturgeon Bay Shipbuilding and Dry Dock Corporation, Leathem D. Smith Shipbuilding Corporation, Peterson Builders and Palmer Johnson all grew to become big names in the business. When World War II broke out it fired a new demand for ships, and Sturgeon Bay willingly obliged, supplying the military with PT boats, cargo boats and other vessels. After the war, the shipyards turned out freighters and ore boats, and the pleasure boat industry grew, with local yards producing luxury yachts for private use. The S.S. Badger, last of the great carferries that now runs between Ludington and Manitowoc, was built here along with its sister ship, the Spartan. This center of maritime activity is also responsible for the invention of today's

A marina at Sturgeon Bay.

"Safeway" shipping containers used for packing everything from shoes to furniture for transport across oceans. Though not as active in shipbuilding as it once was, Sturgeon Bay's proud activity is evident in the huge ocean- and lake-going vessels at dry dock for repair or refurbishing.

Visitors can explore the town's marine legacy at the **Door County Maritime Museum** (920-743-5958) on Business 42, just south of the bridge that goes across the channel. Chris Craft fans will enjoy seeing the 1928 classic wood boat whose basic design was popular for decades. There is also a replica of a naval design shop that was part of Peterson Boat Works as well as a real pilot house from a Great Lakes ore carrier. Other exhibits include models of ships that were built at Sturgeon Bay, a collection of antique outboard motors, and a display about the lighthouses of Door County. One of the most fascinating things to do at the museum is to watch original film footage of ship launchings that occurred in Sturgeon Bay. Most boats were launched sideways into the water, tilting them at precarious angles – for several breathtaking seconds these dramatic events look certain to end in disaster. The museum is open seven days a week, year round.

Other facets of local history are explored at the **Door County Historical Museum** (920-743-5809), 4th and Michigan Streets near the downtown historical section north of the bridge. The museum takes visitors from the days of the earliest known Native American inhabitants to a look at the modern tourist industry, with long stops at the rural lifestyle of the county's largely Scandinavian settlers. Several replicated storefronts – a seamstress shop, grocery, bank, pharmacy and others – give visitors a taste of earlier times. Other local traditions — quarrying, fishing, fruit growing and even the famous Door County fish boil – are depicted in museum displays. A new exhibit also depicts the natural life of the area showing indigenous birds and plants in seasonal settings. The museum is open daily May through October.

Down the street at 107 4th Avenue is the **Miller Art Museum** (920-746-0707), featuring 20th-century Wisconsin artists and changing exhibits on a variety of themes. The museum is open year round, every day except Sunday.

While you're in the area, take the time to stroll around the downtown historical district, much of which is undergoing restoration. There are more than a dozen shops selling gifts, paintings, candy, clothing and more. Down the street at 341 N. 3rd Avenue is the **Cherryland Brew Pub** (920-746-7611), where visitors can take a tour through a brewery that was once the local train station. The on-premises pub is open in the evenings.

Several parks near the center of town make pleasant places to walk or picnic. The best view of the west side of the Sturgeon Bay waterfront is from **Bay View Park**. This one-acre park sits on a narrow peninsula that juts into the water. From here you can sit and watch the harbor activity, bridge traffic and the shipyards at work. There is a viewing area with picnic tables, grills and benches. No parking is set aside specifically for the park, but there is adequate public parking nearby. **Sunset Park**, off North 3rd Avenue, on the north side of the bridge, has a life-guarded beach, picnic shelter, tennis courts, basketball court, exercise course, boat launch, a short all-purpose trail and playgrounds. **Otumba Park**, on the south side of the bridge, also has a guarded beach, picnic shelter, tennis courts basketball court and playground equipment.

Another great place to picnic is at **The Farm** (920-743-6666), four miles north of town on Route 57, though you won't just be picnicking – you'll pet sheep, feed baby piglets, even milk a goat if you want. In addition to live animals, The Farm has gardens, field crops, farm antiques and nature trails. It's open daily, Memorial Day through Labor Day.

More animals – horses, cows, rabbits and chickens – are headliners at the annual **Door County Fair** held in Sturgeon Bay each August. This old-fashioned country event also features plenty of home-baked treats.

WHERE TO STAY:

Bay Shore Inn, 4205 Bay Shore Drive, Sturgeon Bay, WI 54235; 920-743-4551; 800-556-4551. One of three large, modern resorts under the same management (the others are Bridgeport Waterfront Resort and Westwood Shores), Bay Shore Inn is located just under three miles north of Sturgeon Bay on Green Bay. All rooms have at least some water view, and range from one-bedroom suites with living room and balcony to two-bedroom "supreme" suites that include two baths and a wrap-around deck. All suites have whirlpool tubs and full kitchens. Other amenities include indoor and outdoor pools, tennis court, game room, playground, small sand beach, grills, and free bikes, paddleboats and row boats.

Bridgeport Waterfront Resort, 50 West Larch Street, Sturgeon Bay, WI 54235-2503. A large, new upscale resort, the Bridgeport is located on the waterfront just south of the bridge, within easy walking distance to restaurants and the maritime museum. The accommodations consist of one-, two- or three-bedroom condos, each with kitchen or wet bar, living room and dining area, fireplace, sleeper sofa, double whirlpool and cable TV/VCR. On the grounds are indoor and outdoor pools, whirlpool and sauna, playgrounds, game room, exercise facility and walkway along the water. Continental breakfast is included. It is a smoke-free resort.

Glidden Lodge Beach Resort, 4676 Glidden Drive, Sturgeon Bay, WI 54235; 888-281-1127 or 920-746-3900. Located about 10 miles north of Sturgeon Bay right on a beautiful Lake Michigan beach, the Glidden Lodge Beach Resort is truly "away from it all." It has been a resort since 1937, but modern construction has transformed it into one-, two- and three-bedroom condos, all with water views. Each unit has a gas fireplace, double whirlpool tub, kitchen and private patio. The property is entirely smoke free. Other amenities include an exercise room, pool, whirlpool and sauna. The lodge is about two miles south of Whitefish Dunes State Park.

Inn at Cedar Crossing, 336 Louisiana Street, Sturgeon Bay, WI 54235; 920-743-4200. This charming historic inn in downtown Sturgeon Bay was built in 1884. It once housed a tailor shop, apothecary, clothing store and soda fountain. Now it's a comfortable romantic getaway with nine guestrooms, a pub and fine dining. Guest rooms are furnished with antiques, and some have gas fireplaces or whirlpool tubs. All have private baths, phones and television. Breakfast is hearty continental fare – homemade muffins and scones, fresh fruit, cheese, coffee and juice. The inn is three blocks from the waterfront on the north side of the bridge.

Leathem Smith Lodge, 1640 Memorial Drive, Sturgeon Bay, WI 54235; 920-743-5555. This was Door County's first country club, established in 1928 and named for the Leathem Smith of shipbuilding fame. The property sits on 14 acres of landscaped grounds near the water on the shipping canal between Green Bay and Lake Michigan. There are two buildings: the Lodge, which has rooms and two-room luxury suites, and the Harborside building, which has rooms only. In-room amenities and décor vary; the suites feature a gas fireplace, double whirlpool tub, wet bar with refrigerator, microwave, cable TV and more. The guestrooms have cable television and private patios or balconies. A complimentary continental breakfast is served. The lodge has its own power boat, the 39-foot Leathem

Lady, available for waterfront or sunset cruises. Other outdoor facilities include a 9-hole golf course, heated pool, marina and two tennis courts. First-class dining is also available in the lodge's restaurant (see "Where to eat").

Little Harbor Inn, 5100 Bay Shore Drive, Sturgeon Bay, WI 54234; 920-743-3789. Away from the bustle of town this quiet, romantic inn is right on the waterfront in Little Harbor, about six miles north of downtown Sturgeon Bay. There are eight suites, all overlooking Green Bay, and all with a waterfront porch or veranda. Each room has a private bath, fireplace and cable television. Four of the rooms have double whirlpool tubs — by the fireplace for an extra romantic touch. Buffet breakfast is served. An added bonus for boat owners: there's docking available at no extra charge.

The Scofield House Bed & Breakfast, 908 Michigan Avenue, Sturgeon Bay, WI 52435. If your weakness is Victoriana, you've just hit pay dirt. This 1902 mansion built by prominent citizen Herbert Scofield is a study in Victorian elegance. From imposing walnut furniture down to the last little ruffle on fine bed linen, owners Fran and Bill Cecil have aimed for perfection. The most extravagant room is "The Room at the Top," occupying the entire third floor of the house. Modern touches like skylights, a double whirlpool tub, wet bar and refrigerator blend with traditional elements such as an embossed tin ceiling and fireplace with carved cherry mantle to make a private haven most people wouldn't want to leave. Breakfast at the Scofield is no less elegant: a formal gathering in the oak-paneled dining room where guests enjoy entrees like apricot-stuffed French toast or smoked turkey and cheddar omelets. As you might have guessed, the Scofield House is for adults only. It's located within walking distance of downtown shops and restaurants.

Westwood Shores, 4303 Bay Shore Drive, Sturgeon Bay, WI 54235; 800-440-4057. Like the Bay Shore Inn nearby, Westwood Shores is a large, modern resort on Green Bay about three miles north of Sturgeon Bay. The one- and two-bedroom suites each have a water view, double whirlpool tub, living room with fireplace, porch, TV/VCR and a fully equipped kitchen. There is a small sandy beach, as well as indoor and outdoor pools, whirlpool, exercise facility, sauna, grills, game room, laundry facilities and free use of paddleboats and rowboats. Smoking is not permitted.

WHERE TO EAT:

DJ's on the Bay, 129 Madison Avenue; 920-743-9935. This is the hot spot for waterfront dining, indoors or out. Located next to the marina, across the street from the maritime museum, DJ's offers burgers, wraps, salads and fish in a casual atmosphere. Wood-fired pizzas are a specialty. If you happen to be on your boat moored at the marina and get a craving for slow-baked ribs, just give DJ's a call – they've got a water taxi that will pick you up and take you to the restaurant. Want to dine on board? They'll even deliver.

Inn at Cedar Crossing, 336 Louisiana Street; 920-743-4249. Built in 1884, the Inn at Cedar Crossing is listed on the National Register of Historic Places. In addition to its nine guest rooms (see "Where to stay"), the inn serves gourmet country fare in its Victorian dining rooms. Open for breakfast, lunch and dinner, the inn prides itself on items made from scratch using fresh local ingredients. Try grilled hazelnut French toast, or for dinner, roast duck confit cassoulet or wild boar chops with gorgonzola polenta, wild mushroom shallot ragout and sun-dried tomato jam. Save room for dessert – they are reputed to be sinfully good.

Leathem Smith Lodge, 1640 Memorial Drive; 920-743-5555. Lunch and dinner are served here in the lodge's dining room overlooking the shipping canal. The Door County traditional fish boil is featured every Friday, June through October. Reservations are required. (If you're not familiar with fish boils, see the sidebar elsewhere in this chapter. They may sound unappetizing, but give them a try – they're delicious!) The rest of the week there are plenty of other scrumptious things to choose from – filet with Irish Mist oyster mushroom pepper sauce, for example, or roasted duck with bing cherry sauce. Sunday brunch is also a popular tradition.

*For more information contact the Sturgeon Bay Community
Development Corporation, 23 N. 5th Avenue, Sturgeon Bay, WI
54235; 920-743-6246.*
Internet: http://www.sturgeonbay.org

Door County Resort Towns

Driving north from Sturgeon Bay you know immediately that
you are in farm country — silos, fields and cows provide the
scenery. Apple and cherry orchards bloom brightly each spring;
in the winter this countryside setting is blanketed in peaceful
white. Along the shoreline you'll find picturesque little towns
with populations barely topping 500 in the winter, but swelling
mightily in the summer. This is hands-down one of the loveliest
areas along Lake Michigan. Yes, it's full of tourists, but it has
maintained its quaintness and beauty. You'll find no fast food
here, nor a pharmacy or discount store sprouted on every corner. Even the food markets are tastefully designed. You will not
find chain restaurants; instead, independent restauranteurs take
center stage and get a chance to show off their talents.
Likewise you won't be sleeping in a cookie-cutter hotel room.
From simple rooms at quaint inns to cottages or luxury suites,
there are accommodations to suit every preference and pocket-
book, and each is unique.

Likewise, there are activities to suit every whim. Outdoor
enthusiasts will enjoy cycling, kayaking, sailing, parasailing,
hiking, swimming and horseback riding. Gourmands will find
plenty of restaurants and gourmet food shops to explore.
Shoppers will be enthralled with the variety and quality of specialty boutiques and galleries. Arts lovers will enjoy live theater
and concerts. And anyone who loves water will delight at the
constantly changing shoreline, the beautiful deep green water
and the dramatic sunrises and sunsets over a watery horizon.

Traveling north from Sturgeon Bay along the Green Bay side of
the peninsula, the first town you'll arrive at is **Egg Harbor**. No
one knows for sure how the town got its name, but there are plen-

ty of good stories. Some people say it came from the shape of the harbor; others contend that it has to do with the endless supply of duck and gull eggs that early settlers found there. A third story places the blame squarely on frolicking fur traders who engaged in a good-natured egg fight as they approached the bay. Regardless, you will find neither more nor fewer eggs in Egg Harbor than anywhere else, but you *will* find a pretty little town tucked into a peaceful bay where sunset watching is a ritual.

The town was settled in the 1850s, and though there were modest business attempts, Egg Harbor has always been known primarily as a resort town. Not quite as busy as Fish Creek and Ephraim to the north, Egg Harbor has a similar eclectic mix of shops and restaurants, and plenty of places to stay. The town sits on a hill above the water; in summertime the bay can barely be seen from the main street because of the trees. **Harbor View Park** offers the best place to sit and watch the water. At sunset each evening, it becomes a gathering place for visitors and families who quietly sip coffee or eat ice cream while waiting for nature's grand performance.

Performances of a different kind are enjoyed each summer at **Birch Creek Music Center**, about three miles east of town. Birch Creek draws talented young musicians and professional performers and educators together for music studies during the daytime and public concerts at night. Offerings vary, from symphonic to jazz, pop and even Caribbean steel drum band. For information and tickets call 920-868-3763.

A few miles north of Egg Harbor is **Fish Creek**. Unlike Egg Harbor, Fish Creek stretches right along the water. This is one of the primary tourist hubs in Door County, with dozens of galleries, arts and crafts markets, clothing boutiques and other specialty shops.

The first settler arrived at Fish Creek in 1842 and gave it its name. Its development, though, was primarily the handiwork of Asa Thorpe, a New York businessman. Thorpe built a pier and cordwood business to supply passing ships, and the village grew rapidly around this enterprise. Lumbering, milling and fishing became important, but it was fishing that emerged as the mainstay. After the forests and the fish were depleted, the town turned to tourism, where its livelihood remains today.

In addition to being a hub for Door County shoppers, Fish Creek is the center of arts activities on the peninsula. The **American Folklore Theater** (920-868-9999), a professional musical theater company, offers family fare at their outdoor theater located in Peninsula State Park, at the north end of Fish Creek. Lively, zany productions are the hallmark of this entertaining company. **Peninsula Players** (920-868-3287), the oldest professional resident summer theater in the United States, was founded in 1935. Its home is an all-weather pavilion beside Green Bay just south of town. Offerings here may be classics, such as plays by Noel Coward, or contemporary farces and who-dunits. The **Peninsula Music Festival** (920-854-4060) brings together artists from orchestras across the country for three weeks each August. Now nearly 50 years old, the festival is the primary venue for classical music performances in the county. The festival location is the Door Community Auditorium in Fish Creek, which also hosts special performances throughout the year. At the **Peninsula Art School** (920-868-4355) students – adults and children alike – can spend a week learning anything from paper making to pottery, with some 217 choices of classes. Likewise, **Peninsula Dance** (920-868-3371) has classes for both adults and children, in areas ranging from ballet and jazz dance to fitness, yoga and tai chi.

Like Fish Creek, **Ephraim** is right on Green Bay. It was founded in 1853 by Norwegian Moravians led by Reverend Andreas Iverson, who brought his flock of 40 to the peninsula from the town of Green Bay. Life proved difficult for the Moravians, who had to contend with poverty and soil ill suited to farming. Furthermore, the only way to Ephraim was by water, which meant that the townsfolk had to be well stocked for winter, for no supplies could get in until the ice broke in the spring. Hard work and persistence paid off, and eventually the settlers of Ephraim (which, ironically, means "fruitful") were able to eek out a living by fishing, farming and selling lumber.

Today tourism is the main draw, though some of Ephraim's Moravian legacy remains. It is the only dry town on the peninsula, and many of the historical buildings are still standing. Some of these, now the **Ephraim Foundation Museums** (920-854-9688) can be toured. The **Anderson Store**, built in 1858,

DOOR COUNTY'S ANSWER TO THE CLAM-BAKE

Part show, part culinary delight, the fish boil is a Door County tradition you shouldn't miss. Here's how it works: large chunks of freshly caught Lake Michigan whitefish, whole small potatoes and onions are thrown into a huge stainless steel pot over an outdoor woodfire. Salt is the only seasoning. The ingredients are boiled for a set period — 30 minutes for the potatoes, 12 minutes for the onions and 10 minutes for the fish. Then come the pyrotechnics. Kerosene is thrown onto the fire, making it boil over and causing a wall of flames to shoot tree-high around the pot. All the fish oil, and its "fishy" taste, disappears over the edge into the fire, leaving the whitefish sweet and mild. The contents of the pot are drained and served with plenty of melted butter, tartar sauce, lemon wedges and coleslaw on the side. Homemade Door County cherry pie a la mode is the usual finale.

Fish boils have taken place in Door County for over a hundred years. No one knows their exact origin, but they seem to have come about through the combination of an abundance of fresh fish and the necessity of feeding large numbers of hungry lumbermen. Whatever the reason, fish boils today are a unique experience you won't find elsewhere.

The first commercial fish boils were at the **Viking Grill and Lounge** in Ellison Bay (920-854-2998). They still have them every night, May to October. Not all restaurants, however, have them daily. They are popular, and seating is limited, so make a reservation a few days ahead.

has much original merchandise still in the boxes, showing the original prices. Even though the Andersons no longer operated the store at the time its ownership passed to the foundation, the store fixtures, including the cash register, and the goods were found stored in the family's barn. The Andersons, being good Scandinavians, never threw out anything. The **Anderson Barn** also belongs to the foundation and features an unusual square silo, one of only a few in the county. (Silos were generally round because grain in corners tends to spoil.) The **Pioneer Schoolhouse**, down the street, was used into the 1940s. The fourth building, the **Thomas Goodletson Cabin**, was built in the mid-1800s on an island in Green Bay, where the family lived in isolation. It was later moved to Ephraim. These buildings are open to the public during the summer. Call for specific times.

For those with a special interest in local history, there is an hour-and-a-half walking tour of the town given periodically during the week in the summertime. Call the museums for a schedule.

South Shore Pier near the center of the town is the hot spot for water activities. Visitors can sign up for sailing tours of the

The fishing village of Gills Rock.

bay, go parasailing, or rent jet skis, pontoon boats or power boats.

Like Fish Creek, Ephraim is full of interesting shops, galleries and restaurants. Don't miss **Wilson's Restaurant**, a famous red and white landmark in the town. Established in 1906, this casual eatery has the atmosphere of a diner, where burgers, soups, sandwiches and gigantic ice cream cones are the fare.

A few miles farther north is the town of **Sister Bay**. Though largest of the towns north of Sturgeon Bay, it is not as busy with tourists as Fish Creek or Ephraim. It was settled in 1857 by Norwegian immigrants, who set out to work in the lumber industry. But like the rest of the peninsula, Sister Bay is now engaged primarily in tourism.

Beyond Sister Bay are the small towns of **Ellison Bay** and **Gills Rock**, both sleepy little hamlets perched at the edge of the water. Gills Rock, which is still active in commercial fishing, is almost at the tip of the peninsula; from here ferry passengers embark across the passage to Washington Island. (This ferry also makes limited trips to the historic ghost town of Fayette in Michigan's Upper Peninsula. Call 920-854-2972 for more information.) It's not called Death's Door for nothing – many ships have been lost here. When conditions are good, recreational scuba divers explore the many hulls and artifacts remaining on the bottom. Non-divers can learn about the shipwrecks and the local fishing industry at the small branch of the **Door County Marine Museum** in Gills Rock. For more information call 920-743-5958.

At the very tip of the peninsula is **Northport**, which is little more than a ferry dock for people wishing to take their cars to Washington Island. (The ferry at Gills Rock takes passengers only.) The Northport ferry runs year round. To find out about ferry schedules and fees call the **Washington Island Ferry Line** at 920-847-2546.

Twenty-two-square-mile **Washington Island**, the largest of the smattering of islands in Door County, lies seven miles north of the peninsula tip, but it is much farther away in ambiance from the busy towns of Egg Harbor, Fish Creek or Ephraim. Though it has 100 miles of roads, it's primarily rural. Much of what was once farmland has been allowed to go back to nature.

Long inhabited by indigenous Indians, Washington Island wasn't occupied permanently by Europeans until fishermen settled at Washington Harbor in 1858. Originally named Colonel John Miller Island, its name later was changed to honor George Washington. Though a group of black fishermen settled on the island in the 1800s, it was the Scandinavians who took root permanently. The late 1860s saw a large influx of Danes, Norwegians and Icelanders who quickly became the dominant ethnic group. Farming and dairying were the main occupations for many years. These have declined, and today the island is largely a low-key tourist attraction and a popular spot for summer homes. It is the oldest Icelandic community in the United States. This is also the place of departure for those wishing to travel by ferry to Rock Island State Park. (See "Natural Attractions.") The Karfi ferry leaves from Jackson Harbor on Washington Island's northeast corner for the 10-minute ride to Rock Island.

Though the island may be quieter than much of Door County, there are plenty of things to do. With little traffic and miles of smooth, paved roads, Washington Island is a great place for cyclists. Bring your own bike on the ferry, or – if you don't mind a one-speed model with coaster brakes – you can rent one once you get there. Mopeds are also available.

During the summer there is a 90-minute tram tour of the island offered to visitors debarking from the ferry. The tour takes you to an ostrich farm, a farm museum, the main shopping district and beautiful **Schoolhouse Beach**.

This protected beach is located at Washington Harbor on the north side of the island. Composed of smooth white stones, the beach provides the perfect showcase for the bay's crystal clear water. Those who prefer not to venture into the cold water may enjoy picnicking in this scenic spot instead. Grills and tables are provided.

Several other public beaches offer places to relax or swim. On the east side is **Percy Johnson County Park**, with tables and grills. **Sand Dunes Beach**, at the south end of the island, is accessible by a short sandy trail off South Shore Drive. Just to the west is **Red Barn Park** and **Gislason Public Beach**, 13 acres with picnic tables and grills, play equipment and nature trails. A nature trail is also part of **Jackson Harbor Ridges**, a State of Wisconsin Scientific Area that includes a beach, dunes and other shoreline habitats.

Other outdoor recreational possibilities are golfing on a 9-hole course, charter fishing in Lake Michigan, tennis at either of two public courts or horseback riding. Washington Island has a group of rarely seen Icelandic horses, slightly smaller and more gently tempered than most other breeds.

The island has several small museums. The **Jackson Harbor Maritime Museum**, located on the northeast corner of the island near Jackson Harbor Ridges, has artifacts, photographs and videos relating to maritime history and commercial fishing. The museum, which is housed in two old fishing shanties, is open weekends Memorial Day through Columbus Day, daily in July and August. The **Jacobsen Museum**, on Little Lake at the northwest corner of the island, features the log cabin that was once home to local artist Jens Jacobsen, who took a keen interest in the Native American history of the area. The cabin has been restored and furnished with period furniture. Another log building houses displays of artifacts relating to the natural and human history of the island. It is open daily Memorial Day weekend to mid-October. The **Washington Island Farm Museum** highlights the island's agricultural heritage. This open-air museum consists of original buildings on three acres, among them a blacksmith shop, sawmill and log cabin typical of those built by early European settlers. The museum frequently offers demonstrations and children's programs. It is open mid-June to mid-October.

Don't miss the beautiful wooden **Stavkirke** on Town Line

Traditional Icelandic stavkirke.

Road east of the main shopping area and across the street from Trinity Lutheran Church. This hand-built, traditional Icelandic church looks as though it has been transplanted straight from Scandinavia.

Continuing east on Town Line Road, make a left turn onto Mountain Road and stop at **Mountain Park and Lookout Tower**. Built on a higher elevation than the surrounding area, the tower affords a view of the island and the water and islands beyond. There are picnic facilities at the park.

Accommodations on the island are primarily cottages and small motels. There are also two campgrounds. For a listing of places to stay call the Washington Island Chamber of Commerce at 920-847-2179.

Back the on peninsula, the drive down the eastern shoreline along Lake Michigan is mostly rural. This is the quiet side of the peninsula, less developed and far less crowded. It can also be much cooler on hot summer days, with a breeze that blows off Lake Michigan, something the Green Bay side of the peninsula doesn't have.

About midway down the peninsula is **Baileys Harbor**. This quiet town is named for Captain Justice Bailey, who drew his ship into safety here in the 1840s when an agitated Lake Michigan threatened to swallow it. Impressed with the location, Bailey passed the word when he returned home to Milwaukee. The ship's owner purchased the land and began its development. A settlement grew, primarily around shipping, lumbering and farming. Today, with these industries all but gone, Baileys Harbor relies on tourism, though it is much less busy than Fish Creek, Egg Harbor or Ephraim.

Just south of town is **Bjorklunden vid Sjon**, owned by Lawrence University and used as a retreat center for its faculty and students and as an education and performance center for the general public. Situated on 405 acres of waterfront property, the estate was bequeathed to the university by Donald and Winifred Boynton in 1963. Bjorklunden, as it's more commonly called, offers continuing education seminars during the summer on topics such as music, art, drama, religion or nature. Seminar participants can stay in the guest rooms at the beautiful Norwegian-style lodge. The center is also the location for many music and theater performances throughout the year. The lovely *stavkirke*, a Scandinavian-style chapel, is open to visitors for a small fee. This is a popular spot for Door County weddings.

Nature lovers will enjoy the **Ridges**, a privately owned wildflower preserve nearby, also the location of the Baileys Harbor Range Lights, built in 1869. The Ridges has a sand beach open to the public.

Nearby **Cana Island Lighthouse** may be the most famous of the Door County lights. Still a functioning lighthouse, it sits on tiny Cana Island, just offshore from Baileys Harbor. When the water isn't high it's possible to walk across a narrow causeway to the 1869 lighthouse (though you can still walk it when the water *is* high – you'll just get your feet wet). There is a fee to enter the causeway, but this also entitles you to walk around the grounds and tour the keeper's house. Admission to the tower is not permitted.

South of Baileys Harbor is the small hamlet of **Jacksonport**, barely more than a shop, a restaurant and a handful of cottages.

Special events take place in Door County communities year round, but some have become a tradition. One of the most popular is the annual **Lighthouse Walk** in May, organized by the Door County Maritime Museum. This self-guided tour of nine lighthouses includes special boat excursions to several lights that are inaccessible from land. For more information contact the museum at 920-743-5958. Other annual events include the **Door County Antique Show** (July) in Fish Creek, the **House and Garden Walk** throughout the county (July), **Cherry Daze** (August) in Jacksonport, the **Pumpkin Patch Festival** (October) in Egg Harbor, and the **Polar Bear Swim** on New Year's Day in Jacksonport.

WHERE TO STAY:

Alpine Resort Inn and Cottages, PO Box 200, Egg Harbor, WI 54209; 920-868-3000. This 300-acre self-contained resort sits right on Green Bay just south of downtown Egg Harbor. There are three basic types of accommodations. Rooms are available in the main inn and also in the clubhouse above the golf chalet. Housekeeping homes, not located on the grounds but nearby, are fully equipped. Cottages, which are on the grounds, have fewer amenities and require that tableware be brought in. The Hof Restaurant, on the premises, is open for breakfast and dinner. Guests can choose a modified American plan that includes breakfast and dinner, or they may pay only for accommodations and dine at the resort restaurant as they wish. There are many activities available within the resort including a 27-hole golf course, sand beach, tennis courts, pool, game room, playground, bikes and boats. Dockage is available. The resort lounge has nightly entertainment in July and August. Open mid-May through late October.

The Blacksmith Inn, 8152 Highway 57, PO Box 220, Baileys Harbor, WI 54202; 800-769-8619 or 920-839-9222. This 1912 half-timber inn overlooks Lake Michigan at Baileys Harbor, on the "quiet side" of the Door Peninsula. There are seven rooms, each with fireplace, private bath with whirlpool tub, refrigerator, TV/VCR and sliding door opening to a balcony overlooking the water. Guests enjoy a 400-foot private beach. A homemade continental breakfast is served each morning. There is a working blacksmith shop on the premises, as there has been since 1905.

Evergreen Beach Resort, PO Box 170B, Ephraim, WI 54211-0170. Established in 1897, this historic inn is right in the heart of Ephraim. The main building sits across the street from the bay. Four beachside units lack the historical charm of the original building, but are directly on the water. Accommodations are pleasant, simple and affordable. Each room has a water view, private bath, cable TV and telephone. There is a private sand beach, sundeck and outdoor pool. Its location close to shopping and restaurants makes this a convenient spot. Open mid-May to late October.

Gordon Lodge, PO Box 189, 1420 Pine Drive, Baileys Harbor, WI 54202; 800-830-6235 or 920-839-2331. If it's quiet and isolation you're looking for this might be the place. Located in a remote area on the Lake Michigan side of the peninsula north of Baileys Harbor, this tony resort has been around since 1928. There are three types of accommodations available. The main lodge has rooms with water views and private baths. The waterfront "villas" vary, from a bedroom with fireplace and whirlpool tub, to 2-bedroom unit with living room and fireplace. There are also cottages, which are basically rooms, though some have small living rooms but none have kitchens. These are generally the most economical and are located in a wooded setting. (All units are on the expensive side. The villas are beautiful but pricey; the rooms are not much different from standard hotel rooms, but the location is spectacular.) Some units are adults-only. Amenities include an outdoor pool, two tennis courts, two badminton courts, an 18-hole putting green, paddle boats and row boats. The restaurant (see "where to eat") is open for breakfast and lunch. Gordon Lodge is open May through October.

Harbor Guest House and Marina, PO Box 564, Fish Creek,

WI 54212; 920-868-2284. This charming guest house was built as a carriage house in the early 1900s. It is now six fully equipped apartments directly on Green Bay in Fish Creek. Each one- or two-bedroom suite has a wood-burning fireplace (wood supplied), complete kitchen and cable TV. Children are welcome. Those arriving by boat will find slips available at the adjacent marina. This is a good value, especially during the off season. (The guest house is open year round.) No smoking is

BEACONS IN THE MIST

Lake Michigan has more than 100 light towers, beacons or crib lights that protect ships from dangerous shorelines or shallow shoals. Coincidentally they are also pretty to look at and have grown in popularity among tourists in recent years. Though lighthouses are now automated, causing many to be abandoned for more modern structures, there is a growing trend toward restoration of historic towers. Many are open the public or have been turned into museums.

Lake Michigan lighthouses hold some distinctions. Many of them – at Holland, South Haven, Grand Haven in Michigan; Sturgeon Bay and Algoma in Wisconsin – are painted a bright red, a color not seen on lighthouses on any of the other Great Lakes. Lake Michigan also has the Great Lakes' only "candy-cane" striped lighthouse – the 121-foot-tall White Shoal Lighthouse 20 miles west of the Mackinac Bridge. The town of St. Joseph, Michigan, boasts one of two Michigan lighthouses to appear on a U.S. postage stamp.

They come in a variety of shapes – conical, round, square, skeletal or pyramidal – and are built from a variety of materials – brick, cast iron, steel, wood and stone. Some are rumored to be haunted (check out Seul Choix in Michigan's Upper Peninsula, but not at night). But all share a common history as beacons to safety and act as a romantic reminder of days past.

permitted.

Harbor View Resort, PO Box 167, Ephraim, WI 54211; 920-854-1883. This modern resort sits high on a bluff overlooking Green Bay and the town of Ephraim. There are 10 one- and two-bedroom suites, each with wood-burning fireplace, equipped kitchen, cable TV, grill and a private deck facing the water. It is open year round. Rates are quite reasonable. The owners also rent one-, two- and three-bedroom rustic cabins with stone fireplaces and full kitchens in another location; these are open summer and fall only.

Inn at Froghollow Farm Bed & Breakfast, N17W1029 Jackson Harbor Road, Washington Island, WI 54246; 920-847-2835. Situated on five inland acres on rural Washington Island, this renovated 1915 farmhouse is now a bed and breakfast with four guest rooms. The rooms, furnished in antiques and period reproductions, all have private baths. Breakfasts of homemade breads and muffins are served on the wrap-around porch or deck. No smoking.

The Landing, 7741 Egg Harbor Road, PO Box 16, Egg Harbor, WI 54209; 800-851-8919 or 920-868-3282. This 10-unit, reasonably-priced resort is not on the water but is nestled into the woods near the center of town, making it easy to walk to restaurants and shopping. Each condo is different, from a small one-bedroom unit to a three-bedroom, two-level suite. All have fully equipped kitchens, living rooms with TV/VCR, eating area and private deck or porch. The family-oriented resort also has indoor and outdoor pools, a small playground, gas grills, bike rental and laundry facility. There are tennis, basketball and volleyball courts. Open year round.

WHERE TO EAT:

Second Story Restaurant, 10018 Water Street, Ephraim; 920-854-2371. Located on the main drag in Ephraim, this casual restaurant has a great view of the harbor and the sailing, windsurfing and other activities going on there. Breakfast, lunch and dinner are served at reasonable prices. Dinners include items like steak, salmon, chicken, perch and whitefish. In keeping with the town's dry policy, no alcohol is served.

Top Deck Lounge at the Gordon Lodge, 1420 Pine Drive, Baileys Harbor; 920-839-2331. You can't get much closer to the water than this. It's off the beaten path, north of Baileys Harbor on the quiet side of the peninsula. The menu features elegant fare like duck breast with mandarin oranges and coconut, beef Wellington and salmon en croute. Special events include Friday night fish fry/boil and Monday night beach party and fish boil.

Trio Restaurant, Highway 42, Egg Harbor; 920-868-2090. This casual bistro with a French and Italian country theme offers a creative alternative to the usual seafood and meat dishes (though you can get those here too). The menu changes regularly, but items like cassoulet and pasta are regulars. There is no view of the water, but the atmosphere is bright and pleasant. Dinner only is served.

White Gull Inn, 4225 Main Street, Fish Creek; 920-868-3517. One of the best fish boils can be found several nights a week at this historic inn, established in 1896. On other evenings the menu features elegant fare like shrimp and artichoke Romano or honey glazed salmon, served in a candlelit dining room. Fish boils here are extremely popular and fill up quickly. Reservations are essential. The inn's restaurant also serves breakfast and lunch.

For more information contact the Door County Chamber of Commerce, 1015 Green Bay Road, PO Box 406, Sturgeon Bay, WI 54235-0406; 920-743-4456.
Internet: http://doorcountyvacations.com

Natural Attractions

POTAWATOMI STATE PARK

On a peninsula famous for its shoreline and nearly endless swimming possibilities, 1,231-acre Potawatomi State Park is an

Looking at Sturgeon Bay from Potawatomi State Park.

anomaly. There are no beaches. There is, however, a wide range of spectacular scenery here along the rocky contours of Sturgeon Bay, just west of the city of the same name. An added bonus is that it's rarely as crowded as popular Peninsula State Park, its neighbor farther up the Door Peninsula.

The park is named for the Potawatomi Indians who once inhabited the area. They called themselves Bo-de-wad-me, which means "Keeper of the Fire." The name, difficult for Europeans to pronounce, eventually came to be altered to "Potawatomi," which is how it is still spoken and written.

The park has six miles of hiking trails, some along the rugged shoreline. The most popular trail is probably the 3.5-mile

Tower Trail, which winds along the park's highest bluff, offering magnificent views of Green Bay. It passes by the observation tower at the northeast corner of the park. This tower, which was built in 1932, rises 75 feet from the ground making it 225 feet above the water. From the top you get a bird's-eye view of the bay, Sawyer Harbor to the north and Cabot Point across the water. On clear days, the view extends all the way to Michigan's Upper Peninsula.

Near the tower is the terminus of the **Ice Age Trail**, a 1,000-mile National Scenic Trail that traces the route of the glaciers.

The half-mile **Ancient Shoreline Trail** is a good place to learn about the geological origins of the area. The easy walk takes hikers to 14 learning stations that tell about the glaciers that formed the contours of the land as we see it today, along with other natural forces at work over the past thousands of years. In addition to hiking trails, there is a four-mile off-road bike trail. During the winter some of the trails are open to cross-country skiers. The park also has the only downhill ski slope in Door County.

Camping is a popular activity at Potawatomi. **Daisy Field Campground** has 123 sites in two sections at the middle of the park. Twenty-five of these have electricity. The campground is equipped with flush toilets and showers that are open on a seasonal basis. For campers with disabilities there are two options: two accessible campsites or a barrier-free cabin at the edge of the campground.

The park store carries groceries and supplies. Bike and canoe rentals are available at the campground. Pretty Sawyer Harbor is a protected bay that is usually calm, making it a pleasant place for exploration by canoe. There is a boat launch on the bay near the tower.

If you're only going to Potawatomi State Park for the day, consider a picnic in the day-use area at the south end of the park, where you'll find sweeping views of the bay.

For more information contact Potawatomi State Park, 3740 Park Drive, Sturgeon Bay, WI 54235.

PENINSULA STATE PARK

There's something for everyone at this sprawling, popular park — swimming, boating, golf, bicycling, hiking, camping, theater, even a lighthouse and an island to explore.

Established in 1909, this 3,775-acre park is one of the oldest and largest of the Wisconsin State Parks. It is also the busiest of the parks in Door County. Its location is on a small peninsula about three-quarters of the way up the Green Bay side of Door Peninsula, just north of Fish Creek. Most of the shoreline, with the exception of pretty Nicolet Beach, is rocky, and much of the park sits on limestone bluffs rising nearly 200 feet above the water. The scenery is beautiful, whether you see it by foot, bike, car or boat.

One of the best places for a panoramic view is from **Eagle Tower**, a 75-foot wooden structure that towers 250 feet over the water. Originally built in 1914, it was rebuilt in the 1930s. There is ample parking here for the many people who stop to climb the stairs for an eagle's eye view of Green Bay and, on clear days, the Lake Michigan shoreline.

Another popular stop is the **Eagle Bluff Lighthouse**, built in 1868. For nearly 40 years the 43-foot light was maintained by the same family, keeper William Duclon, his wife and their seven sons. In 1961 the Door County Historical Society began restoration of the keeper's house, reverting it to 19th-century appearances. Guided tours are offered June through mid-October for a small fee.

Nicolet Beach, the park's only sandy beach, is tucked into a bay on the park's northeast side. The water is shallow a long way out and tends to be very calm, making this a great beach for small children, though there are no lifeguards. The beach has just about every amenity you'd want: a store, snack bar, playground, picnic area, changing rooms and showers. A con-

Eagle Bluff Lighthouse, Peninsula State Park.

cession rents boats and bicycles.

Various types of bikes can be rented, with speeds from one to 21. Cyclists can ride the park's roads or the popular **Sunset Bike Trail**, a 9.7-mile round trip ride over packed gravel and asphalt. The scenic trail winds through pine and cedar forests and meadows, along rocky shoreline and past the lighthouse. The terrain is rolling, with no long hills, though there are some short, steep inclines that make it nice to have a multi-geared bike. There are also several places to rent bikes and mopeds (which can't be ridden on the bike trail) just outside the park entrance, near the beginning of Sunset Trail. There are also eight miles of trails designated for mountain biking.

Boats available at Nicolet Beach include sailboats, paddle boats, canoes, windsurfers and kayaks. An especially pleasant excursion is to paddle over to **Horseshoe Island**, also part of the park, about a mile away. The island consists of woods and rocky shoreline with a protected area for beaching a boat. For those with their own boats, there are two launching ramps in the park.

Nicolet Beach at Peninsula State Park.

Hikers will find 20 miles of trails of varying difficulty. The scenic **Eagle Trail** is a two-mile loop that winds along the shoreline and up Door County's highest bluff, making it steep in places. The **Sentinel Loop** is another two-mile trail on easier terrain, accessible from the Eagle Tower. A trail brochure describes plants and trees along the way. A map showing all the trails is available at the park entrance.

The park's **White Cedar Nature Center** has displays and exhibits about park history and the natural history of the area. The center has many programs for adults and children, including guided hikes.

The park has 469 campsites in four campgrounds. The small **Weborg Campground** (12 sites) is located near the park entrance by a rocky beach. **Welcker's Point Campground**, with 81 sites, is at the far north edge of the park. The 188-site **Nicolet Bay Campground** is closest to the swimming beach; some sites are on the water and a boat launch is nearby. **Tennison Bay Campground**, with 189 sites, is enclosed in a large loop near the other of the park's two boat launches.

The view from Eagle Tower at Peninsula State Park.

The **American Folklore Theater** has live stage productions in the park June through October. These original musical programs include comedy, storytelling and folk music for the whole family. For information call 920-868-9999.

The park's scenic par 71, 6,200-yard golf course is open daily May to mid-October. Reservations are recommended (call 920-854-5791). The grounds include a pro shop with restaurant. On the course stands a 30-foot carved pole commemorating the Potawatomi and Menominee Indians. The original pole was dedicated in 1927. In attendance were 6,000 spectators, among them 32 full-blooded Potawatomi. It was unveiled by Potawatomi chief Simon Kahquados, who was later buried here. The pole deteriorated and in 1970 a new, weather-resistant pole was erected. On it are replicas of the original carvings along with additional new ones.

Activity doesn't cease at the park during the winter. Eighteen miles of snowmobile trails are groomed January through mid-March, weather permitting. There are 20 miles of cross-country ski trails and two miles of marked snowshoe trails. The hill on the 17th fairway on the golf course is open to sledders. A portion of the Tennison Bay Campground is plowed, with water, electrical hookups and pit toilets available.

For more information contact Peninsula State Park, PO Box 218, Fish Creek, WI 54212-0218; 920-868-3258.

ROCK ISLAND STATE PARK

It takes a little planning and effort to get to this beautiful park. Located off Washington Island, Rock Island is entirely state park land. Unless you're already on Washington Island, you must first take the ferry there (see "Washington Island" section), which docks at Detroit Harbor. Then you must get to Jackson Harbor on the opposite side of the island, where the Karfi ferry departs for Rock Island.

If you're on bicycle, you'll have to leave it at the ferry dock in Jackson Harbor; no vehicles of any kind are allowed on Rock Island — which is one of the things that make it so special.

The 906-acre island was once the private haunt of Icelandic-born businessman Chester Thordarson. He bought the island in 1910 and set out developing 30 acres on its southwest side. The rest he left untouched, the way it remains today. The most striking legacy he left behind is the imposing great hall and boathouse, a massive stone structure at the water's edge near the ferry dock. The hall, where he once housed his 25,000-volume library, still has some of its original furnishings, including wooden furniture carved with scenes from Icelandic mythology.

Long before Thordarson, the island attracted many others. Scientists have verified the presence of Indian peoples from the early centuries A.D. At later times it supported the Potawatomi, Fox, Winnebago, Menominee and other tribes. There is some speculation that René-Robert Cavelier de La Salle's trading post was located here, and that this was the last port of the Griffin, the first sailing ship on the Great Lakes that was mysteriously lost in 1679.

Today's visitors come to the island with something less serious in mind — hiking, swimming or camping. There is a beautiful half-mile sandy beach, not far from the ferry dock, with changing rooms and toilets nearby. Water is available on the island, but no food or other supplies; be sure to take whatever you will need.

Ten miles of hiking trails wind through the island. The main one is the 6.5 mile **Thordarson Trail**, which circles the island's perimeter. Other trails intersect in various places, making it possible to reach different sites without having to walk around the entire island.

The Thordarson Trail leads through pine and birch forests, along a bluff high over the water and past historic sites. The ruins of an old fishing village remain, as well as two old cemeteries. On the north tip is the **Potawatomi Lighthouse**, Wisconsin's oldest lighthouse. Built in 1858, it is still a working light, though now automated, and its interior is not open to the public.

There are 40 campsites on the island, 35 of them close to the ferry dock, the others a longer hike away. Some sites have beautiful water views. Vault toilets, fire rings and tables are provided, but all supplies must be carried in and all refuse packed out. The campground is open Memorial Day through Columbus Day.

There are few places as pristine and serene as Rock Island. The only sounds you are likely to hear are from birds and crickets, wind and water. Over 200 species of birds have been spotted here, along with deer, coyotes, foxes, rabbits and occasional bears. Visitors have heeded the request to carry out all trash, and you are likely to spend your entire visit to the island without once seeing a reminder of previous campers or hikers.

For more information contact Rock Island State Park, Washington Island, WI 54246-9728; 920-847-2235 (in season) or 920-854-2500 (off season). For ferry information call 920-847-2252.

NEWPORT STATE PARK

If the crowds at Peninsula State Park get to be too much, head

Newport State Park.

to the other side of Door County to Newport State Park. With 2,370 acres and 11 miles of Lake Michigan shoreline, there's plenty of space here, and usually few people. The park has been left undeveloped, with only a mile and a half of road running through it.

It was not always so quiet and rugged. Once the site of a logging village, it was briefly a thriving area. But when the wood was gone, so were the people. Though traces of the old post office and store remain, there is little else to remind visitors that this beautiful wilderness tract was ever anything else.

The park has 30 miles of hiking trails through forests and along Lake Michigan and diminutive Europe Lake. You can learn about the history of the logging village on the **Upland Loop**, a two-mile self-guided trail with interpretive signs along the way. Hikers can also expect to see a wide variety of wildlife such as deer, coyotes, porcupines, raccoons, and foxes. Bikes are permitted on some of the park's trails, though strictly the mountain bike variety since the paths are unpaved. During the winter, most of the trails are open to cross-country skiers.

The park's long, uncrowded shoreline is one of its primary attractions. The sandy swimming beach on Newport Bay is 3,000 feet long. There is little in the way of amenities, but changing stalls and toilets are available. There are no lifeguards. Picnic facilities, including a shelter, are nearby

In keeping with the park's wilderness designation, camping is by backpack only. The 16 sites are remote, requiring hikes up of to 3.5 miles to reach them. Drinking water is available at the park office, but not at the sites, so all water must be carried in. Likewise, all trash and refuse must be packed out. Pit toilets are located nearby.

For more information contact Newport State Park, 475 County Road NP, Ellison Bay, WI 54210; 920-854-2500.

WHITEFISH DUNES STATE PARK

Located on the Lake Michigan side of the Door Peninsula, Whitefish Dunes State Park has some of the relatively few dunes on the Wisconsin side of the lake. Though nothing like the towering dunes found on Michigan's Lower Peninsula, such as Warren Dunes or Sleeping Bear Dunes, these 3,000-year-old dunes are nonetheless some of the highest in Wisconsin. The tallest of these, **Mt. Baldy**, rises 93 feet over the lake. It is the only dune in the park that visitors are permitted to climb, and a wooden walkway has been built for that purpose. An observation platform at the top makes for a pleasant view of the water and surrounding dunes.

There is no campground, making the primary activities hiking, picnicking and swimming. Fourteen miles of trails wind through the park, which is long and narrow, perched on a strip of land between Lake Michigan and Clark Lake. The trails, many of which intersect, take hikers through hardwood and pine forests, along both lakes, into wetland areas and through forested dunes. Some are open to cyclists, and during the winter they are open to cross-country skiers. The **Brachiopod Trail** has 16 learning stations along the way, for which there is a booklet available at the park interpretive center. One of the

The highest dunes in Wisconsin, at Whitefish Dunes State Park.

stations is a fossil wall where brachiopods can be seen. During the summer the park has regularly scheduled naturalist programs and guided hikes.

There are three accesses to the Lake Michigan beach: two just off the park road near the office and interpretive center, the other about midway along the beach off one of the hiking trails. Dangerous rip currents that run out into the lake are often found in the area closest to the ramp by the office, and this section of beach has been cordoned off.

However, these currents can occur elsewhere, especially after a storm, and swimmers are warned to take extra caution when waves are high, the condition during which rip currents are most often spawned. Park officials urge swimmers to note that if they should get caught in a rip current, the best defense is to swim parallel to the shore, since the currents are rarely more than 30 feet wide. Swimmers are also warned not to go into water more than waist deep because of long shore currents that run parallel to shore and can carry them into the dangerous rip currents.

The picnic area is located near the beach, by the interpretive center and parking lot. The area is equipped with tables, charcoal grills and a shelter.

Within the park boundaries is tiny **Cave Point County Park**, where small stone cliffs drop directly to the lake, which over time has carved caves and fanciful shapes into the relatively soft rock. It's easy to see how this has occurred if you happen to be there on a day when the lake is in a nasty mood. Water crashes into the flat face of the rock, spraying up and over the cliffs and the trees at their edge. It's one of the more dramatic locations on the Door Peninsula. If you've got small children be aware that there are no barriers between the cliffs and the water; a fall here could be fatal.

For more information contact Whitefish Dunes State Park, 3701 Clark Lake Road, Sturgeon Bay, WI 54235; 920-823-2400.

Cave Point County Park, where the lake has carved into the soft rock.

Some Favorites

It's always an author's pleasure, after writing a book like this, to share some personal favorites. I spent two months traveling along the shores of Lake Michigan doing research for this project. I stayed at many of the inns and B & Bs written about in this book, ate in many (too many!) of the restaurants, walked beaches and wandered through museums. I hiked, biked, kayaked and rode on horseback. In short, I had a ball, and I'd like to let you know some of very special places and experiences that made this work memorable and enjoyable for me. These choices are, of course, wildly subjective. Try them out, but explore others as well – you'll find your own favorites!

FAVORITE PLACES TO STAY:

- The **BaySide Inn** in Saugatuck, Mich., for its bright airiness and for being right on the Kalamazoo River with up-close views of ducks taking off and landing on the water.
- The **Boardwalk Inn** in St. Ignace, Mich., and the **Nahma Hotel** in Nahma, Wis., because I am a sucker for historic hotels. Neither of these places is fancy, but they evoke the past in a very special way.
- The penthouse suite at **The Last Resort**, South Haven, Mich., because I loved waking up beneath a stained glass window.
- The **Tall Oaks Inn** in New Buffalo, Mich., for its utter peacefulness and, yes, tall oaks.

MOST MEMORABLE MEALS:

- **Bistro on the Boulevard**, St. Joseph, Mich. Expert preparation, fresh (and often local) ingredients and excellent service made this among my favorites.
- **Boathouse Blue Water Bistro** in Bower's Harbor on Michigan's Old Mission Peninsula. Picture yourself enjoying scrumptious food while sitting outdoors watching the sunset over the water and sipping a glass of excellent wine made just a few miles away. This place combines the best of expertly prepared food with nature's finest show.

- **Café Bliss** in Suttons Bay, Mich. This tiny, intimate restaurant doesn't have a scenic view or an elegant décor. It just has some of the most imaginative, creative food I encountered anywhere along the lake.
- The fish boil at the **White Gull Inn**, Fish Creek, Wis. Fish boils are always dramatic, with the burst of flame that signals its climax, but the White Gull Inn goes beyond drama, to melt-in-your mouth perfection.

FAVORITE BEACHES:

There are so many fantastic beaches on Lake Michigan that it seems almost subversive to pick favorites, but here goes...

- **Good Harbor Beach** in Sleeping Bear Dunes National Lakeshore. This is not perhaps one of the more beautiful beaches. It is narrow, and tends to be stony. But it is long and quiet, and often glassy calm. Petoskey stones abound here, seen easily while walking through the crystal clear water.
- The public beach at **South Haven**, Mich. This beautiful sandy beach stretches all along the town's shoreline, making South Haven the quintessential beach town. On a day when the waves are really rolling in, you'd swear you were in Southern California.
- **South Manitou Island**, Sleeping Bear Dunes National Lakeshore. The beach rings the island, and if you've got the time, you can walk the whole thing. Framed by dramatically blue water, this beach is wild and gorgeous.
- Along U.S. 2 west of **St. Ignace** in Michigan's Upper Peninsula. Miles and miles of pristine beach stretch along this northernmost portion of Lake Michigan. There are no facilities, giving it an atmosphere of wild, unspoiled beauty.

FAVORITE STATE PARKS:

- **Rock Island State Park** in Wisconsin's Door County. No vehicles, no paved roads, no noise and no trash, combined with stunning views of the lake, a sugar sand beach, towering forests and the hushed tones of nature on a sunny summer day – need I say more? It takes some effort to get there, but oh is it worth it.

- **Silver Lake State Park** near Pentwater, Mich. Mountainous dunes offset by the deep blue of Silver Lake on one side and Lake Michigan on the other combine to create scenery that is exotic and dramatic.

FAVORITE TOWNS:

- **Door County, Wis**. All these little towns – Fish Creek, Egg Harbor, Ephraim and the rest – are picture perfect enclaves of charm. No ugly architecture, no unattractive signage and no fast food!
- **Manistee, Mich**. Perhaps the best-preserved Victorian town on the lake. Kudos to the citizens of Manistee for spending the time and money to keep it so.
- **Sheboygan, Wis**. Of all the small cities covered in this guide, Sheboygan has, hands down, the most attractive, lively waterfront – shops, restaurants, a boardwalk, bike paths, greenery, parks and a beautiful beach. And away from the waterfront, the town's John Michael Kohler Arts Center is an amazing treasure.

FAVORITE HISTORIC SITES:

- The **Straits of Mackinac**, Mich. Nowhere else on the lake is the legacy of the voyageurs, the traders, the early settlers and native peoples so evident. This area at the crossroads of the Great Lakes – Mackinaw City, Mackinac Island and St. Ignace – is a gold mine for those who want a look at this rich history.
- The ghost town of **Fayette** in Fayette State Park, Mich. Company towns were a common thing at one time in the Upper Peninsula, but Fayette is the largest and best preserved one remaining. It's hard not to get goose bumps while walking the streets here.

FAVORITE SHOPPING:

- **Saugatuck, Mich**. There's more to this art town than galleries (though those in themselves are well worth the visit!). Saugatuck has boutiques, antiques shops and gift shops galore in a pretty setting to boot.

- **Door County, Wis**. One after another the Door County resort towns, especially on the Green Bay side, are shopping heaven. *And* there are plenty of ice cream shops when spender's fatigue sets in.
- **Petoskey, Mich**. You can find just about anything in Petoskey's sophisticated downtown gaslight district, including beautiful jewelry made from – you guessed it – Petoskey stones.

Acknowledgments

Doing research for this kind of book may be one of the most enjoyable tasks in the world. Fun as it is, it's still hard work, but many people helped make the job *much* easier. To all of them, I'd like to extend heartfelt thanks. Though there are too many to name here, special gratitude goes to Dianna Stampfler of the West Michigan Tourist Association; Tom Nemacheck of the Upper Peninsula Travel and Recreation Association; Krista Elias of the Wisconsin Department of Tourism; Felicia Fairchild at the Saugatuck/Douglas Convention & Visitors Bureau; Chris Groff of the Michigan Department of Natural Resources; Al Nash and Mark Bluell of the National Park Service at Indian Dunes National Lakeshore; Greg Hokans of the Mackinac State Historic Parks; Mary Jane McBeath and Elizabeth Brockwell-Tillman from the Gillette Natural History Association at P. J. Hoffmaster State Park; Mary Beth Daniels at the Grand Hotel, Mackinac Island; Bob Benser at the Chippewa Hotel, Mackinac Island; Kathy and Frank Wilson at the Bayside Inn, Saugatuck, Mich.; Bob and Pat Elenbaas at the Dutch Colonial Inn, Holland, Mich.; Doug Yoder at the Brigadoon Bed and Breakfast, Mackinaw City, Mich.; and Roland Peterson from Tower Marine in Douglas, Mich.

I also owe a debt of gratitude to the many local historical societies and museums that publish pamphlets and books about their areas; I relied on these for much of the historical background covered here. I also found two books invaluable: "Around the Shores of Lake Michigan: A Guide to Historic Sites" by Margaret Beattie Bogue (The University of Wisconsin Press, 1985) and Milo Quaife's "Lake Michigan," part of The American Lakes Series (The Bobbs-Merrill Company, 1944).

Many steps are taken before a manuscript becomes a finished book. For seeing that process through from beginning to end I extend an enormous thank you to the great folks at Glovebox

Guidebooks of America: publisher Bill Bailey, editor Penny Weber-Bailey, graphic designer Dan Jacalone and the rest of the staff.

Another huge thank you goes to my good friend Nina Sobel, who read the manuscript and offered her comments and suggestions. She now knows more about Lake Michigan than she ever dreamed she would.

And finally, this book would not exist if it weren't for the support and patience of my husband, Tony, and son, Justin, who not once complained about my absence – either during the weeks of travel or the months of intimate communing with my computer. Thanks, guys.

About the Author

Donna Marchetti's articles have appeared in the International Herald Tribune, New York Times, Los Angeles Times, New Jersey Life and many other newspapers and magazines. As a free-lance travel writer, she has traveled to and written about destinations on six continents, but some of her favorite places to visit are much closer to home – on the Great Lakes. Her first book, "Around the Shores of Lake Erie: A Guide to Small Towns, Rural Areas and Natural Attractions," was inspired by a 755-mile bicycle trip around that lake. While she didn't cycle the entire 1,640-mile Lake Michigan shoreline, she did drive, hike, kayak and eat her way along the perimeter in order to write this book. She lives with her husband and son in Cleveland, Ohio.